Exploring Rural
GREECE

Exploring Rural
GREECE

PAMELA WESTLAND

PASSPORT BOOKS
a division of *NTC Publishing Group*
Lincolnwood, Illinois USA

This edition first published in 1989 by Passport Books,
a division of NTC Publishing Group, 4255
West Touhy Avenue, Lincolnwood (Chicago), Illinois
60646-1975 U.S.A. Originally published by Christopher
Helm (Publishers) Ltd., London, England.

Printed in Great Britain

CONTENTS

Acknowledgements   vii

Introduction   1
Getting There/Hiring Transport/Roads and Maps/
Driving and Parking/Where to Stay/Eating Out/Food and
Drink/Shops/Opening times/Public Holidays/Touring
Information/History/The Greek Language/Abbreviations/
Metric Conversion Tables

1. The Peloponnese   13
The Argolid   15
Laconia   22
Messinia   27
Mani   31
Ilia and Ahaia   35

2. Central Greece and Lefkas   41
Etolia and Akarnania   42
Fokida   46
Lefkas   52

3. Epirus   57
Thesprotia   59
Zagoria   63
Arta   67

4. Thessaly   73
Trikala   74
Olympos   79
Pelion   82

5. Evia and Skiros   87
Artemissia   88

Kafirea	92
Skiros	95
Specialities	98

6. Macedonia and Thrace — 99
- Western Macedonia — 100
- Halkidiki — 106
- Thassos — 111
- Eastwards to Thrace — 114

7. Corfu — 121
- Durrell Country — 123
- The North West — 127
- The Southern Tip — 130
- *Specialities* — 134
- *Festivals* — 134

8. Crete — 135
- The Lasithi Plain — 137
- Around the Dikti Mountains — 140
- The Eastern Province — 143
- Festos and the Amari Valley — 147
- Western Crete — The Gorges — 150

9. Rhodes and Karpathos — 155
- Kamiros and the North — 156
- Lindos and the South — 161
- Karpathos — 164
- *Specialities* — 168

10. The Island Groups — 169
- The Saronic Gulf Islands — 169
- The Cyclades — 170
- The Dodecanese — 172
- The North-Eastern Aegean Islands — 174
- The Sporades — 175
- The Ionian Islands — 176

Books — 177

Index — 179

ACKNOWLEDGEMENTS

I should like to thank Thorice and Ron Turnnidge for so generously sharing with me many of their favourite little-known towns, villages and routes; Veta Diamandopoulou for her professional help and advice; Despina Katsirea, Deputy Director of the Greek National Tourist Organisation in London; Olympic Airways; Hertz car hire; Nen Isbell for a far-from-easy typing assignment, and my husband Douglas for providing the driving force and, most of all, the route maps.

INTRODUCTION

Geographically, Greece is a bridge between Europe and Asia Minor, a peninsula covering an area of 131,944 square kilometres and with a population of around 9 million.

Topographically the whole territory, the mainland and the islands, is riven with high mountain ranges and peaks which means that, scenically, it is varied, breathtakingly beautiful — and, in parts, completely impassable. It means, too, that large areas of the country, irrigated by mountain streams or a generous rainfall, are intensely and abundantly fertile — crops of olives, citrus and orchard fruits, nuts and vegetables are an important part of the nation's economy.

Historically, being surrounded by the sea on 3 sides, the country was highly vulnerable to attack. The combination of millennia of immigrant settlers and colonising invaders has left its mark on the architecture we can see today, in Paleolithic and Neolithic sites; the great Minoan palaces of Crete; in Turkish mosques and workshop communities; in Venetian fortresses and stylish mansions.

Artistically, the ancient Greek sculptors and architects gave the world some of the finest, purest temples, monuments and statues it has ever seen.

Politically, Greece is both the home of the oldest European civilisation and the birthplace of democracy, and as such, it has had a profound effect on the shaping and development of every other Western nation.

Emotionally — and it is this fact which makes the country so magnetic — the generosity and hospitality of the Greek people is legendary. Every visitor is treated spontaneously and warm-heartedly as a friend — a fact which can come as something of a surprise, and even an embarrassment, to those of us who come from a more reserved background.

If you stop to admire a cottage or a tub of flowers in a country village and the owner asks you to come in and sit down, recognise this at once for what it is, part of a centuries-old tradition of trust and friendship, and accept graciously. You will be offered a cup of coffee, perhaps a glass of wine or ouzo, a 'spoon sweet' of crystallised fruit or a small cake, and all the while your host or hostess will look on in beaming approval — but not join you. If you smile your appreciation warmly, and show obvious delight in the hospitality, that is enough to fulfil your side of the custom. In practice, a tiny gift, something to offer the children or grandchildren, makes acceptance of such genuine kindness easier.

1

The tours I have planned throughout the country, on the mainland and the islands, will get you far, far from the madding crowd, and almost certainly show you this deep-rooted, emotional side of the Greek character; one that is perhaps no longer apparent in the bustle of city life or the eagerness to serve in tourist resorts. And the estimated journey time allows for the pleasure and leisure of meeting the people, unexpectedly in this way, as well as for normal *kafenion* and taverna breaks.

Use the tours in whole or in part as the mood takes you and time allows. You could, for example, start from Athens, drive to Corinth, enjoy the 5 tours on the Peloponnese and cross by ferry to start touring in Epirus. Or just pick out highlights from one or two tours and build your own schemes and dreams around them.

One more point, a personal interest to declare. For me, a meadow spattered with scarlet anemones and snow-white marguerites; a hillside misty with clouds of mauve lupins; a stone cottage peeping out from a shower of bougainvillea; a valley confetti-pink with almond blossom is so much more evocative than the same scene, 3 months hence, when the sun has declared that the flowering has to stop. And so I have described these scenes the way they are in spring and early summer. If the countryside flowers are one of your interests, too, from early March to late June is the most beautiful time to explore rural Greece.

Getting There

It takes time — 3 or 4 days — to drive from Britain to Greece, and so most people fly there, or go by train and, if they wish, hire transport in the country. From the USA there are scheduled flights as well as charter flights operated by, among others, Pan American, Metro Airlines, Arista Airways and Transamerican.

There are direct scheduled flights from the USA to Athens, and from Britain to Athens, Thessalonika, Corfu and Iraklion (Crete) and charter flights also to Preveza (for Lefkas and Epirus), Alexandroupoli (in Thrace) and the islands of Rhodes, Mykonos, Santorini (Thira), Kos, Samos, Hios, Lesvos, Limnos, Skiathos, Zakinthos (Zante) and Kefalonia, and more destinations are being added all the time.

The Greek national airline, Olympic Airways, uses only the West Airport in Athens (01/989.2111) and all foreign airlines use the East Airport (01/979.9317).

It is at present an offence to travel to Greece by charter flight unless you have accommodation booked for the duration of your stay. A glance at the sometimes negligible difference in price between 'flight only' and packages including accommodation in 'village rooms' indicates that the way to keep on the right side of the law and to enjoy a touring holiday is to buy a package and forgo the overnight-stay part of it.

The regulation was made to prevent an 'undesirable element' sleeping rough. And for just that reason all 'freelance' camping other than on authorised sites is strictly forbidden. But that is no hardship, since there are well set-up sites beside lakes and close to the sea, on wooded hillsides and in lush green valleys all over the country. For a list, contact National Tourist Organisations of Greece in London (address on p. 10) or the regional office when you arrive.

Hiring Transport

Some airlines offer a 'fly-drive' package deal with a car to meet you at the airport, and travel agencies will book a car when making a plane reservation. This can be considerably cheaper than hiring in Greece.

All large towns and tourist centres have a 'car hire street' of competing hire firms. Whether you want to hire a car or prefer the cheaper and enjoyable alternative of a scooter or low-powered (50cc) motor-cycle, make sure the prices are competitive by conspicuously going from one shop to the next.

You need a valid UK, US or international driving licence and, for a hired motor car, must pay 'collision damage waiver' insurance and an 18% government tax on the total cost.

Roads and Maps

Both the road network and the quality of the road surfaces are improving all the time. But particularly in mountainous regions it must seem that the authorities are taking 2 steps forward and 1 back, as rock falls and water deluge destroy large tracts of road each year.

Gradually local roads in main tourist areas, especially around the coasts, are being replaced by new dual-carriageways, designated national highways. These are useful for getting more quickly from one region to another, but where possible the tours in this book have used the more 'friendly' former roads which call at hamlets and villages along the way.

There are only 2 toll roads in the country, Athens-Lamia-Larissa-Katerini, and Athens-Corinth-Patra. The ordinary main roads are proudly known as 'asphaltos'. Just below them in status but often barely distinguishable in fact are the 'macadam' ones. Both are perfectly acceptable.

The problem arises with minor roads. Because both road improvements and natural hazards are on-going, it is often impossible to tell from a map how passable a road is likely to be. As a general rule, never set out on an unrecommended minor road — an unmade one up in the mountains — unless you have sufficient fuel and time to retrace to the main road in daylight, should you come across an immovable lump of rock or a gaping great hole. With better luck, of course, you may come across a steamroller giving the road the red carpet treatment just for your benefit. I have tried to be completely factual about the roads in all these tours so that you can judge what constitutes a challenge.

The Michelin road map No. 980 (red) covers the whole country with a scale of 1:700,000, 1cm:7km. A series of Freytag and Berndt maps produced in Austria covers most regions in more detail, the scale ranging from 1:100,000 to 1:300,000. These maps have place names in both the Roman alphabet and Greek script, which will help you to match up the tour destinations with the sign-posts *en route*. Whilst those on main routes all have a 'Roman' translation many out-of-the-way places have yet to be so helpful.

You can usually buy locally-produced maps at bookshops and kiosks throughout the country. Experience shows them to be useful as a general guide, but subject to inaccuracies.

Much the same may be said of asking directions. People jogging along on a donkey tend to gaze fondly at a map — perhaps the first they have seen — and tell you to go straight on. It is always best to ask a motorist, motor-cyclist or shopkeeper.

When asking the way to a garage, it's still a *garage* you want. Petrol is *venzini* and super grade is *supaire*. If you want the tank filled, *yemato* says it all.

Driving and Parking

Driving is on the right-hand side of the road, and the wearing of seat-belts is compulsory. International highway signs are used. Except on major highways and main through roads it is advisable to drive at a speed that allows for a fully laden mule to be just around the next sharp bend.

Regulations — not always observed by local drivers — restrict overtaking to stretches of road with no marking, with a broken central line, or a solid and a broken line (when overtaking is allowed on the latter side only). Double white lines or a single unbroken line prohibit overtaking.

Parking regulations are clearly marked and may be strictly enforced in cities and large towns. Police have the authority to impound number plates of illegally parked vehicles.

Greek traffic hazard

Where to Stay

Greece must be the easiest country in the world to find somewhere to stay. Their whole culture and tradition of welcoming guests as friends makes the Greeks natural hosts.

Staying with a family in what are termed 'village rooms' can be the most rewarding experience of all. What better way to get to know the people? In tourist areas, islands especially, locals meet the boat or bus and approach visitors with the question *'domatia?'* (rooms?), lead them to their house or cottage and have a pencil and paper handy to write down the room price.

Arriving by your own transport, just ask at a *kafenion* — someone's sister nearly always has a spotlessly clean room to rent, and usually with access to a shower. Alternatively, and if there is one, ask the Tourist Police — a misleading term which simply means 'tourist information'. Wherever possible I have given numbers of the local offices on each route. The Tourist Police compile lists of approved village rooms, pensions — often attached to a shop or taverna — and hotels, and will help you make bookings. In July, August and the week of Greek Orthodox Easter it is advisable to reserve a room in advance.

Hotels are classified as L (luxury) and, in descending order of price, A–E class. Prices for each room are government-controlled, according to season, and (other than in village rooms) must be displayed on an authorised form.

Asking for a *diplo* (double) or *mono* (single) room may be little more than a formality since most rooms have 2 single beds (*theo crevattia*) and the price is normally charged for the room, not the number of persons. Family rooms with 3 or 4 beds are not uncommon.

I have given phone numbers of a couple of (mainly B and C class) hotels along each route. Please take these as suggestions, not necessarily recommendations. I have not stayed at all of them myself.

Hotel breakfasts are usually of the continental type: bread, jam, butter (a luxury item), a slice of cake, and coffee.

Breakfast (*to proino*) is not usually included with village rooms, so it's a question of eating out. Most tavernas and some *kafenions* serve breakfast, or you can buy bread from the baker's and yoghurt from the general store and take it to a café to have with your coffee.

Eating Out

There is a definite pecking order in catering establishments in small towns, villages and rural areas, and anyone who does not know the form can be in for a confusing and frustrating time.

A restaurant — *restoran* or *estatorio* — is what you might expect, a place where you can order a full meal, from the first course through to coffee. A taverna is rather different. Here you can choose a first course and main dish, breakfast or a simple meal such as salad and wine, but usually not a dessert of any kind, not even fruit, and sometimes not even coffee. If you like to finish your meal *in situ* with a coffee and you don't see anyone else drinking it, there's no harm in asking. But don't be surprised if the answer is no.

A *psitaria* (literally a barbecue) is a taverna which specialises in spit-roast lamb, sucking pig and chickens, and may open just for the tourist season. You can usually identify them by the heavenly smell of herbs wafting down the street.

A *kafenion* is the place to go for coffee and drinks at any time of the day — the closest traditional Greek equivalent to the British pub. The café society is very much a male preserve — men sit there for hours with a single drink — but it isn't a club. Women travelling alone need not feel in the least daunted, however heavily they are outnumbered. Cafés serve beer, spirits, liqueurs and soft drinks but not always table wines, not even *retsina*.

One of the delights of a pre-lunch or dinner drink such as an ouzo, an aniseed-flavoured spirit which you dilute with water, is the small plate of *mezethes* (appetisers), that may accompany it — without your asking. This may be tiny pieces of grilled fish, cheese, olives, wedges of cucumber and tomato, anything.

Some *kafenions* rise to these heights, but the specialists in pre-prandials and the *mezethes* to go with them are *ouzaria*, ouzo bars where a range of drinks is served. The smart thing to do, in a harbour for example, is to select your *ouzaria* according to the quality of the tasters. Me, I always go for the one with the blackest slices of grilled octopus.

Desserts are not usually served after a meal, and restaurants generally offer only 'bought-in' cakes and pastries. The place to go for these, again at any time of the day, is the pastry-shop, ponderously called the *zacharoplasteion*. Sticky honey and nut *baklava* pastries, *kataifi* (they're the ones that look like shredded wheat), chocolate and cream cakes, nut shortbreads, ice creams, whatever you order — with a coffee or an alcoholic drink perhaps — will be served with a refreshing glass of ice-cold water.

Take-away food Greek style can be delicious. Many bakers sell hot *tiropitta* (cheese pies), *spanakopitta* (spinach and cheese pies), and *bougatsa* (custard pies), wrapped in paper napkins for tempting instant consumption or picnics. More substantially, *souvlaki* bars sell small skewers of lamb or thin slices of *kokoretsi* (grilled sheeps' entrails or other meats, infinitely more tasty than it sounds) wrapped in warm pitta bread with a sprinkling of salad.

The edges of the centuries-old Greek tradition of catering are becoming blurred, and have been lost forever in some large towns where 'Westernised' fast food and snack bars are taking over. But in rural Greece, it is as well to know the conventions.

Food and Drink

People are apt to say that no one goes to Greece for the food, and it is true that by some national standards, French particularly, the menu is limited. But the country has two great advantages: an abundance of good fresh ingredients — meat, fish, fruit and vegetables — and a long tradition of cooking them simply and well.

Whilst you will find excellent grilled meat and fish, and probably moussaka and stuffed tomatoes — *yemistes* — in tavernas which set out to attract tourists, you are likely to find a wider range — more akin to home cooking — in those that do not. Ask someone in a kiosk or shop to direct you to a local (*dopio*) taverna, and don't be put off if, away from the bright lights of the square or harbourside, it looks frankly scruffy. Peeling paintwork and creaking furniture may well mean that the owner has his priorities right!

You will almost certainly be invited into the kitchen, where you can see for yourself how clean it is, to see what is cooking — *pastitio* (lamb and macaroni casserole), *sofrito* (steak stewed with vinegar), braised rabbit, pork with artichokes, squid casserole, whatever — or to choose meat or fresh fish — pork chops, steak, goat cutlets, mullet — from the cold cabinet.

In both tavernas and restaurants the most expensive ingredients, red and grey mullet, swordfish and goat for example, are usually priced by the kilo. You select the item or stipulate the weight you want, and know exactly how much it will cost. If the price of *barbounia* (red mullet), expensive all over the country, horrifies you, do a double-take and order *marithes* (whitebait), instead!

The Greek pattern of eating a meal requires a little, well, understanding. No matter how carefully you might order *tzatziki* (yoghurt, mint and cucumber), *hummous*, aubergine, and *taramasalata* (cods' roe) salads as a first course, your main dish is likely to arrive at the same time and sit there getting chillier and chillier until you are ready for it. But this would never worry a Greek — they prefer their 'hot' food almost cold, anyway!

It's no good, incidentally, looking around for the waiter to bring side plates. Except in the very best of circles they are never used. You take an extra paper napkin and put your bread on that.

Greek coffee takes a little getting used to. The very finely ground powder is boiled in a small long-handled jug-like vessel, a *briki*, with sugar if you want it. So when ordering *elliniko cafe* you need to specify *gliko* (very sweet), *metrio* (medium) or *sketo* (without sugar). The coffee comes in tiny cups, and always with a glass of iced water. On no account attempt to drink it straight away — a very gritty experience. Allow a couple of minutes for the grounds to settle, then sip it carefully without disturbing them. There is a very good reason why Greek coffee is never served with a spoon!

All *kafenions* and tavernas offer 'Western-style' coffee as a (more expensive) alternative. Ask for it by the accepted generic term Nescafé, or just *nes*. If you answer yes to the query '*me gala?*', the milk is likely to be tinned. Sugar is usually served in individual sachets, some of them highly decorative and collectors' items among children.

Retsina, the resinated white wine that is almost the national drink, is an acquired taste — one which many visitors find it all to easy to acquire! If you have only tasted *retsina* in a restaurant at home and not been too impressed, give it another chance. For one thing, this inexpensive wine doesn't travel well, and for another it tastes a whole lot better in its natural environment.

Eating times, particularly in recognised tourist areas, are flexible, but tavernas in out-of-the-way places tend to adhere to the Mediterranean 'siesta' time, and close between around 2.30 and 5pm, with 'last orders' taken around 9pm. In large towns and popular resorts the customer tends to call the tune and meals are served all day, and well after midnight.

Shops

There is all the difference in the world — literally — between shops in the cities and tourist areas — just like those in any Western town — and those in small rural towns and villages, where there seems to be a total lack of window dressing and interior lighting.

Your nose will probably lead you to the baker's, *to fourno*, and the red or green cross over the door will indicate the *farmakeion*, the chemist's Should you need it, the doctor is *to yiatros* and the dentist's, the tooth doctor', *to odontoyiatros*. The grocer's and general store, which in many villages is the only shop, is the *pandopoleion*. The butcher's is the *kreatopoleion* and the greengrocer's the *oporopoleion*. If you fancy grilling your own morning-fresh mullet, most fish — and a good many other provisions and household goods — are bought from travelling vanmen who come round shouting their wares through a megaphone. A bookshop is a *vivliopoleion* and a stationer's a *hartopoleion*. You will find maps in both.

Post offices are indicated with a yellow sign saying 'Post' in 'international' areas, *tachidromeion* elsewhere, and post boxes too are bright yellow. You can usually buy postage stamps where you buy postcards, in stationers, bookshops, and the all-purpose yellow kiosks, the *periptero* — where there is also a phone.

You will soon notice that Greek postcards are an art form which raises photography — and the national culture — to the heights. The 'I was here' type of local-view cards are being edged out by beautifully evocative, moody, often unidentified scenes — a cat snoozing under a table in front of a bright blue door, or the sun sinking rosily behind a dome on Santorini. There are 2 postage rates for postcards so you need to specify whether your cards (*hartes*) are *megales* (big) or *mikres* (small) when asking for stamps (*grammatosima*).

To make an international telephone call, go to an OTE (telephone corporation) office, where there are metered kiosks — look for the blue-on-silver signs in cities and towns — or ask at a hotel or *periptero* kiosk. Some have meters geared to register overseas calls and some don't.

Opening Times

Shopping hours, like restaurant hours, are becoming more flexible, and in many tourist resorts it seems to be a case of 'we never close'. It is a trap for the unwary, though, to travel away from a busy hotel complex, only to find that traditional 'siesta' hours are rigidly adhered to. A recent move to 'Westernise' office and shop opening hours in Athens was met with a firm *ohi* from the workers, who reinforced their negative attitude with a one-day strike.

Shops The standard opening hours on Mondays, Wednesdays and Saturdays are from 8am to 3pm, and on Tuesdays, Thursdays and Fridays from 8am to 2pm and again from 5.30pm to 8.30pm. Non-food shops — chemists', fashion stores, electricians' and so on — may trim half-an-hour off each opening session.

Banks Official banking hours are from 8am to 2pm on Mondays to Fridays. Having said that, some banks in some places will open again in the late afternoons and on Saturday mornings but you can't rely on it. Major airports have a round-the-clock bureau-de-change service, and hotels, restaurants and shops in large centres will take travellers' cheques and major credit cards.

Museums and archaeological sites In an ideal world there would be standard opening times, they would be comprehensively listed in this book, and you would arrive at the gates confident of finding them open. Life isn't like that. As the times are constantly being changed, I decided it is better to give none than to risk being infuriatingly out of date.

In general, archaeological sites open at 8pm and close at sunset in the summer, with earlier closing in winter and on Sundays. Some close for 2 hours at lunchtime, and some (without warning) close at 3pm.

Museums tend to be more predictable, opening from 9am to 3pm or 4pm.

That isn't much help, I know. Contact the nearest NTOG office when you arrive, or play safe and aim to visit your top-priority sites early in the day.

Public Holidays

Shops, offices and banks officially close on the following public holidays:

1 Jan.	New Year's Day
6 Jan.	Epiphany
	Last Monday before Lent
	Good Friday
	Easter Monday
25 Mar.	Greek Independence Day
1 May	May Day, the spring festival
25 Aug.	Assumption of the Virgin Mary
28 Aug.	'Ohi' Day, when the Greeks said 'no' in 1940 to the Italian ultimatum
25 Dec.	Christmas Day
26 Dec.	Boxing Day

Note: The Greek Orthodox Easter does not necessarily coincide with the Easter festival in other Christian churches — it is calculated in a different way.

Touring Information

The National Tourist Organisation of Greece provides one of the best free information services in the world — colourful brochures and maps of every region and island group in the country. NTOG in Britain is at 195–7 Regent Street, London, W1R 8DR (01-734 5997); in the United States at 645 Fifth Avenue, Olympic Tower, New York, NY 10022 (421 5777); 611 West Sixth Street, Los Angeles, California 90017 (626 6696), and 168 North Michigan Avenue, Chicago, Illinois 60601 (782 1084).

There are regional NTOG offices throughout Greece, and many of these are listed with the tours. The head office (it is EOT in Greek) is at 2 Amerikis Street, Athens (01/322.3111–9). Call them for all touring information, opening times, any details you want and cannot find locally.

History

Books on Greece tend to bandy about terms such as Archaic and Hellenistic as if everyone knows their Greek and other European history like the back of their hands. This isn't meant to be a history lesson, just an at-a-glance guide to the chronology and the terms:

Paleolithic and Mesolithic Age	260,000 to 7000 BC
Neolithic	7000 to 2800 BC
Chalcolithic/the Bronze Age/the Minoan Age*	2800 to 1000 BC
Palatial	
Pre-palatial	2600 to 2000 BC
Proto-palatial	2000 to 1700 BC
Neo-palatial	1700 to 1400 BC
Post-palatial	1400 to 1100 BC
Helladic	
Early Helladic	2800 to 2000 BC
Mid Helladic	2000 to 1580 BC
Late Helladic or Mykinean Period	1580 to 1100 BC
Minoan	
Early Minoan	2500 to 2100 BC
Middle Minoan	1950 to 1750 BC
Late Minoan	1550 to 1400 BC
Iron Age	1100 to 67 BC
Geometric Period	1100 to 700 BC
Archaic Period	700 to 500 BC
Classical Period	500 to 323 BC
Hellenistic Period	323 to 146 BC
Roman and Byzantine Period	146 BC to AD 1453
with Arabic occupation	AD 824 to 861
Post-Byzantine Period	AD 1453 to 1821
with Turkish occupation of varying periods throughout the country	
Beginning of 6-year War of Independence	AD 1821

---

* There are various accepted ways of subdividing this important period in the history of Greece, and particularly of Crete. We give 3 of the principal theories.

The Greek Language

If only the Greeks didn't use a different alphabet, there would be no problem! So many English words are derived from Greek and sound so similar that one can quickly gain confidence. But the alphabet! Even when characters look identical to Roman ones, you can't rely on them. The Greek *b* is pronounced like *v*, *p* like *r*, and so it goes on.

If you have an hour or so to spare, it really is worth buying a small phrase book (see bibliography) and getting to grips with the alphabet. Then at least you can read shop and street signs, bus destinations and all the other written paraphernalia that makes getting about easier.

Another slight local difficulty is that there are several ways to interpret some Greek sounds into their closest equivalent in English. Think about it. As a simple example, the sound for *f* can be written as *f*, *ff* or *ph* — and, take my word for it, if you have 3 Greek maps you will come across one place name 'translated' in all 3 ways, as in the modern Festos and the ancient Phaistos. The back-of-the throat sound represented by *x* in Greek is another example. It isn't said as *ex*, but *ch*, or *kh*, or simply a guttural *h*. And again you will come across all 3, as in Chora, Khora or just Hora (for an old town).

One more nasty. The Greeks have, or had, a habit of putting place names in the genitive case. We won't go in depth down that path, but what with one thing and another it can mean that Gytheio (in the Peloponnese) can be spelt Gytheo, Gythio, Ytheio, Ytheo or Ythio; Gytheion or any of the other variables, with an *n* on the end.

I have tried to use spellings which are the simplest, most logical and most often used on local signposts. If you come across a place name that looks *nearly* right, give it the benefit of a long hard look. It could well be the rose you want, by any other name.

Abbreviations

Ag.	*Agia*, *Agios*, Saint
C	century
km	kilometres
leof.	*leoforos*, avenue
m	metres
Mon	monastery
Mt.	mountain, mount
NTOG	National Tourist Organisation of Greece
Pan.	Panageia, Virgin Mary

Metric Conversion Tables

All measurements are given in metric units. For readers more familiar with the imperial system, the accompanying tables are designed to facilitate quick conversion to imperial units. Bold figures in the central columns can be read as either metric or imperial: e.g. 1 kg = 2.20 lb or 1 lb = 0.45 kg.

mm		in	cm		in	m		yds
25.4	1	.039	2.54	1	0.39	0.91	1	1.09
50.8	2	.079	5.08	2	0.79	1.83	2	2.19
76.2	3	.118	7.62	3	1.18	2.74	3	3.28
101.6	4	.157	10.16	4	1.57	3.66	4	4.37
127.0	5	.197	12.70	5	1.97	4.57	5	5.47
152.4	6	.236	15.24	6	2.36	5.49	6	6.56
177.8	7	.276	17.78	7	2.76	6.40	7	7.66
203.2	8	.315	20.32	8	3.15	7.32	8	8.75
228.6	9	.354	22.86	9	3.54	8.32	9	9.84

g		oz	kg		lb	km		miles
28.35	1	.04	0.45	1	2.20	1.61	1	0.62
56.70	2	.07	0.91	2	4.41	3.22	2	1.24
85.05	3	.11	1.36	3	6.61	4.83	3	1.86
113.40	4	.14	1.81	4	8.82	6.44	4	2.48
141.75	5	.18	2.27	5	11.02	8.05	5	3.11
170.10	6	.21	2.72	6	13.23	9.65	6	3.73
198.45	7	.25	3.18	7	15.43	11.26	7	4.35
226.80	8	.28	3.63	8	17.64	12.87	8	4.97
255.15	9	.32	4.08	9	19.84	14.48	9	5.59

ha		acres
0.40	1	2.47
0.81	2	4.94
1.21	3	7.41
1.62	4	9.88
2.02	5	12.36
2.43	6	14.83
2.83	7	17.30
3.24	8	19.77
3.64	9	22.24

Metric to imperial conversion formulae

	multiply by
cm to inches	0.3937
m to feet	3.281
m to yards	1.094
km to miles	0.6214
km^2 to square miles	0.3861
ha to acres	2.471
g to ounces	0.03527
kg to pounds	2.205

1 THE PELOPONNESE

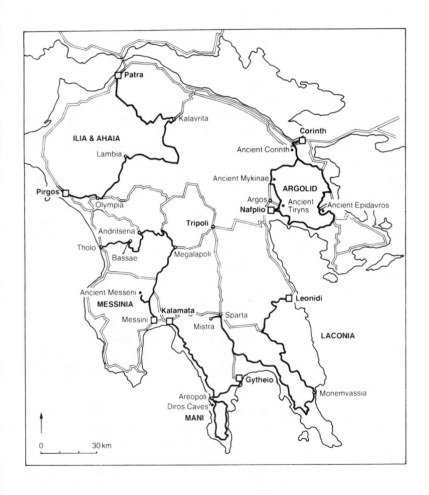

If travelling around the Peloponnese, the 21,463 square kilometres which forms the southern extremity of the Balkan peninsula, gives all the sensation of being on a Greek island, then that is not surprising. And it is nothing new. It is joined to mainland Greece by no more than the narrowest of margins — an isthmus 23 metres wide — and in ancient times it was known as the Island of Pelops. In the Middle Ages, in deference to the crop that flourished there in such profusion, the Peloponnese became known as the Morea, or mulberry.

The idea for the construction of a canal was not a new one either. It had been on the drawing board since 7C BC, and the Roman emperor Nero is said to have made the first serious attempt to build it. It was not, however, until engineering knowledge was well advanced, towards the end of the last century, that the dream became reality. And it is not until one sees ships passing through the canal, tiny moving specks on the strip of water far, far below the road and rail link, that one can appreciate the scale of this strategic waterway.

To cross the bridge into the Peloponnese — a good, fast road links Corinth to Athens — is to enter if not an island, then almost a separate world. The peninsula, which is shaped rather like a hand with three fingers and (in the Argolid region) a thumb, is highly mountainous and split by massive ranges which sweep down to the sea in almost all directions. This makes for beautiful scenery on a grand scale; and, for much of the way, driving which to say the least requires due care and attention.

The peninsula is divided into 7 regions (called *nomes*) — the Argolid (to the east), Corinth (north east), Achaia (north), Elis (north west), Messenia (south west), Laconia (south east) and Arcadia (central) — which roughly correspond to those formed by the ancient inhabitants and, naturally, by the mountain ranges. Their respective rises and falls are dealt with in more detail as each tour is introduced.

The first settlers on the peninsula, tribes who probably came from Asia, date back to the 3rd millennium BC, known as the Early Helladic period. A thousand years later they were joined — after a struggle — by warring groups of Indo-European origin whose culture and (Greek) language continued unbroken into the Mykinean period, the area's golden age. It is remains of these later Middle Helladic communities, excavated at Asini, Mykinae and Lerna, which can be seen on the sites of the ancient cities and in the archaeological museum in Athens to this day. The Dorian invasion by a new wave of Greek-speaking people from the north wrought death and destruction on the peninsula, and brought civilisation to a standstill for centuries. This was the region's own Dark Ages, from which it eventually rose decisively to take a hand in international affairs. Sparta contributed significantly to the defeat of Persia 5C BC and, after the Peloponnesian War, gained a short-lived ascendancy over other Greek cities.

The Goths and Alaric ravaged the area AD 3C and 4C and the Ostrogoths attacked the western shores 6C; earthquakes and Avar and Slav incursions in turn devastated the area 6C; plague took its toll 8C; the

Byzantine influence arose early 9C; Venetians developed trading privileges 12C — the history of the Peloponnese has always had a high and changing profile. That profile was raised even higher after the fall of Constantinople when, in 1205, the area was divided up by William de Champlitte and Geoffrey de Villehardouin among the barons of France, Flanders and Burgundy.

The see-saw effect continued. The Byzantine influence was reinforced; the Albanians threatened ascendancy; the Turks turned this situation to their advantage; in 1460 the region was taken and held under the orders of Mehmed, until in 1699 it was ceded to Venice. In 1715 Ali Pasha retook the peninsula for Ahmed and it was returned to Turkey.

The pages of the history book turn again. The War of Independence was begun in the Peloponnese in 1821 and one by one the cities fell. In 1825 Ibrahim Pasha advanced with an Egyptian army. In the 1827 battle of Navarino (recorded in the film *The Guns of Navarone*) the Turko-Egyptian fleet was sunk with Allied help and the Turks withdrew. An uprising by the inhabitants of Mani (in the south west), determined outsiders and party to no union, was suppressed with help by Bavarian troops in 1830.

In the sites of ancient cities; in the plays performed at the summer festival in the theatre at Epidavros; in the style of architecture influenced by the Venetians, the Turks and others who temporarily formed colonies there; and in the individual characteristics of the people one meets, the turbulent history of the Peloponnese is deeply etched, tangible and clearly visible to even the most casual holiday visitor today.

The Argolid

1–3 days/215km/ from Corinth (about 100km west of Athens)

Ancient Corinth ... Epidavros ... Asini ... Tiryns ... Mykinae ... some of the richest archaeological treasures in the whole of Greece are here, in the Argolid region of the eastern Peloponnese.

Meandering through countryside painted vividly with orange groves and speckled for much of the year with wild flowers and alongside an uninhibited — and largely uninhabited — shoreline, it would be possible to visit these sites and even more in a long day. But not everyone has the capacity to absorb an almost overwhelming wealth of past glories, millennia of early civilisations and many exhilarating changes of scenery in so short a time. And, it has to be said, the grandeur of the sites and the surrounding countryside is magnetic. If on your schedule time is not of the essence, be prepared to linger and let the hours slip by.

The tour starts in Corinth just a few kilometres from the Isthmus and, going in a clockwise direction, strays far from the good new roads which now link many of the principal places of interest. Two of the minor roads do make progress slow and interesting; and in so doing give even the driver the opportunity to appreciate the rich variety of the terrain.

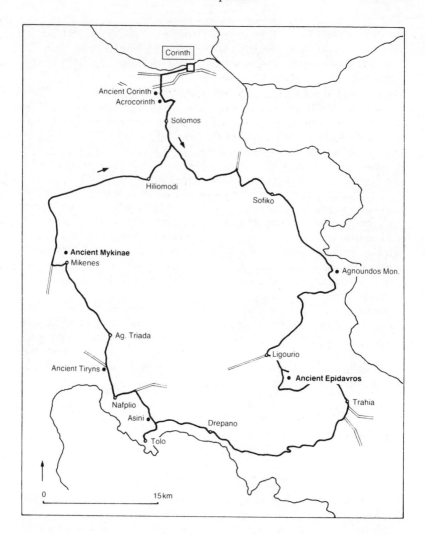

CORINTH (or KORINTHOS) (pop: 20,800) The modern town, with a
long sea front on the Bay of Corinth, is an important industrial and
commercial centre which has been rebuilt twice, after earthquakes in
1858 and 1928. With its bustling shops, tavernas and choice of hotels, it
makes a suitable — though not a scenic — stepping stone for the quintet
of tours in the region. Hotel: **King Saron**, Isthmia, 0741/37.201.

We leave the town on the Patra road, going due westwards along one of
the many urban routes in Greece that should aptly be named 'mechanical
engineering street'. It improves. In 5km, where sheep wander along the
beach, turn left on to the Argos road, signed to **Ancient Corinth**, 4km
away. The road takes a modest incline to reach the site of the ancient city

built on the northern slopes of Acrocorinthos (628m). The 'long wall' started from the summit of the mountain, enfolded the city and terminated at the port of Leheo, an artificial harbour to the west of the Gulf and once a vital link between Europe and Asia.

Geographically the site is impressive, backed by formidably rocky peaks and dropping down to a leafy valley of vines, oleander, almond and citrus trees. In its day (6C–5C BC) it boasted a population of over 300,000 with, it is said, slaves numbering half as many again. The ancient inhabitants, who took Aphrodite as their divine goddess, were renowned for their profligacy even in so licentious an age. It was here, during the 18 months he spent in the seemingly unfertile midst of the vice-torn community, that St. Paul founded a church. It is here, in the sun-soaked fertile valley where grapes grow so freely, that the production of currants has its origins. And it was here, according to Vitruvius, that Kallimachos created the Corinthian capital, an architectural style that was widely copied and has become almost a household term.

The principal surviving ruins of the ancient city are the two-storey agora (forum) dating from Roman times, when its massive area (150m by 90m) was taken up by arcades, shops (one still retains its roof), temples and shrines. On a mound to the north, 7 of the original 38 columns of the 6C BC Temple of Apollo, of the Doric order and one of the oldest in Greece, stand erect. There are also notable remains of the sacred Fountain of Glauke, which was linked to the Sanctuary of the Oracle; the 5C BC theatre, built to hold 18,000 spectators, and the small Roman Odeon, dating from 1C AD. (Corinth Tourist Police: 0741/23.383.)

The road to **Acrocorinth** is well signed, through the old pottery district and a Turkish quarter. The ruins, which were in turn a Greek acropolis, a Roman citadel and a Byzantine fortress, stand in isolation on a sky-scraper of a rock and, after parking the car, are reached only by a steep climb. The effort of the ascent is rewarded by the exploration of the Peirene spring in a Hellenistic underground chamber, the site of the famous Temple of Aphrodite on the highest point of Acrocorinth, the remains of the Frankish Castle and three fortified gates; and — it goes without saying — by a breathtaking view as far as Mt. Parnassos in Central Greece to the north.

From Acrocorinth, take the due-east road through the villages of Examilia and Hirokeriza to join the coast road. Turn right, going south, where in about 3km you pass close by another archaeological treasure, the Baths of Helen, Loutra Oreas Elenis. Turn inland at the cross-roads in the village of Kato Almiri to Rito (2km) and then — first through the valley and later on to a steep, narrow road — to **SOFIKO**.

In the centre of the village past a small basilica and its separate bell tower, there is a *kafenion* with a large, square, shady, raised terrace. It is not as grand as it sounds, but the owner serves the crispest, driest of minute fish as a snack, even with a coffee. Bear left in the village. You pass a sturdy red-pointed stone basilica which demands a double-take: the river runs so close to its foundation that it appears to be moated. Fork right and in 2km, joining a more major road, bear right, heading south.

Spectacular views of red rocks, bays and islets on the left give rise to many a pull-in for vehicles, almost to x-marks-the-spot places for photography, while on the land side olive groves give way to pines. You pass **Agnoundas Monastery** and, in 4km, turn right towards Nea Epidavros. Keep on this road for 16km, ignoring the sign to the left for Paleo (old) Epidavros. (Old, in this context does not mean ancient.)

At Ligourio, turn left where it is clearly signed to **Ancient Epidavros**. There is ample parking for cars and an efficient one-way-in, one-way-out road system.

The site opens at 8am and in the tourist season here, above all, the early bird catches the majesty and tranquillity that is hard to discern once the eager coach parties arrive.

What can one say about this most awe-inspiring of sites, that in antiquity was a sanctuary of Asklepios, the god of medicine, and is now, from June to September, the very heart of Greek drama? The open-air theatre, the most impressive in the ancient world, was designed in 4C by the Argive architect, Polykleitos the Younger. The massive fan-shaped theatre held 14,000 spectators, every one of whom would benefit from acoustics which were perfect in all weather conditions. That has not changed. Stand centre-stage and it is as well to remember that your slightest whisper will be clearly heard in the farthest reaches of the semi-circle.

The same architect raised the Tholos, or Rotunda, which may have been used for mystic rites — in those days man was not healed by medicine alone.

The main monuments are contained within a wall which confined the

The ancient theatre at Epidavros

sacred serpents. The doctor, the son of Apollo and a Boeotian princess, and who was said to be suckled by a nanny goat, had become a cult figure by 6C BC, and in 4C BC a Doric temple — the outlines of the foundations remain — was raised at Epidavros to house his statue, in gold and ivory.

The Temple of Artemis, the Temple of Themis, the Greek Baths, the Roman Baths, the portico (enlarged by the Romans) where the sick slept in hopeful anticipation that the god would appear to them in their dreams, the Stadium and the museum housing a collection of Roman medical instruments — the serious and even the casual visitor needs a guide book to bring Epidavros excitingly to life. Hotel: **Xenia**, 0753/ 22.003.

Retrace the 2km to the road, turn left and in 16km you come to **TRAHIA**. This could be a temporary parting of the ways. Take the left fork and in 41 km you come to **GALATA**, the long strip of mainland fishing village connected by almost constant ferries to the Ionian island of **Poros**, just an admiring glance away across the Gulf of Epidavros. A right fork 2km south of Trahia leads to **ERMIONI**, the ferry-boat port for Idra and Spetses. Our tour does not take up these options, but when time is on your side they are almost irresistible (see p. 169).

Continuing the route from Trahia, fork right in less than 1km (signed to Kranidi). It is a pleasant ride in any season, with the road running beside the river. In spring and early summer, the strips of wheat and globe artichokes shimmering their alternate shades of ripening gold and silver green, and banks and fields of dazzling poppy-red anemones, brilliant yellow Jerusalem sage and lime-green euphorbia, it is stunning.

The road passes through Karnezeika and crosses the river at **KANDIA**, where there are camping facilities and distracting views of the Bay of Tolo with, in the hazy distance, a picturesque chapel on an islet.

The road continues to **DREPANO** (7km from Kandia). Fork left for **Ancient Asini**, a wild site scattered with the remains of Hellenistic ramparts, a gate, a paved road and Roman baths. Just below the site there is a beach and a grassy knoll where mallow and sow-thistle grow. I take no responsibility for its seclusion or lack of it in high season.

For a similar reason, there is a decision to make at **ASINI**. You can take the southern road (a mere 3km) to the 'Westernised' resort of **TOLO**, but I believe that you cannot put a pin's head on the beach or the footpaths in summer. There are certainly more hotels — by far — than typical Greek *kafenions* and tavernas. From Asini, rejoin the Drepano road, turning left for **NAFPLIO** (pop: 9,300), which the Venetians called the *Napoli di Romania*. It may have been, in Mykinean times, the naval station of Argos, to which city it fell in 7C BC.

Nestled on the northern slopes of a craggy peninsula, the present town has all the appearance of a sea-faring one, its narrow streets protecting tall houses against the elements; although in fact, since the port — which does a brisk freight trade in tobacco, cotton and currants — faces away from the open sea, it provides an unusually safe harbour. Examples of medieval military architecture are impressive. Nafplio Tourist Police: 0752/27.776. Hotels: **Xenia's Palace**, 0752/28.981; **Amphitryon**, 0752/ 27.366.

Take the Argos road north from Nafplio and in 2km, the right turn (it is well signposted) to the citadel of **Ancient Tiryns**, situated high on a series of knolls rising on the seaward side from reclaimed marshland and on the other from extensive citrus groves.

Tradition has it that **Tiryns** was founded before Mykinae, and it was certainly inhabited before the Bronze Age. Like that other great ancient city (the next archaeological stop on our tour) it came under Perseus' rule. In 13C BC it was subject to Mykinae, and it took part in the Trojan war. When the Dorians invaded (12C BC) Tiryns was an independent kingdom supporting about 15,000 inhabitants. It flourished until 468 BC when the Argives breached the massive military defences, captured the city and effectively razed it to the ground. In the *Iliad*, Homer refers to 'wall-girt Tiryns', and that wall, 750m of irregular red and grey limestone blocks up to 18m thick, still stands today. Pausanias was impressed. He compared the structure of the wall to the Pyramids. Students of military tactics and defensive operations will find much to interest them in the overall plan and design of the fortress. The ruins encircled by the wall date mainly from 13C BC covering an area 300m by up to 100m, and include, on the upper storey, the royal palace, with the great hall, a porch, the base of the throne and parts of the painted floor intact. On the lower level a precinct encloses military, religious and domestic buildings. A flight of 80 massive stone steps winds down to one of the 2 postern gates.

Impressive? Oppressive? Whatever your view of Ancient Tiryns, there is a huge time-gap to leap as you emerge into the busy activity of the citrus groves. Pruning, spraying, hoeing, harvesting, packing, tractor-ferrying the fruit to the near-by soft drinks factory and the wholesalers or, a temptation for the visitor, offering a bargain buy of bright pink plastic bags of mandarines and oranges — the life of a fruit farmer is a busy one.

Return to the main road, turn right on to it, and almost immediately right on to the 'back' road to Mikenes — it's oranges, oranges most of the way. Go straight over the cross-roads to Ag. Triada (4km) following the sign to Ireo. You will pass through the village of **PLATANI** slowly enough to admire its pretty, Swiss-style-chalet houses because the road is (at the time of writing) severely pitted with pot-holes. Turn right in the village of Anifi (the signs are now helpfully consistent to Mikenes), and left just past the petrol station. The familiarity of the citrus groves is relieved now. They are lined with almond trees, a 'picture' of shell-pink blossom in spring. Go over a staggered cross-roads in Honikas, through lush market gardens, to (in 4km) a right turn to **MONISTRAKI**. Go uphill through the village and turn left on the Mikenes road, past a reverie-shattering new building that lacks something of the style, if none of the imagination, of Sir Arthur Evans. No Knossos Palace, this one!

The village of **MIKENES** is ready. (Hotel: **Agamemnon**, 0751/66.222.) The visitor runs the gauntlet through a bright parade of tavernas, bars, gift and souvenir shops and precious few establishments that would be there if Ancient Mykinae were not. (To attempt to clarify the confusion, the modern village is spelt locally as Mikenes, the ancient city as Mykinae.) After a right-hand turn at a T-junction, you arrive at the site, a short walk from the car park.

Ancient Mykinae is straight from the history books. Evidence shows that the city was inhabited as long ago as 3000 BC, and its unique importance — indeed much of its visual character even today — lay in the fertility of the surrounding plain. Legend (in a country where myth was ever as powerful as fact) has it that the city was founded by Perseus, son of Zeus, who raised the massive city walls with the aid of massive city builders — Cyclops, the giants who had but a single, central, eye. Between 16C and 12C BC, when the city was destroyed by the Dorians, Mykinae was the richest and most powerful state in the Mediterranean, its influence embracing both Crete and Egypt. Homer described the city as, variously, well-built, broad-streeted and rich in gold. Just how rich in gold did not

The Lion Gate, Mykinae

21

become apparent until the late 19C when a German amateur archaeologist, Heinrich Schliemann, unearthed a circle of 19 royal tombs dating
from 16C BC, the men wearing gold face-masks and breast-plates and the
women, heavy gold jewellery. These relics are displayed in the National
Archaeological museum in Athens.

The Acropolis, triangular in shape and enclosed by ramparts, was built
on the summit of a 278m hill to house, thus fortified, the royal family, the
noblemen and the royal guard, with the town clustered around the
foothills.

What remains of this legendary and powerful civilisation is majestic
and awe-inspiring. The Lion Gate with the (now-beheaded) symbolically
powerful lionesses, the massive gateway and the grain store where carbon-
ised cereal grains have been found; Schliemann's first circle of royal
tombs (a torch is helpful) and the 'royal way' leading to the 15C BC
palace and the later Temple of Athena; Clytemnestra's Tomb, a 14C BC
round communal funeral chamber, the 17C BC circle of 24 tombs, and
the 13C BC Tomb of Agamemnon, or Treasury. Allow time to absorb the
importance and scale in both time and place of this ancient city where tablets
inscribed with the only recently deciphered Linear B script were found.

Return to Mikenes through the village. In 3km, after a triumphal drive
through an archway of silvery eucalyptus, turn right at the T-junction, on
to the Corinth road. In 23km you bump over the level crossing at
HILIOMODI where goats munch beneath the almond trees and the
crossing keeper, sheltering from sun and wind in a sentry box, fills in the
gaps in the train timetable with a crochet hook. This is an unremarkable
but useful little town, attractive only in its verdant setting, not in its
architecture. In 18km, passing through Solomos, the road returns to
Corinth.

Laconia

2 days/260km/from Leonidi (70km South of Argos) to Sparta

The massive but friendly shadow of Mt. Parnon presides over this south-
eastern finger of the Peloponnese. The range rises to 1950m and is tipped
with snow at least until early May. Wolves still roam its more impenetrable slopes, and there is a large, wooded game reserve.

The icy mountain waters ensure a prosperity of crops and wild flowers
in the valley below, and a huddle of busy little agricultural villages where
tourists are rarely seen; and made the more welcome, for that.

Perhaps even fewer visitors might explore this most rural and remote of
regions, were it not for its hidden gem, the Byzantine town of
Monemvassia, completely concealed, from the landward side, by the face
of the towering rock in which it was built. Here is a time-capsule of social
history (most closely resembling, perhaps, Mont St Michel in France)
completely unexploited and unspoiled. It is almost as if one is discovering

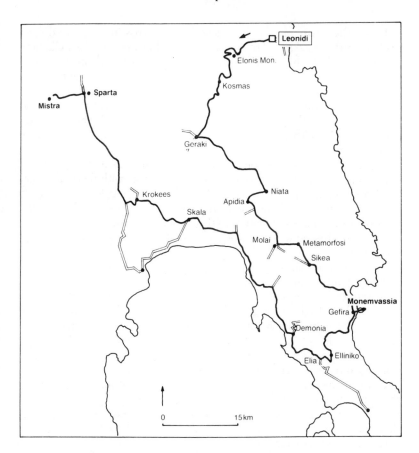

the near-deserted, cliff-hanging town for the first time.

Continuing through a criss-cross of functional (just!) rural roads, one has time to file away, so to speak, one almost forgotten township before exploring another. Mistra is tucked into the foothills of the neighbouring range, Mt. Taigetos, a maze of churches, palaces, mansions, smaller dwellings and a fortress set among figs and vines.

LEONIDI (pop: 3,200) is on the estuary of river Dafno and lies at the eastern foothills of **Mt. Parnon**. The people make their living from fishing, merchant trade and goat-keeping. Luckily that leaves room for romantic eccentricity. An old fisherman enjoying the sunshine on a café wall had a string of white anemones tucked behind his ear. Why? 'Because it's spring, of course!' It has all that is needed for a lunch-time stop: banks, shops, *kafenions* and tavernas. (The one facing the Shell garage has been known to serve generous portions of small fried fish straight from the sea.) The narrow streets make close study of the houses, with their stone arched doorways, overhanging upper storeys and elaborate balconies, something of a neck-aching pastime.

Leave the town on the road leading west, passing a multi-domed basilica on the outskirts. The road, fairly level at first but then climbing steeply, runs through the mountain valley, and is washed by streams and a waterfall. After 13km, it passes the almost forbiddingly steep entrance to **Elonis Monastery**. Just beyond that, the road surface deteriorates considerably, but for only 1km. After a further 17km of spectacular scenery and variable but entirely passable road conditions, we reach the mountain village of **KOSMAS** (about 1¼ hours driving from Leonidi and 1213m above sea level).

A cheerful sign of welcome (literally translated meaning 'good you have come') greets the visitor. The grey stone houses with their slate roofs and iron balconies are almost camouflaged as they straggle up the equally grey mountainside. There are plenty of *kafenions* around the square, catering for the male population as they while away the time at the backgammon boards, and for visitors, too — but these are an infrequent distraction.

We continue on the road from Kosmas through Christmas-card scenery of mountain tops and pine trees, refuge huts and picnic-table sites, terraced slopes and — with warning signs — tumbling rocks. The countryside is a haven for game and birds, and colour-washed with wild flowers. There are a few landmarks; 11km out of Kosmas, a series of rock-caves on the left of the road; here and there a pretty way-side chapel, and everywhere devotional boxes of various styles. At a cross-roads, 16km from Kosmas and signed to **GERAKI**, turn left (there's a little stone devotional box on one corner). The road continues, straight and level, for the 3km into the centre.

Geraki is a working agricultural village with streets so steep and narrow that there are wall-mirrors for traffic safety. The houses, with wooden balconies and shady terraces, are stepped up the hillside, and there is an air of relative prosperity accounted for by the abundance of olive, nut and fruit trees and the extensive market gardens along the valley.

Take the road going south-east to (in 7km) **ALEPOHORI**. Turn right at a mini T-junction there and continue (crossing a bridge and then with the river on your left) to **AG. DIMITRIOS**. Turn right and then left out of the large village square, following the sign to Monemvassia. Almost at once you will see the twin towers of the basilica at **NIATA**, where you turn right, and in 5km come to **APIDIA**, following the distant town signs in both villages. In 2km you turn left, on to a more major road, and 12km further on, with Molai on your right, fork left (signed **METAMORFOSI**) through the apple orchards that lead to the village. In the square, lively at seemingly all hours of the day with children playing volley-ball, turn right, taking the road to **SIKEA**. The village, high on a hill, is then ahead of you. The road passes it by, about 1 km to the left. Take a major left turn and follow the road (signed Monemvassia again) to the coastal village of **GEFIRA**, the mainland springboard to the Byzantine town.

Gefira is a workmanlike coastal town, more cheery than some, with a few tourist facilities beyond the local everyday needs, tavernas, gift shops and reasonably priced places to stay (**Malvasia Pension**, 0732/51.323,

Monemvassia Pension, 0732/61.381). But we haven't travelled from Leonidi to visit Gefira!

MONEMVASSIA is special. Its name means 'only entrance', indicating that the town is reached by the narrow causeway and bridge linking it to the mainland — or from the sea, of course. You can drive right round to the entrance gate, or enjoy the anticipating build-up of a 30-minute walk towards and around the 300m high rock. No wonder it is called the Gibraltar of Greece! The town was fortified by the Byzantines against the Slavs and fell in turn to the Franks, the Pope, Venetians (who fortified it further) and Turks. Besides being a strategic trading post, Monemvassia was famous from the Middle Ages through to 19C for the export to Britain and France particularly of Malmsey, the sweet white wine which was produced locally and in the Aegean islands. The fortifications consisted of a 13-arch bridge, a castle a-top the rock and a circuit wall with sentry posts, which enclosed the town on 3 sides. There was a population of 300,000 (which is reduced to less than 100 today) and over 40 churches.

Walk part-way around the sentry wall; climb up (it's steep going, but worth it for the view) to the remains of the citadel; wander through the town stopping here or there for refreshment; pause by the tiny gardens of deserted houses spilling over with colourful shrubs and aromatic plants gone wild; visit some of the deserted or restored churches (such as the white-painted Pan. Chrysafitissa, 16C, beside the parade ground) and the museum housed in Ag. Pavlos (956 AD), and above all allow time to soak up the atmosphere and get lost in the maze of steep, narrow, winding, cobbled streets.

We leave Gefira on the coast road going south and after 4km, at Nomia, take the right, minor road. The views of waterfalls, terraced mountainsides and old vineyards (shades of Malmsey wine?) compensate for the condition of the road. After another 4km, with the road going steeply uphill, fork right again — the surface shortly improves — to **LIRA**. Turn left at the village square (perhaps after stopping for coffee and a plate of feta cheese and olives). The road surface and the scenery are both variable, and suddenly the countryside softens.

You soon see **ELLINIKO** on a hillside, one of those villages with houses straight out of a Greek postcard, all flaking blue shutters and doors. Go through the village and after 1km take the right fork, the upper road. A graffiti sign on a wall reads Neapoli.

At 1km intervals take 2 more right forks. After another 1km — civilisation! — you come to some houses. Take the left fork at the next junction (1km) — you're down to the medieval paved surface by now, which is actually a slight improvement — through the extremely rural hamlet of Criovrissi. Turn right when you come to the 'main' road, to Pandanassa and (in 6km) Elika — sparing a moment for coastal views of massive rock formations. A glance at one's watch shows that it's 1½ hours since leaving Gerifa.

Continue on the road to **DEMONIA**, a friendly, busy little village with an infectiously bright mood. Dried sausages are the local speciality — you see them hanging everywhere, in shop windows and over kitchen stoves in houses. One butcher (his corner shop has a *psistaria* taverna-grill sign outside) cooks his chunky and highly-spiced sausages in the back of the shop. Enjoyed with chunks of bread, a salad and a glass of the local red wine, there's no better lunch to be had; at least, not in Demonia.

Take the left, minor road out of the village. It is signposted Papadianika and Asopos; take that route. At Asopos turn left, past the large basilica and immediately right, behind it, to **ELIA** (9km, with mountain views along the way). Take the left, coastal, road (the surface improves at this point) at Elia, the hive of local market gardening industry, with tomatoes and strawberries the main crops.

The road leads in 11km to **KATO GLIKOVRISI**. Turn left at the cross-roads (no signpost) and fork right at the sports ground. Go on through **ASTERI**, where prehistoric remains have been found. After 5km take a left fork, on to a road fanned on either side by curtains of parchment-coloured reeds, to **ELOS**. Turn right at a T-junction in the village. In 3km turn left on to the road for **SKALA**, the modern market town (pop: 2,500) of the plain.

Take the Sparta road, which at this point heads almost due west, as far as **KROKEES**, famous in antiquity for little more than its stone quarries. Turn left there. In 4km, at Hania Vas, the minor road joins the main Gytheio-Sparta highway. Turn right. In 25km, through olive groves and mulberry plantations, crossing first one and then another tributary of the Eurotas, and coming increasingly under the shadow of **Mt. Taigetos**, the road reaches **SPARTA**.

Modern **SPARTA** (pop: 10,500), the capital of Laconia and an important agricultural centre — figs, olives and citrus are fruitfully farmed through the valley — dates from only 1834. Its straight streets lined with orange trees are built on the site of **Ancient Sparta**, the city of 10,000 warriors and their many slaves who (9C to 4C BC) dominated the Peloponnese (except Argos) and eventually the whole of Greece. Little exists of this once-powerful state but the remains of the Acropolis (north of the modern town and signposted), the base of a temple and, screened by oleanders and rushes on the river bank, the remains of the Sanctuary of Artemis Orthia. It was here that the young Spartiates undertook the stringent ritual endurance tests which made them such all-conquering heroes. There are many hotels in the town, eg: **Xenia**, 0731/26.524; **Lida**, 0731/23.601. Tourist Police: 0731/28.701.

With its glorious past so far behind it, modern Sparta is (as far as this tour is concerned) but a stepping-stone to Mistra, 5km to the west and well signposted.

MISTRA lies peacefully at the foothills of Mt. Taigetos, the ruins of a medieval city, once a glittering outpost of the Byzantine Empire. It stands in magnificent ruins, an open-air 'museum' of churches, monasteries, palaces and houses lining narrow, winding streets. The city was (and still is) dominated by a castle (built 1249). A modern road ascends the hill and stops just short of it. Within the rugged walls which defended both the upper (*Ano Hora*) and lower (*Kato Hora*) towns are some of the finest examples of 14C and 15C Byzantine architecture to be seen anywhere.

The setting is perfect, the golden stone buildings, many of them capped by intricate tiled rooflines, outlined against a background of thickly-wooded mountains. Plasterer bees build mud nests in the mouldings, butterflies brush the scenery with brilliant colour — lemon-yellow brimstones, dappled whites, large tortoiseshells and swallowtails are all there for the spotting.

The lower town comprises many of the ecclesiastical buildings, the cathedral (early 14C, bas relief 2-headed Byzantine eagle on the floor), the church of the Evangelistria (14C, sculpture decoration) and the monastic complex, the Vrontokhion with 2 churches, Ag. Theodori, the oldest in Mistra (late 13C and recently restored), and Pan. Hodegetria (early 14C, frescoed portraits).

Among the treasures of the upper town are a small mosque, a Turkish bath and a rare Byzantine civic building, the great Palace of the Despots (grand hall well preserved) with its church, Ag. Sophia.

At a short distance are the Pantanassa, the church built in 1365 and now belonging to a nunnery (external staircase, fine frescoes) and the Perivteptos monastery (its church, 14C, fine frescoes).

In late May each year a Paleologia, sound and light show, is held in the city. Hotel: **Byzantion**, 0731/93.309.

Return to Sparta, 5km. There are good, easy roads to both Gytheio (47km to the south) and Kalamata (60km to the west) for Messini, where other tours begin.

Messinia

2 days/175km/from Messini (21km west of Kalamata) to Tholo

This is a tour of exhilarating contrasts; an exciting overland voyage of discovery. The route starts in the flat-as-a-pancake fertile plain around the new town of Messini, well-watered by the Pamisos river and crisscrossed by agricultural roads which we take to reach the ancient site of Messeni (whose name was borrowed, confusingly, centuries later by its southern neighbour).

Soon the topographical and architectural contrasts begin. We strike off into the mountains, visiting hillside villages on the way to Karitena, a glorious medieval town which seems to encapsulate the whole magic of Byzantine architecture.

The craggy, uncompromising mountain scenery (much the same description could be applied to the road) leaves the visitor ill prepared for the magnificent elegance of the Temple of Bassae, surely one of the most majestic and least acknowledged wonders of Ancient Greece. The road

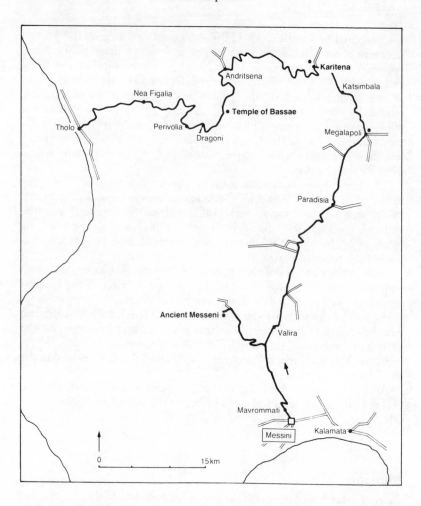

presents a difficult climb, but choose a good day, take your time and a picnic and you wouldn't have missed it for the world.

After Bassae, anything is an anti-climax. The track, linking scattered, isolated and friendly villages, belongs to the animals — sheep with black-patched faces, curled horns and long, floppy ears, and shaggy-coated goats attending bell-ringing practice as they leap from rock to rock.

The tour ends, as it began, in a green and fertile valley close to the coast in this fascinating south-western region of the Peloponnese.

MESSINI (pop: 6,000) principal town of the Markaria Plain, is an important agricultural centre. Rice is the main crop of the well-watered fertile plain, with olives, figs, grapes and citrus fruits all plentiful. Hotel: **Drossia**, 0722/232.48.

Leave Messini by the Triodos road, going north up the Pamisos valley.

Keep straight on at Triodos (5km), through Eva to Lambena (7km) and there turn left. Fork right after 3km and in 5km turn right on to the Ithomi road, which climbs quite steeply. These by-roads can be confusing, and if in doubt ask for Ancient (or *archaea*) Messeni, and be sure you are travelling generally northwards.

At **ITHOMI** turn left to **MAVROMMATI**, a pleasant village occupying part of the site of Ancient Messeni. (This *is* confusing. There's a Mavrommati a couple of kilometres north of the new town of Messini, 30km south of here.) At the far end of the village the footpath leading to the ancient city is clearly marked, archaeological site.

Ancient Messeni was built in AD 369 in a hollow in 3 hills, a magnificent setting for the ruins we can explore today. The 9km city wall, well preserved, is a fine example of military architecture complete, as it is, with gates and towers. The footpath leads down to the Sanctuary dedicated to Asclepios, the foundations of a temple and the wall of a theatre (corbelled archways). A small theatre has been restored. To the west, a group including the Temple of Artemis Orthia and to the south, remains of the Stadium. From Laconia Gate a steep path leads to the summit of **Mt. Ithomi** (798m), the Citadel and Voulkano Convent, on the site of an Altar-sanctuary to Zeus Ithomatas, where human sacrifices were made. Allow 1½ hours return. As always, the steeper the climb, the more rewarding the views.

Return to the main road and take the one which crosses the Pamisos to **VALIRA** (8km). Prickly pear bushes line the road, not one of the smoothest in Greece. Turn left in the village to **SKALA** (5km) where take the right fork. At the next T-junction, turn left on to a more major road, signposted to Tripoli and with a rash of exclamation marks and double-S-bend signs. The road crosses the railway and later climbs sharply. The plain looks even flatter. **DERVENI**, on a high ridge, is 15km from Skala, and has a two-table *kafenion*. A welcome stop. The road continues to **PARADISIA**, a village surrounded by rocky outcrops, and thence to **MEGALAPOLI**, a small modern town in the upper Alfios Valley and now best known for its thermal power station. Turn left in the town, following signs to Andritsena, and on the left (1km) you come to the ruins of the ancient city (4C BC). In guidebook shorthand, **Ancient Megalapolis** is worth a squint, if only because the theatre was the largest in Ancient Greece, built to hold 20,000 spectators. Only the first few rows remain, the rest are cushioned with grass and the whole arena is attractively ringed with trees. The assembly hall, which held 10,000, has a new thick-pile carpet — of blue speedwell.

Continuing in the same direction, the road is less than scenic, but matters soon improve. At **KATSIMBALA** (after 8km) there are beckoning views of mountain peaks; 7km farther on, fork right to **KARITENA**. In the distance, you can see the medieval town, built on an isolated hill, in all its glory. Stop in the square.

A steep, stepped path climbs to the Frankish castle (built in 1254 at

583m) on the summit of a high rock (vaulted hall, cisterns). During the War of Independence Ibrahim Pasha was defied by its fortifications. Back at street level, 2 churches, Panageia (11C Frankish belfry) and Ag. Nikolas, a multi-domed Byzantine church in a deep hollow. Ask for the key — the interior is covered with 11C, 13C and 15C frescoes, many in good condition. The old houses climbing the hillside are mostly abandoned in favour of a new village built at the foothills.

Turn right out of the village on to the Andritsena road, passing the villages of Kotilio (in 10km) and (in another 8km) **THISSOA**, with pretty stone houses trickling down the hillside. Turn left for Andritsena. We are now in lonely shepherd country, and climbing. The scenery is majestic. Another 12km brings **ANDRITSENA**, a mountain village whose charm has almost survived the centuries. There is a folkloric museum in the square, and shepherds' crooks are the main item on the shopping list. Hotel: **Theoxenia**, 0626/222.19.

Take the right fork out of the village. Drive with great care because the road follows a high, narrow mountain ridge. Fork right again in 14km. There is a sign to **The Temple of Bassae**. At a height of 1,141m it stands, on a narrow, rocky terrace of **Mt. Paliavlakitsa**. This magnificent Temple of Apollo Epikourios is larger than the Parthenon in Athens, matches it for grandeur and, experts think, predates it. The temple (c425 BC) is built of dark grey local limestone, 38.5m long and 14.75m wide with 6 by 15 columns. Perhaps because of its remoteness — a more wild and rugged setting is hard to imagine — the Temple is in a remarkable state of preservation. (Currently enclosed in a tent for restoration, but accessible.) The site of **Ancient Bassae** (also Vasses), with an easily discernible floor plan, walls and column bases, is extensive. Dotted with oaks and almond trees and sprinkled with wild flowers it is pleasant as well as engrossing in summer; carpeted with snow into late spring and watched over by hooded crows, a bleak prospect but still not to be missed.

With due care and attention take the track south and then west from Vasses (the modern name), passing through (in 7km) **DRAGONI**. Here the road crosses a stream, a useful aid to food preparation. Women sometimes gather under the shade of fig trees, winding offal around vine twigs for *kokoretsi*, the *souvla* of family and taverna meals. From a distance, they seem to be wool spinning. Fork right 2km beyond there — a stream of bright blue irises shows the way in springtime — for **PERIVOLIA**, where remains of a Doric temple were recently found. Bear right out of the village, and bear with it. The track — rough in places — winds through terraced fields and a lengthy community of stone shepherds' huts. At 8km from Perivolia, fork left on to the lower road, signed to **PETRALONA**, which is reached in 3km. Turn right in front of the church, and suddenly the scene changes. The wild landscape is transformed. It becomes soft and gentle, and the views are amazing. There's a cross-roads 7km from the village. Go straight across, taking the road to **NEA FIGALIA**. After about 1½ hours of mountain track, it seems like the metropolis! A general store serves coffee, and the owner wants to know how many eagle owls one has spotted *en route*. Turn right at the

T-junction in the village and follow the now-improved road, through Lepreo, to **THOLO**, on the main north-south coastal road, where this tour ends.

You can turn right here for **PIRGOS**, 40km on a good road, where another tour starts. (Hotel at **ZAHARO**, 7km from Tholo: **Nestor**, 0625/312.06.) Or turn left to **KIPARISSIA** (Hotel: **Artemis**, 0761/221.45).

[Anyone not wishing to undertake the mountain driving involved in this tour has a pleasant alternative. Take the coast road from Messini round the south-western point, through Methoni and the port of Pilos, to the legendary Nestor's Palace (1300–1200 BC) with its throne room and furnished bathroom. Continue on this road to Tholo.]

Mani

1–2 days/200km/from Gytheio (on the Laconian Gulf) to Kalamata

Wild. Remote. Timeless. Barren. Fascinating. Anachronistic. Photogenic. The Mani is all of these things. And, on a good day, it is beautiful.

The region forms the southern spur of Mt. Taigetos extending between the Messenian and Laconian Gulfs, and in fact represents the most southerly point of mainland Greece. The terrain is uncompromisingly rugged — impenetrably so in places — but our route takes to roads which make light work of the gradients.

Mani has a troubled past. Its inhabitants, pagan until late 9C and probably descended from the Spartans, were driven from northern Laconia in 7C by the Slavs, an indignity they were not to forget. They eventually settled in tribal villages in this austere region, trusting no one and clinging to their autonomy — not an easy task in the face of the advancing armies of Franks, Byzantines, Venetians and Turks, against whom they fought savagely in the War of Independence. It was only in 1834 that the Maniots reluctantly agreed to become part of the new kingdom.

The domestic scene was no more harmonious than the political one. Living under the dominance of tribal chiefs, families confronted families in bitter feuds which were avenged for centuries. In 17C Sir George Wheeler wrote that the Maniots were 'famous as pirates by sea and pestilent robbers by land'.

Their houses reflected their isolationism: square towers, some 25m tall, built of irregular blocks of stone and with the minimum of small, high windows serving 3 or 4 storeys. Like castle keeps, the towers rise in groups on the hillsides, most now deserted, some still occupied, and a few being carefully restored. Some, open to the elements, are thus also open to visitors and one (in Areopoli) is converted as a comfortable guest house.

Our tour starts at the sea port of Gytheio, crosses to the west coast and explores first Inner or Deep Mani, south of the valley at Areopoli, and

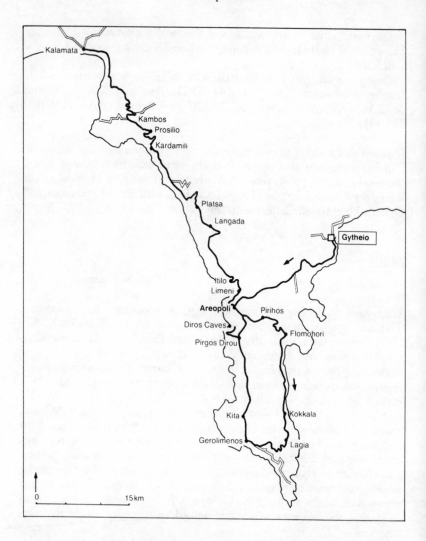

then Outer Mani, to the north. For good measure and an exciting boat trip the tour takes in the famous Diros caves.

One last word on the subject — the Maniots today are as warmly welcoming people you will find anywhere in Greece.

GYTHEIO (or GITHIO) (pop: 4,900), the port of both ancient and modern Sparta, is connected to Athens by a regular ferry-boat service, and is a popular port of call for international cruise ships (whose passengers can be in Mistra within half an hour). This is when the water-front comes alive, with donkeys and bicycle-carts laden with oranges, cakes, bon-bons, peanuts, rusks, trinkets and sponges turning the cobbled landing-stage into an instant and noisy market-place. At other times the town seems to sink into reverie. The neo-classic-style houses, painted in sun-bleached pastel colours, are built in tiers on a steep, rocky hill — a dramatic contrast to the unrelieved grey stone architecture of the Mani. The site of the ancient city — Herakles and Apollo were claimed as joint founders — is 1km from the shore (small theatre; museum). Hotel: **Lakonis**, 0733/22.666. Tourist Police: 0733/22.236.

Take the Areopoli road parallel to the coast and heading west — good views across the Gulf to the island of Kithera. Just beyond Mavrovouni (5km) there are Mykinean chamber tombs on a sandy hill to the right. The road crosses the **Passava** plain and passes the village of that name (ruins of a Frankish castle), and soon there are the first sightings of grey, gaunt Mani towers. Continue until (25km from Gytheio) the road joins the north-south coastal road.

AREOPOLI is the main village of Mani, with tower houses on the outskirts and 'conventional' stone houses, shops and cafes around 2 squares in the centre (18C church, primitive reliefs of martial saints). One of the towers, on a windswept hillside, has been converted by the National Tourist Office of Greece as a guest house, **Kapetanakos**, 0733/51.233.

To reach Deep Mani, take the Kotronas road, south out of Areopoli. In 3km, at **PIRIHOS**, there's a typical cluster of towers, an architectural taste of things to come. One's impression may depend on the weather. On a warm, spring day when the towers, shafted with sunlight, rise from a wide moat of snow-white marguerites, mauve anemones and yellow aconites, the scene is pastoral and mellow. On a grey and drizzly day, the word sombre comes to mind.

At **FLOMOHORI** turn right. The road, on a ridge cut low down into the mountainside, follows the coastline, through Nifi, to **KOKKALA**. A little domed chapel, a voluptuous contrast to the cubist towers, stands on a promontory on the wild and stony shore, its slender iron bell tower a separate silhouette.

LAGIA (pop: 80!) comes next, in 8km. Some towers around the stony square are being restored; shiny-bright sailing boats beached in the court-yards strike an incongruous note. Wander off-centre for close-up and distant views of tower-houses in — it seems — equally well fortified gardens. With enormous restraint, one refrains from mentioning the wild flowers again: campion, hellebores, sea stock, cranesbill ... An olive farmer issues a cheery invitation for coffee and a chat about current affairs. The big thing is the telephone. Old ladies swathed in black long to phone their sons and daughters in Athens, for this area has suffered more than most from migration to the cities. He puts them through.

Turn right at Alika, across a desolate rocky plateau to **GEROLIM-ENOS**. A small, pebbly bay is closely guarded by watchful towers and, rising steeply, the backdrop of rocks is pitted with caves. Continue on the road to (in 4km) **KITA**.

This is fertile ground for exploration, with a primitive, barrel-vaulted chapel and dozens of towers to wander around, some used now as donkey shelters and shepherds' huts, others as summer houses by city folk. If the season is right, banks of wild asparagus colonise the track, and rock nuthatches chirp noisily from their nests in the rocks. Go through the village and turn left on to the old road (a new house faces the entrance).

Back on the modern road, turn left. A sign at **MEZAPOS** points to sea sports in the bay. Continue for 13km, then take the road on the left, signposted to **PIRGOS DIROU** and the caves. The village, on a bay of the Messenian Gulf, was famous even before the caves were discovered. In 1826, anticipating an invasion, the women of Mani lay in wait with their sickles. The intruders chose the easy way out, and jumped into the sea.

There are 2 **Diros caves**, the Alepotripa, discovered only in 1958 and covering an area of 6,500 sq.m, and Glyfada, or Vlychada, which extends to 16,700 sq.m through more than 2,800 waterways and over 300 dry passages. Alepotripa has been closed for restoration and further exploration, and so one can only read of the magnificent 'grand hall', the simulated statues, the lake and the rock drawings of this outstanding Neolithic find.

Glyfada is a subterranean wonderland of vividly colourful stalactites, and stalagmites rising, red, pink, yellow, blue, from the slow-flowing river which carries the semi-salt water out to the sea. The interior decoration of alabaster arabesque compositions includes areas known as the 'cathedral', the 'dragon's cavern', the 'sea of wreckage' and others. The tour, by paddle-boat with a guide, takes 30 minutes.

Snack bar, taverna, bathing with changing rooms near by. Tourist Police: 0733/52.222.

Retrace 5km to the main road and turn left, towards Areopoli. Go through the village, keeping to the coast road (signposted Kalamata) and in 5km turn off left to **LIMENI**, a truly picturesque Maniot fishing port, the cottages turning their backs on the open Gulf and the long main street a curiosity of tiny shops. It's the perfect place to while away an hour or so.

Back on the Kalamata route, the coastal scenery becomes spectacular, the road a friendly meeting-place with wandering donkeys, sheep and goats. **ITILO**, viewed from above, nestles on the side of a ravine, the towers mellowed by the warmth of tiled roofs and dwarfed by slender rockets of cypress trees. Its name has remained unchanged since the days of Homer, and a potent, reddish-brown wine is still made there.

The road continues, through Ag. Nikon, to (5km beyond) **LANGADA**, its tower-houses rising in terraces. Shortly after, you can see **TRAHILA** (cave) on the deserted coast below and then there is **PLATSA**, one of the many Upper Maniot villages with little rounded Byzantine churches. In 20km of diverting coastal scenery and the scent of wild thyme, a bird's-eye view of **KARDAMILI**, a seaside village set in olive groves and with a fortified off-shore island (medieval castle, Mykinean rock-cuttings). There are bright shops, cafés and an air of comparative sophistication.

In another 8km, **PROSILIO** seems designed for photography, the village crowned by a large basilica, making a compact triangle on the hillside. At **STAVROPIGI** the road forks and in the shade of high mountain peaks, take the upper road, inland and to the right, crossing (in 1km) a stone bridge at **KAMBOS**, where turn left, soon to pass a huge, heavily wooded ravine. At **ALMIRO** the route joins the coast road again (camping facilities near by) and continues, through the dreary city outskirts, to **KALAMATA**. Hotels: **Elite**, 0721/250.15; **Filoxenia**, 0721/231.66. Tourist Police: 0721/231.87.

Ilia and Ahaia

2–3 days / 235km / from Pirgos to Patra

The tour through this north-western region of the Peloponnese represents a microcosm of much of what Greece has to offer. It sets out in the fertile

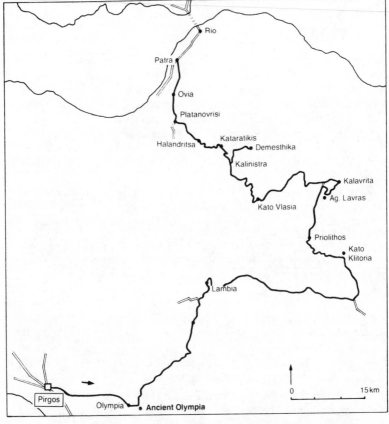

plain that creates such a verdant and leafy setting for Olympia, one of the most magnificent treasures to have spanned the centuries and be spread before us, giving a glimpse and understanding of the ancient world.

After so thought-provoking a visit, the route takes to the hills — high mountains, to be exact — through out-of-the-way villages to Kalavrita, set among spectacular scenery and close to a ski resort, before gradually descending to another green and fertile plain colour-washed in springtime with fruit blossom and wild flowers.

A suitable caption to parts of this tour could be 'exploring extremely rural Greece'.

PIRGOS (pop: 20,600) Busy market town, centre of the currant trade. It has large, open squares and neo-classical public buildings (market, municipal theatre). Hotels: **Alkistis**, 0621/236.61; **Olympos**, 0621/236.50. Tourist Police: 0621/236.85. Near-by (11km west) at **KATAKOLO** submerged ruins of the ancient city of Fia can be seen.

Leave Pirgos going eastwards, on the road signposted to **OLYMPIA** (17km). Take the Tripoli road from the new village to the archaeological site. Another much-visited inheritance from the ancient world, which was already flourishing in Mykinean times, this is a site most appreciated out of the high season, or in the early morning.

Ancient Olympia is situated in the lush, green valley of the Alfios, the largest river of the Peloponnese, well shaded by olives, pines and deciduous trees. It was a sacred precinct (not a city) of temples, ecclesiastical and official residences and buildings connected with the Olympic Games. For the duration of the Games, held regularly every 4 years from 776 BC to AD 393 when, with other pagan festivals, they were banned, there was a truce between warring city-states so that young men could leave the battlefield to compete. (The Games were first revived in Athens, 1896.)

Zeus was the sovereign god of Olympia and his statue in gold and ivory housed in the temple in his honour was one of the 7 wonders of the ancient world. Also see: the Temple of Hera, the Echo Portico, the treasuries, the wrestling school, remains of the running track, council house and museums. Hotels: **Amalia**, 0624/221.90; **Hercules**, 0624/225.32. Tourist Police: 0624/225.50. Archaeological Museums: 0624/227.42 and 225.79. Large car park, comprehensive bookstall (a site plan is helpful) and refreshments.

Turn left out of the car park, going eastwards, and in 1km fork left, taking the road signposted to Lambia. A feature of the road, which soon starts a gradual ascent, is the larch trees hung with cocoon-like birds' nests. Bear left at Miraka and continue through the modern village of **LALA** (17km from the site). Clusters of sky-blue beehives are placed to take advantage of the rich vegetation, and soon there are choose-your-superlative views of mountains filling the horizon. The road continues through copses of

The Temple of Hera, Ancient Olympia

evergreen oak with only an occasional shepherd's hut; 15km from Lala the surface changes from asphalt to rough, and 3km farther on, where it improves again, there is a T-junction. Turn right, signposted to Tripoli. The route, a joyful one because of the scenery, is lined now with broom. **LAMBIA**, a village nestling in the mountains, is picturesque, the houses having painted wooden balconies and deep overhanging roofs to protect them from snow. There is a bustle of *kafenions* and tavernas and even the butchers' shops are open on Sundays. (Just before and just after the village, monasteries sometimes open to visitors.)

The road continues on a low ridge over the mountains. I wish you could meet, as I did, an elderly man leading a donkey carrying 4 small canvas panniers. Snugly tucked up in each one — a tiny baby goat. In 14km, through lush grazing land, **TRIPOTAMA**, the main feature of which is the petrol station, and in another 14km a junction, at which, straight on. This section is the main Patra to Tripoli road, easy riding through gentle pastures. A sharp left turn, a U-bend, 13km from the junction, is signed to Kato Klitoria on a minor road through fields of maize. In another 3km, turn left at a major junction, along a river valley sheltered by mountains (can there be a more pleasant picnic spot?). Go straight on at the next junction (4km) and take the right fork, the lower road, at the next (3km).

Known locally as Mazeika, **KATO KLITORIA** is a market village at the junction of 2 valleys, its large square the centre of agricultural and horticultural trade and well supported by cafés and tavernas. Home-made sausages a speciality.

Leave the village by the Kalavrita road, going west, and passing a tempting sign (1km, left) to Ancient Klitoria. The full extent of the track, 2km and crossing a river and watercress beds, is not always passable by vehicle or on foot, but it makes a delightful detour. The road soon passes Ano Klitoria high on a hill, and opens out to spectacular views of mountain peaks rising like pyramids from the plain. There is a well signposted (to Kalavrita) right fork and, in 4km, the road descends to **PRIOLITHOS** at the head of the Vouraikos valley, a pretty village set among fruit trees, splashed by waterfalls and with a chirpy air of well-being. **LAGOVOUNI** is the next landmark along the valley. In 14km take a right turn signposted to **Ag. Lavra Monastery**. Pass the building on the left to approach by the front entrance. The monastery was founded AD 961, some buildings burnt by the Turks in 1821 and again by the Germans in 1943. See: 17C church, museum (icons, manuscripts, gold and silver ware). Open mornings and evenings, and there is a guest house. A path signposted Paleion Monasterion leads (30 minutes return, on foot) to the original hermitage. A near-by hillock bears a War of Independence monument.

This loop-road continues to **KALAVRITA** (pop: 1,950), situated at 763m on the Vouraikos at the foot of **Mt. Velia**. A narrow-gauge railway, connecting the town with Diakofto on the north-eastern coast of the Peloponnese, is nominated by railway and landscape buffs as one of the most beautiful stretches of track anywhere. The modern town of Kalavrita, more appreciated for its surroundings than for its contrived new architecture, is overshadowed by its past, and has become a place of pilgrimage. A monument on a hill, a simple white cross, commemorates the massacre in 1943 of 1,436 males by the German occupying forces. The metropolitan church clock stands, poignantly, stopped for ever at 2.34 when the tragedy began. Part of the town was then burnt to the ground.

A baker's sells deliciously varied and unusual country breads — stand in the centre of town and your nose will guide you — just the thing for a picnic. There is a good choice of cafés and tavernas and, 15km from the town, a ski centre. Hotel: **Chelmos**, 0692/222.17.

Leave the town on the Patra road, heading west across the valley through the gap between **Panakhaion** and the rugged peaks of **Erimanthos**. Mountain villages offer an occasional greeting: Flamboura (in 16km) and **BOUMBOUKA** (7km farther) with its distinctly Turkish appearance. The road is steep. It reaches 1,076m before slowly winding down (in 9km) to **KATO** (lower) **VLASIA**, and then as surely climbing again. There are magnificent mountain views around every turn — and plenty of those. The villages of Kombigadi and then **KALINISTRA**, which is 18km from the village in the valley, and the route in springtime is alight with sunshine yellow Jerusalem sage and broom and blue streams of wild iris. A minor road to the right leads (10km) through vineyards to **DEMESTHIKA** where the Achaia-Clauss wines are produced. The village is way, way off the beaten track, and visitors are greeted like old friends, with much clinking of glasses.

Back on the road, **KATARATIKIS** (6km) lies in a valley bursting with greenness. Houses high on the hillside hide behind window-box geraniums and sheep graze under almond trees. At **HALANDRITSA** (8km), once a Frankish barony, rugs and blankets hanging over iron balconies to dry turn the village into one big tapestry. Fork right, on to the top road. The high-peak views are stunning. From **PLATANO-VRISI** (5km) one has a bird's-eye view to the west, over the patchwork fields of the plain. In 3km turn right on to the main Patra road. **OVIA** looks like — and is — a suburb of the city, now only 6km away.

PATRA (pop: 141,000) Third largest city in Greece, rebuilt in 1821 after the Turks had razed the medieval town. It is designed on a grid plan (which does not facilitate route-finding). Heavy industry includes the manufacture of cotton and motor-tyres, and the port handles the export of olive oil, currants, wine and sheep and goats' hides which are processed there. At pre-Lenten carnival time, Patra takes the lead in local merry-making. King Carnival heads a long procession, the people wear fancy dress and on the last Sunday (be prepared!) it is the custom to throw chocolates from car windows on to balconies and the passing crowds. Hotels: **Agropole**, 061/27.98.09; **Galaxy**, 061/27.88.15. Tourist Police: 061/22.09.02. Automobile Touring Club: 061/42.54.11. Archaeological museum (Neolithic, Mykinean and Roman finds): 061/27.50.70.

[The ferry port of **RIO** (8km east of Patra) has half-hourly car-ferry connections to Antirrio, across the Gulf in Central Greece. The crossing takes 20 minutes. Hotel in Rio: **Georgios**, 061/99.26.27.]

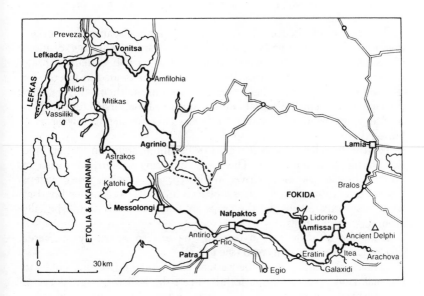

The official name for the diverse and widespread area of Central Greece, the region that is left when one has divided off the Peloponnese to the south, Epirus and Thessaly to the north, and Macedonia and Thrace farther north and to the west, is Sterea Ellada. Its popular name, the one insisted on by the inhabitants, proud of their Roman heritage and the many battles fought here, is Roumeli, the land of Rome.

This region more than any other is divided by high mountains, a fact that has had a significant effect on its political and military history. The southern Pindos chain running north-south effects a formidable barrier between west and east, separating regions to either side that have few common characteristics. Indeed, only one road has the temerity to cross the massive southern group, the spectacular helter-skelter route between Agrinio in the west and Lamia to the east.

Just south of Lamia is the Pass of Thermopylae, which in antiquity was the only practical route from Athens for a sizeable land force. The gap, just over 6km long, ran between the sea and precipitous mountains — erosion and eruption have since considerably altered the lie of the land. It was narrow at both ends and widened in the middle, where the hot springs were that gave the pass its name. History was made here. In 480 BC Leonidas, commanding 300 Spartans against the massive forces of Xerxes, was asked to surrender because it was feared that the Persian arrows would eclipse the sun. 'All the better, then we can fight in the shade', he retorted. But his gallantry was not rewarded with victory. His troops were attacked from the rear, and buried there.

Throughout the centuries forces have marched on and through this territory, many of them on their way to claim the rich prize of the Thessalian plain.

This history of Greece is heavy with its resistance against the Turkish invasion, and Sterea Ellada, and one town in particular is no exception. Messolongi, strategically situated on the Gulf of Patra, is virtually a shrine to the memory of Lord Byron. It was here that he landed in Greece for the second time; where he joined the citizens in their struggle, and perhaps gave them the moral courage and organisational know-how to hold out against the Turks for two years after his death. His heart is buried there.

For the traveller, this is a region of beautiful mountain scenery and rich, fertile, verdant plains. The cool, refreshing western peninsula of Etolia is host to the longest river in Greece, the Achelos, which widens into a fertile basin where olives, tobacco and early vegetables flourish, while eastwards, in Fokida, the crops are cotton, cereals and, especially around Amfissa, olives.

Evia, the off-shore island forming the eastern boundary of Sterea Ellada, has a section all its own (see p. 87).

Lefkas, the island just off the western coast of the region and linked to the mainland by a causeway, forms part of the Ionian group. Its access from Central Greece is so easy, however, and its allure so irresistible, that a tour is included in this section.

Etolia and Akarnania

1–2 days/240km/from Antirio to Agrinio, with optional excursion, 72km, around Lake Trichonis

This far-western peninsula of Central Greece, composing the side-by-side districts of Etolia and Akarnania, seems to be almost slipping into the waiting arms of the sea, ever anxious to claim another island in the Ionian group. From Messolongi, the town turned shrine, where Byron died of a fever fighting for the cause of freedom, north to Amfilohia, the military base established by Ali Pasha, where fish are farmed and water-birds conserved, the territory is rippled with large lakes and lagoons. One large wave (the Piscean imagination runs riot) and the whole territory would drift off towards Lefkas!

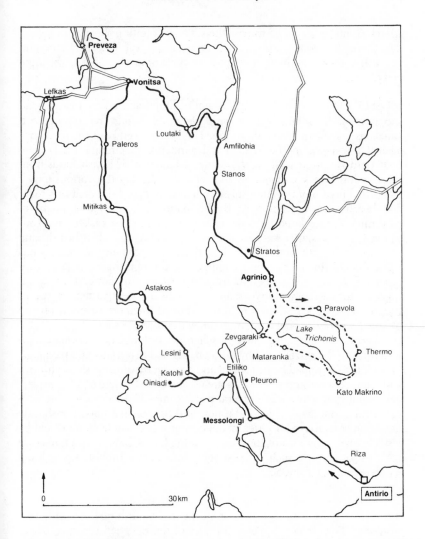

This is a route to take at leisure, to spot countless species of birds on the wing and waders, and enjoy a meal of fresh farm trout in a waterside taverna.

ANTIRIO, the port linked by a frequent 20-minute ferry service with Rio, across the 'Little Dardanelles' on the north coast of the Peloponnese, is all hustle and bustle, bright new buildings, busy cafés — and quick exit roads. See: impressive medieval fortress, known as Roumeli Castle. Turn left, direction Ioanina, through the narrow coastal plain. Olive groves, copses of cypress and ribbons of pink and white oleander paint the landscape for a while. At **RIZA** (5km) the road starts a long ascent and winds round a mountain ridge. This isn't the most exhilarating of stretches, but gives scope to pass the time by counting sheep. On a clear day there are good retrospective views across the bay to Patra and beyond, even to the high, wide peak of the Erimanthos. Cross the wide bed of the river Evinos and in 11km turn left.

MESSOLONGI (pop: 11,500) Capital of Etolia and Akarnania, a good shopping and banking centre with plenty of hotels, restaurants and *kafenions*; excellent pastry-shops too. This was the centre of the resistance against the Turks in the War of Independence (beginning 1822). The poet Lord Byron arrived on the scene in January 1824 with funds from the London Greek Committee and set about uniting the various Greek factions. Three months later, mission unaccomplished, he died of a fever and became, as he still is, a British national hero. Three weeks of mourning was declared, and his embalmed body (in a casket in a 180-gallon barrel of spirit) was despatched to London via Zakynthos. Facing an impossible task and 10,000 Egyptian reinforcements 2 years later, 9,000 Greeks (including whole families) fled through the town gate, since named Exodus, only to be ambushed by Albanians. Fewer than 2,000 made it to the comparative safety of Amfissa. See: garden; statue of Byron erected 1881 where his heart is buried; memorial garden on site of house where the poet died, museum with a Byron room.

There is another, quite different side to Messolongi, the vast lagoon on which it stands, surrounded by salt marshes and fish farms and navigable only by flat-bottomed boats. Sheep and goats graze on tiny islands fringed with beds of reeds and rushes; the area is a wildfowl sanctuary of considerable significance; there are several gypsy camps like kaleidoscopes, with colourful garments draped on bushes, and fishermen's huts, ramshackle affairs on stilts, have an Oriental appearance. The whole scene would be visually idyllic were it not for the infuriating Greek habit — on a massive scale — of turning such isolated spots into public rubbish tips. Hotel: **Theoxenia**, 0631/28.050.

Leave the town by the Exodus Gate and take the lower coastal road on the left, going westwards. Look out for the unusual fishing boats with long whip-cord-flexible net supports, a legacy of the Egyptian presence. After 4km of mud and salt flats and more gypsy camps, **PLEURON**, close to the road but accessible only to the persistent, owing to waterworks and a steep gradient. The reward: the 3C BC circuit walks of 'New' Pleuron, some 15 courses of stone with 36 towers and 7 gates; ruins of theatre, agora, cistern, acropolis towers. (The city of Old Pleuron was destroyed in 234 BC.) Continue on the coast road through fields and fields of rice and take the left turn, signposted Etiliko, crossing a bridge over calm water. The medieval refuge town, strategically built on an island between 2 lagoons, is joined to the mainland by a stone bridge at each end. See: 15C church of Panageia (wall paintings).

Turn right out of the village, signposted Astakos, through flat landscape of the spot-the-crops kind — cotton, oranges, olives and maize — and the villages of first Neohori and then **KATOHI**, crowned by a ruined medieval tower. Ignore (temporarily) if you wish the Astakos road and, 2km beyond the village, take, in turn, 2 tracks to the ruins of the ancient city of **Oiniadi**, wildly overgrown, surrounded by marshes and belonging now to the wildlife. Many a battle was fought here 5C–3C BC, until the Romans took it 211 BC. See: well-preserved fortifications, acropolis, and gates with arched openings on one site, late 3C BC theatre (inscriptions record freeing of slaves) on the other. Maritime enthusiasts will want to see, to the north, remains of ancient docks around a basin hewn in rock. Return along the track and now rejoin the Astakos road, through intensely agricultural villages where tractors are more numerous than motor-cars. Follow the signposts, turning right at **LESINI**, a village wrapped in cotton plantations.

The road climbs inland with vineyards increasing in ratio to the height, and there are good and extensive misty-island views to the left. The pretty (of the peeling-paintwork kind) fishing village of **ASTAKOS** (pop: 3,000), at the head of a small bay seems itself to be on an island. There's a mini fish market in the smallest of cottages with a blue door, seabirds wade in the harbour, massive watermelons are piled high on the pavements, mulberry trees cast dappled shade along the sea front and the tavernas are crowded with fishermen enjoying the fruits of their labours — and encouraging visitors to eat herring-sized fish head-first and whole.

Leave the village by the coastal road going westwards. Turn left by the Eko petrol station, over the bridge, and the road bears left. There are good views back to the fishing village and an assortment of middle-of-the-road obstacles ahead, sleeping goats, black pigs and cattle. The 'asphaltos' road surface deteriorates alarmingly, but only for 500m. Detour to the left (31km from Astakos) to **MITIKAS**, a small and absolutely delightful fishing village with pretty little cottages hanging their balconies over the pebbly beach. One taverna even has tables and chairs along the whole length of a breakwater. Return to the main road, turn left and marvel at the views: gorse-covered sand dunes for miles, fiery yellow against sea blue. **PALEROS** comes in 19km, a fishing village with a yachting station and good facilities. Continue on the road, now following the signs to Vonitsa. Women working rhythmically across a field scatter seed by hand from shallow trays, and the scene is pastoral.

At **VONITSA** there is an important cross-roads. One road leads to Ag. Nikolaos and the road to the Ionian island of **LEFKAS** (see p. 41); one to the ferry for **PREVEZA**, the southernmost tip of Epirus (see p. 61) and the other, which this tour takes, to Amfilohia on the right. Vonitsa has neatly-laid-out gardens of oleander along the wide promenade, large hotels, smart shops and 2 elegant squares. It also has a small, tidy port and a Venetian citadel (1676).

The road from Vonitsa to **AMFILOHIA** (37km) sometimes hugs the coast, sometimes tacks through marshes and cotton fields and all along keeps a low profile. The town (pop: 4,700), deep-set in a narrow inlet in the gulf, was founded by Ali Pasha as a military base. There are extensive fish farms near by and good fish tavernas. The road continues southwards over rolling hills and along the shores of 2 lakes, both sanctuaries for water birds, passing through **STANOS** and **RIVIO**, both waterside villages, to **STRATOS**, which has seen better days. The new village sits humbly on the ruins of **Ancient Stratos**, once the capital of Akarnania. See: remains of 4C BC Doric Temple of Zeus; well-preserved 429 BC walls. A folk-dancing festival is held there in September. The road continues, crossing the **Achelos**, the longest river in Greece (215km), which rises in the Pindos mountains, forms a natural boundary between Etolia and Akarnania, and discharges into the sea west of Oiniadi, facing the tiny Ehinades islands. Its power has been harnessed for energy and irrigation. **AGRINIO** (pop: 31,000) is an important tobacco-growing centre, the capital of the region, linked by air to Athens and Ioanina. It is linked by road through the pretty mountain village of Karpenisi to **LAMIA** in the east (where another tour starts, see p. 48) by a spectacular pass across the Pindos range, and to **ANTIRIO** to the south, where this tour began.

Decision. Finish this tour at Agrinio, and be poised to take one of the 2 suggested exit roads, or add an optional excursion around **Lake Trichonis**, a round trip of 72km.

For the excursion, take the Karpenisi road from the town and turn right at the cross-roads (direction Thermo). The villages are rural and pretty, some high above orange groves and splashed by mountain streams (Mt. Vlohos rises to 615m to the east), others spread out along the lakeside and ringed by holm oaks. In 26km **THERMO**, the spiritual centre of the Pan-Aetolian League, who held elections of magistrates and an annual festival of fun and games here. Philip V of Macedon sacked the sanctuary 218 BC, destroying 2,000 statues. See: remains of Temple of Apollo Thermios (6C BC) and fountain, still working. Also, substantial remains of houses of prehistoric village. Museum, with Bronze Age, Mykinean and Geometric finds.

The road, rough in places, continues around the southern shore of the lake, a tranquil route pierced by the shrieking of birds and adorned by a brilliant palette of wild flowers. **KATO MAKRINO**, just off-shore, marks the southern tip. Take the left fork to Gabalo, where the road surface improves and **MATARANKA**. Continue to **ZEVGARAKI** (also known as Sikia) where the lakeland road meets the main route. Turn right to Agrinio, 11km to the north.

Fokida

2–3 days/270km/from Lamia

Two natural elements dominate the start of this tour, the towering Mt. Parnassos which rises sharply to 2,457 metres and presides, in this direction, over the whole of the Gulf of Corinth, and the site of the ancient Oracle of Delphi, situated in a remarkable stone amphitheatre facing the sea and harbouring at its base the Sanctuary of Apollo.

A pretty route through citrus and olive groves carpeted with wild flowers does nothing to prepare the visitor for the breathtakingly beautiful

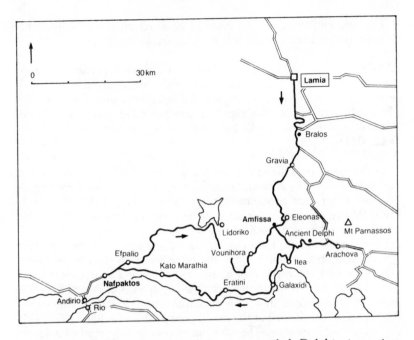

situation of the Oracle. Legend has surrounded Delphi since time immemorial. Ancient Greeks believed it to be the point where earth touched the divine. Zeus made two eagles fly in opposite directions, to locate the centre of the earth. On their return the eagles landed, together, here. In dangerously declining numbers but symbolic and majestic as ever, golden eagles still nest in the highest crags, as if they have been there for ever. The Sacred Way, the theatre, temples, the stadium that housed the Pythian Games, the museum — a whole day would scarcely be enough for a comprehensive study of this most evocative Classical inheritance. Even at a superficial level, Delphi in this wild, mountainous setting is absorbing and unforgettable.

The route continues to the mountain and ski resort of Arachova, bristling with energy and, for much of the year, with snow. It is bright, lively and fun, and a tempting market-place for local handicrafts and food specialities. A souvenir-hunter's paradise!

No apologies for the fact that Delphi and Arachova, two destinations that could scarcely contrast more vividly, form a turn-round-and-come-back detour totalling 40km.

After that, much of the pleasure derives from the journey, up hill (mountain, to be exact) and down dale through olive groves, craggy peaks, fertile valleys and coastal bays dotted with tiny fishing hamlets and fringed with good beaches.

The jewel of this stretch of the coastline is Galaxidi, a proud maritime town that has retired now into the shell of a picturesque fishing village. Charming, unassuming and unspoiled, it is the ideal place to let the world go by.

The tour ends in a sea of a different kind, returning to Amfissa, the pleasant market town in the fertile plain known as the sea of olives.

LAMIA (pop: 38,000) In Central Thessaly, a flourishing provincial market town in the heart of a fertile plain producing cotton, cereals and vegetables. Sheltered by 2 densely wooded hills, the town is dominated by a Frankish castle whose walls were built on Classical foundations. Of great ornithological interest: storks build their nests on house roofs. Hotel: **Delta**, 0231/21.600.

Take the minor road going due south (signposted Bralos), a scenic route that is however almost monotonously straight for the first dozen or so kilometres and then twists and turns its way to **BRALOS**. There is a British Military Cemetery for allied soldiers who died there in 1917. The route passes the neat, well-maintained entrance (stone pillars and 2 massive cypress trees). Turn right in the village and in 500m turn right again (direction Gravia). In 5km, the cemetery is on the left. In 11km, **GRAVIA** — a hotch-potch of houses and shops and a large taverna on the left. Lucky the customer who lifts the lid on a casserole and finds the most delicious octopus stew, in a thick tomato and local red wine sauce. And appreciative the one at the neighbouring table who filled a *vrac* with 6 litres of the heady wine. The road climbs ponderously; marked poles on each side indicate that it is frequently impassable in winter, and can be tricky even in spring — a signpost to the mighty Mt. Parnassos on the right explains why. Bear left in 12km, signposted Amfissa. Photographers will be fretting to record the fantastic views across the valley. Patience is rewarded in 4km, where parking space is thoughtfully provided. The road is dappled with the confetti-like effect of marguerites and red campion as it gently descends, with many a gushing waterfall, into the valley. **ELEONAS**, 2km to the right of the road, is a sprawling hillside village crowned by a large church and with a light, bright welcome. The coffee is almost waiting for you!

Back on the main road, it's 5km into **AMFISSA** (pop: 6,600), at the north-western end of the Krisean Plain and the foothills of the Locrian mountains. The town has twice risen from the ashes of destruction, by Philip of Macedon (4C BC) and by the Bulgars in the Middle Ages, after which it was rebuilt by the Franks, who called it Salona. Its turbulent past still shows. See: remains of ancient walls, towers and cistern; ruins of 1205 Frankish castle (Frourion) built on walls of ancient acropolis on a wild site shaded by larch and cypress; fine arcaded Turkish fountain; 12C church. And the town's exceptionally favoured position on this fertile plain, extending some 17km around the Gulf, bears fruit. Amfissa is known as the sea of olives. Hotel: **Amfissaeum**, 0265/22.161. Large restaurant at foot of castle remains.

Take the Delphi road from the town (direction south-west and well signposted), through olive and orange groves. Blue-painted beehives are clustered like miniature cubic villages, and there are so many wild flowers that species-spotting is a busy pastime. Bear left (9km) at the junction with the Itea road. Camping facilities, and a splendid view to the west of Itea and distant Galaxidi. The road climbs steeply as it approaches the modern village of **DELPHI**, where visitors are eagerly catered for. Hotels: **Xenia**, 0265/82.151; **Hermes**, 0265/82.318. Tourist Police: 0265/82.220. The ancient site is south of the village.

Ancient Delphi occupies a spectacularly beautiful site, so well endowed with natural attributes — springs, crevasses, ravines, olive groves and a dramatic, theatre-like bowl — that it was once considered the centre of the world. The precinct which, under the name of Pytho, was sacred to numerous deities — Mother Earth, Gea and Poseidon among them — is situated in a seismic area beneath the precipitous slopes of Mt. Parnassos, within the angle between 2 peaks descriptively known as the shining rocks. Shortly before the end of the Mykinean period the cult of Apollo was adopted from Dorian Crete, and Apollo became the sole guardian of the Oracle. As its fame grew, the sanctuary became an international diplomatic centre; by 6C BC it was a cultural and athletic forum and, some say, the national conscience of the entire Ancient Greek world. The Pythian Games, commemorating Apollo's slaying of the serpent Python, attracted competitors and spectators from far and wide. The Oracle attracted the smart money, too. City-states from Marseilles to Asia Minor vied with each other in bringing rich votive offerings such as priceless statues, and king Croesus, last king of Lydia (6C BC) was a major benefactor, although the Oracle repaid him with disastrous advice.

The Tholos at Delphi

Pilgrims (men only) consulting the Oracle had to sacrifice an animal, then write their question on leaden tablets. The priestess of the Sanctuary (Pythia) went into a trance and her utterings were interpreted in verse by resident priests and poets. Her political pronouncements included good omens for Xerxes during the Persian invasions; Athens, Sparta and Thebes 4C BC; Philip of Macedon, and Alexander the Great. See: Sacred Way (Roman paving flanked by treasuries and votive offerings); the Tholos Sanctuary of Apollo; ruins of Doric Temple of Apollo (rebuilt 4C BC; the 6C BC Temple partly financed by Croesus destroyed by earthquake); the Theatre, Stadium, Gymnasium and Hippodrome of Krissa, all used during the Games; Agora (Roman dwellings and baths); Castalian spring (pilgrims cleansed themselves, priestesses drank from it); Museum with relics from Archaic, Classical, Hellenistic and Roman period, especially life-size silver Archaic bull (6C BC) and bronze Charioteer (478 BC). Museum: 0265/82.312.

A festival of plays is performed in the Stadium in the summer.

Leaving Delphi, the road climbs to (in 10km) **ARACHOVA** (pop: 2,800), an attractive mountain town constantly bustling with activity. It is the starting point for climbers and skiers on **Mt. Parnassos** (the ski centre, 16km) and for visitors to Delphi. The stone houses, rising in terraces on the mountainside, are decorated with colourful window boxes; shops stocked with local specialities are an attraction. Shop here for multi-coloured hand-woven woollen rugs, blankets and garments, suede garments, embroidered linens and cloths, copper and brass ornaments and utensils, Mt. Parnassos honey, crystallised fruits and sheeps' and goats' cheeses, especially *formaella*, a bland goats'-milk cheese. There is also a local red wine.

Festival of Ag. Georgios, in April: villagers in traditional dress dance the Tsamiko and Panigiraki in main square, the old men of the town race over the slope above the church in honour of the victory charge of the Greek forces over the Turks (1826), and lambs are spit-roasted in the street. Hotel: **Xenia**, 0267/31.230.

Return through Delphi; 10km beyond, take the left fork, and turn left at the junction in 3km. The road leads in 2km to **ITEA** (ancient Chalkian), a bright, pleasant and busy resort at the head of the Corinthian Gulf and the port of call for cruise ships bringing passengers to Delphi. Accordingly, visitors are welcomed with enthusiasm (gift shops, *kafenions*, tavernas). **Xenia Motel**, 0265/32.262.

Turn right on to the Antirio road, which follows the shoreline. Sorry about the blot on the horizon — the bauxite excavations which make brick-red craters in the landscape. Torches of lime-green euphorbia lighting up the rock headland try hard to compensate. From a distance **GALAXIDI** looks almost too pretty to be true, a fine old sea-faring town that even improves on closer acquaintance. The imposing mansions, sea-facing, fortified and built to last, are a relic from 19C, when the town boasted 50 shipping magnates and had trade throughout the Mediterranean. Now it is a tranquil resort that seems content to doze behind its blue shutters. Basketwork and pottery are specialities. See: small maritime museum; church of Metamorphosis (fine altar screen); forest planted by schoolchildren. Hotel: **Ta Adelphia**, 0265/41.110.

Continue on the coastal road around the bay of Vitrinista, passing through Eratini (good beaches), a trio of fishing hamlets facing the islets of Trizona (more good bathing beaches) and then Kato Marathia. Just beyond is the pretty seaside site where Herodotus located ancient Erythrai. The route will soon turn inland, but not before calling in on **NAFPAKTOS**, a picturesque little seaside town not to be missed. High above the pine trees, a well-preserved Venetian fortress dates from the Middle Ages when, as Lepanto, this was the scene of the battle of that name (1571) — the last and greatest one in which oar-propelled boats were used, and the subject of paintings by Titian and Tintoretto. The castle walls descend to the harbour — others divide the town into compartments — which is protected by twin keeps. There are fine views from the citadel and good waterside tavernas. Above all, as an old sailor put it, Nafpaktos 'is as Greek now as it ever was'. (10km farther along the coast is Antirio, connected by ferry to Rio, in the Peloponnese.)

Return along the road going eastwards and in a couple of kilometres fork left, away from the coast, signposted Efpalio. The road crosses the **river Mornos** close to its mouth and climbs gracefully through orchards and undulating hills. Streams cross its path, and the route sparkles. So does a radar station, a giant silvery disc high on a ridge, keeping watch over the Rion strait. Just off the road, to the left, the village of **KARDARA** has a fine vantage-point, too, and a pleasant situation. It is almost impossible not to stop and gaze in admiration at the profusion of geraniums and carnations in gardens. And yet to do so is almost asking for the generosity that comes so spontaneously to the Greeks. The result, an armful of flowers to gladden the journey. The road begins a descent, through Filothei, and on the left is the turning to the large **Varnakova Monastery**, rebuilt 19C on Byzantine foundations. The road wends its way farther inland at the dictate of the mountain ridge it follows, dropping slowly down into the Mornos valley and at times apparently heading straight for the foothills of forbidding-looking mountains. The meeting of 2 rivers, a pretty, peaceful spot, is an assembly point for countless butterfly species. And sitting thoughtfully on a tangle of branches not far away, there's the graceful outline of a stork.

Almost inevitably in this helter-skelter region, any road that descends gently into a valley will shortly start another ascent. This one does. It closely follows the course of the river, gaining height on it for a time, with views across immaculately terraced hillsides and isolated farmsteads, only to be drawn down into a valley once more, crossing first the Kokkino and then, beside an old packhorse bridge, the Mornos again (tourist pavilion). Collectors of old bridges are in luck. In 2km, there are the remains of an arched stone one too.

The river widens into a lake and the road sticks closely to its side, with the large village of **LIDORIKO** on its eastern bank. As the road bears southwards towards the Gulf the scenery becomes soft and pretty.

Continuing in the shadow of Mt. Parnassos, fork left to **VOUNIHORA** (at a height of 767m). Just after the village there is a view of the best of both worlds — mountains covered with thick pine-forests, and snow-capped for almost half of the year, and the port and villages around the bay. As the road approaches **AMFISSA** (26km), the capital of Fokida, the landscape is transformed to a dense, soft silvery-green, and it's olive groves all the way. The tour ends here, or return on the main road to Lamia.

Lefkas

1–2 days/140km/from Vonitsa, in Etolia, Central Greece, plus optional excursion (48km) to Cape Dukato

Lefkas is an enchanted island, an impressionist canvas painted with fruit blossom, colourful shrubs, wild flowers and butterflies; a geographical chart dominated by a central mountain group and ringed by deep, sea caves and tiny off-shore islands, Aristotle Onassis' Skorpios among them.

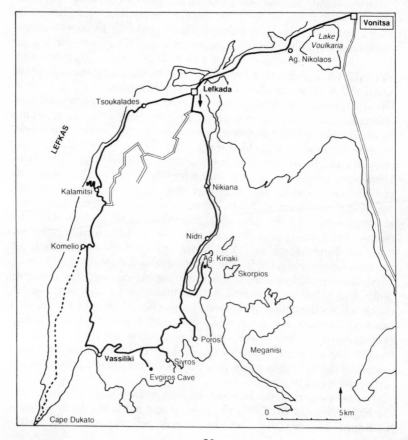

In parts, the island offers a nostalgic backward glimpse into a centuries-old way of life. Not all the villages have mains water, not all the cottages are 'on the electric' and not all the considerable number of beauty spots have been discovered. But some of them have, and it can't be long ...

This tour gives you the joy of exploring a Greek island without ever leaving dry land. One of the Ionian groups (which includes Corfu and Cephalonia), Lefkas is linked to the mainland by a long, narrow causeway which pursues its course through salt flats, sand spits, marshland and lagoons.

The island was colonised by the Corinthians 7C BC and joined Sparta in the Peloponnesian War and was devastated by first the Corcyreans and then the Athenians, both 5C BC. 'Leucas' was made the capital of the mainland province of Akarnania 3C BC but fell to the Romans. It became a political football between the Venetians and the Turks, suffered four crippling earthquakes in 18C, was taken by the French, and liberated in 1810 by the British.

Local folklore gives Lefkas important literary credentials, insisting that this, and not the island of Ithaca, was Homer's birthplace. At the beginning of this century, in an attempt to put fact on the theory, a German archaeologist led an extensive excavation on the tranquil plain of Nidri, in the north east. In unearthing Early Bronze Age circular tombs, he succeeded in putting 'Leucas' firmly on the map of antiquity.

VONITSA (see p. 45). Leave the village by the south-west road (sign-posted Lefkada, the local name for Lefkas). The road runs alongside **Lake Voulkaria** and, in 11km and at the western edge, watery **AG. NIKOLAOS** with sea on one side, the lake on the other. A castle looms in sight, the last-ditch fortification on the mainland. The road rumbles over a bridge, turns right, drifts past a cloud of mimosa, puffs past windmills, sails past yachts in the harbour, crosses a causeway and lands on the Ionian island of **Lefkas**. The port (or *limni*) of **LEFKADA** (pop: 6,800) is surprisingly large, busy and modern with a sufficiency of shops and hotels. Down in the harbour a fisherman turns over octopus on a line, like so much unruly washing. In the *kafenion* next door you get tiny plates of the grilled-until-it's-black octopede, tender and delicious, with an ouzo. Hotels: **Santa Mavra**, 0645/22.342; **Lefkas**, 0645/23.916.

Leave the port by the southern road and fork left to follow the eastern shoreline. Small fishing villages glide by, inviting you to stop where you will. **KALAGONI** (10km) a hamlet of huddled cottages, then a sparkle of salt works close to the site of **Ancient Leucas** where a few traces of walls post-date its 7C BC beginnings. **LIGIA** (4km), where life is earnest. Fish is being unloaded and noisily sold on the spot, a loud hand-slap sealing the transaction. The houses are built on stilts, living quarters above, a few lazy tables and chairs comprising *ad-hoc* café bars below. Olive trees have their feet practically in the water, and so do fishermen's wives, hanging the family laundry on rope-lines along the beach.

NIKIANA in 3km is effectively screened from the coast by a curtain of cypress trees. Look out for a particularly well-stocked nut shop. A track leads uphill to **ALEXANDROS**, a steep climb, where there's a monastery. Across the Bay of Drepano, the mainland appears as a collage of overlapping misty mountains. Lemon trees line the coastal road, so flat and easy-going that cycling would be a doddle. In the stone cottages at **PERIGIALI** (5km) the living quarters are upstairs again, but the lower floor, level with the pebbly beach and the incoming waves, belongs to the animals.

Until now the villages have belonged to the inhabitants. **NIDRI** (in 2km) is for the tourists who congregate like bees round a honey-pot. There are smart tavernas, night clubs, Western-style coffee bars and pubs, boat chandlers and gift shops. Day-tripper boats chug off to the islands of Meganisi, Ithaca and Kephalonia, and fishermen vie with each other to fill up their boats, destination the best bathing beaches. Nidri, my notebook reminds me, is the 'Mykonos' of Lefkas!

Only 3km beyond, **VLAHO** belongs to the people again, with its tiny fishermen's chapel by the roadside, its little gardens covered in vines. Fork left just past the village, on to a track exploring the prettiest of peninsulas, **Ag. Kiriaki**, it couldn't be more backwoodsy if it tried. Fields and fields of mauve and white, anemones and marguerites; terraces teeming with olives (with an oil-pressing plant in a small stone cottage); groves of lemon trees; pergolas covered with vines; strip-fields of broad beans, their flowers perfuming the air; oh, and even banana trees. Take a picnic on to the grassy hillsides, or climb down to the little quay at **GENIO**. I can't call to mind a taverna in a more delightful situation.

Return to the main road, which climbs on a ridge around the foothills of the mountain and looks down over heaven knows how many olives and pines. It just by-passes **KATOHORIO** (4km from the junction). Turn left in 2km to **POROS**, nestling in the hillside. Women in the island dress of dark brown skirts and overskirts, shawls and overshawls carry trays of bread, tin baths of washing and pitchers of water on their heads. And still find time for a chat.

Reluctantly, we must get on! Return to the main road, passing **Poros Beach**, a beautiful sandy cove with authorised camping, and in 3km turn left to another one. **SIVROS**, a hamlet tucked into **Sivota Bay**, has just the kind of fish taverna that 'makes' a trip. Back to the main road again, turn left and in 3km left to **Evgiros Cave** (signposted) set deep in the hillside. Beyond that (you have to walk) is **Chrisopilia Cave**, a deep but not spectacular shelter at the head of Afteli Bay. Much of the island's coastland is pitted with caves, some reputedly large enough to shelter a submarine.

Continue on the main road, passing ribbons of strip-cultivated fields with their crops — wheat, dried beans, whatever — stored in stylish round stone houses with tall, thatched-cone roofs. Time has almost passed **MARANDOHORI** by, though a few new villas show signs of reawakening. **KONTARAINA** (3km) rising from an orange grove, may be beyond recall.

VASSILIKI, 4km across the flattest of plains, is a lively village at the head of a bay, pebbly of beach and warm of welcome. Water-sports organisers and villa operators are moving in, so hurry! Dinner in a harbour-side taverna crowded with 2 small card tables is cooked by an old lady swathed in brown and presided over by her husband, a genial stranger to the razor blade. She offered us *sviritha* (rare and relatively expensive white fish) steaks, the equivalent of rolling out the red carpet, with slices of feta cheese, olives, *horta* (wild greens from the mountains, simmered in olive oil and lemon juice) and a bottle of potent red Santa Maura wine. I suppose you could get a portion of cod and chips at home for the same price ...

Don't believe anything you read about the road around the west coast lurching from bad to terrible. It has been resurfaced. The road continues around the bay and turns inland to **AG.PETROS**, a shabby agricultural village undergoing a face-lift. People sit on donkey saddles in the street, chatting. A rotisserie gives off sparks of aroma, *rigani* from the mountainside on baby lamb. Fork left in the village. Pine forests vignette the outlines of **Mt. Stavrotas** (1,145m) and the hillsides are terraced with vines.

In 6km there's a left turn signposted to Komelio and Athani which leads, in 24 rough and tumbling kilometres, to the south-westerly tip of the island, **Cape Dukato**, protected by a lighthouse. I make this an optional excursion. The earlier remark about the quality of the road surface does not apply, and it's a there-and-back road. Here's legend for you. In antiquity the precipitous 61m rock saw many an impassioned leap into the turbulent waters, all hope of love's requital lost. Sappho was one such victim, but Cicero turned a potential crisis into a drama and had live birds strapped to the performer and rescue boats at the ready. Childe Harold 'saw the evening star above Leucadia's [Lefkada's] far-projecting rock of woe', the white cliff once marked by a Temple to Apollo.

Back in the real world, and on the main road, continue to **HORTATA** (3km after the junction) where the term kitchen garden takes on a new meaning. The cottage gardens *are* the kitchens. In 3km, turn left on to a minor, shingly road to **KALAMITSI**. It's the first time in my life I have seen elderly Greek ladies invading that most masculine of male preserves, the *kafenion*. It's unheard of. There has to be a reason. There is. It's pension day, and the official comes to the café to pay out.

With time on your hands, turn left in the village (clearly marked 'beach' in English) for another there-and-back excursion. The track, a centipede of steep S-bends, winds down through indescribably beautiful countryside — olive and pear groves, terraced vines, banks of thyme, carpets of wild flowers, clusters of blue and green-striped beehives, clouds of blue, white and yellow butterflies — to a fabulously sandy and rocky cove 8km away.

Back in Kalamitsi the still-stony road descends, but more gently, into the valley. Fork left in 3km, signposted **AG. NIKITAS**. Breath-taking coastal views. A new road under construction. Mulberry trees dripping all over the old one. Banks of camomile. Inquisitive flocks of sheep. Bear left, towards the coast, in 1km, and go straight over the junction 1km farther on. Just before the village turn right. The signpost reads, Lefkada, 12km.

The road follows a clean sweep of sandy shore with a pine-covered arc, the lower slopes of **Mt. Meganoros**, to the right. **TSOUKALADES** is ripe for development, hotels and tavernas springing up from the olive groves. One day, I suppose, it will be a suburb of Lefkada, where the tour ends.

The island goes *en fête* in August each year. In the mountain village of Karia there's a 2-day festival of folk songs and dancing on the 11th and 12th in honour of St. Spiridon. And in Lefkada town there's a 2-week prose and art festival with theatrical performances, folk concerts, lectures and exhibitions.

Food specialities of the island: Santa Maura wine, smoked salami-type sausages, an unusually large variety of sea foods. Handicrafts: hand-made lace and colourful embroidery.

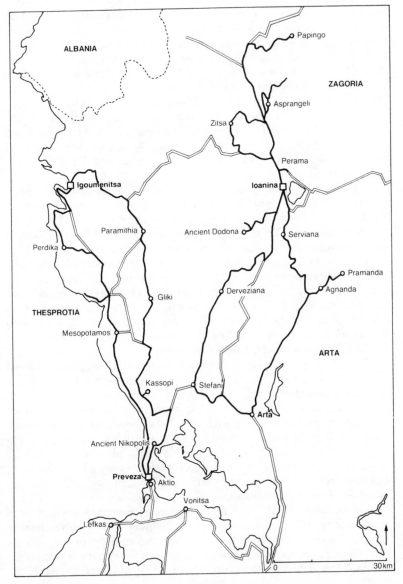

Epirus is scenery on a majestic scale; archaeological sites that stand comparison with any in the whole of Greece; craftsmanship that shows the stamp of centuries of unbroken local tradition, and wildlife — from exotic lilies to wild boar, ramonda (mountain gloxinias) to bears and wolves — that is a source of both national pride and active conservation.

The region, the most mountainous and also the most humid in the country, occupies the north-western corner of the Greek peninsula, to the south of an artificial border with Albania ('who is always watching us', as one shepherd put it). To the west is the Ionian Sea with its miles-long beaches, lagoons and river estuaries — a haven for waterfowl — and on the east, separating Epirus from Thessaly, the massive Pindos range, the backdrop against which hills and valleys, towns and villages are seen.

The region was originally inhabited by 14 warring tribes and united after the victory of one of them, the Molossians, whose king, Pyrrhus, won doubtful, costly (Pyrrhic) victories in Macedonia and Italy, and came within 24 miles of Rome. ('Another victory like that and we are lost', Pyrrhus exclaimed on one occasion.) Epirus was ambivalent in the Macedonian wars, joining first the Macedonians, then the Romans and finally (170 BC) turning — unsuccessfully — against them again. In falling to Rome, 70 towns in Epirus were destroyed and 150,000 inhabitants enslaved.

In the Middle Ages Epirus endured a succession of rulers. The region became a despotate when the Crusaders captured Constantinople in 1204, a dynasty that survived until late 13C. The Orsini, the Byzantines, the Serbs and the Turks — who took Ioanina in 1431 but failed to subjugate many of the most mountainous communities — have all left traces of their architecture and their culture. Epirus stood aside from the War of Independence, and Arta was liberated from the Turks in 1881. The Greek army took Ioanina in 1913 and subsequently occupied the whole of the north of the region. Much of this territory was given to Albania — and so the present border is not a natural one. In the Second World War the Greeks repulsed the advance of the Italian army, but Epirus still bears scars of German occupation.

Throughout the ebb and flow of varied cultural influences, the thread of traditional Epirean arts and crafts has remained unbroken. The arts flourished with the original Byzantine style of painting. Wood-carving attained a high artistic standard, as can be seen on the elaborately ornate altar-screens in the village churches and the woodwork on sale in the shops. Goldsmiths and silversmiths work late into the evening in workshops mainly in and around Ioanina, a good place to buy holiday souvenirs, and weaving, particularly of brightly coloured woollen rugs, blankets and shawls (in consideration of the harsh winters) continues centuries of tradition in mountain villages.

The outstanding feature of the mountain settlements is the grey local stone used for building. It is a form of slate found in successive layers of varying thickness, easy to chisel and shape and convenient not only for exterior work but for floors and decorative features besides. The combination of the slate-grey stone and the deep, rich red and blue of the woollen furnishings epitomises the village houses.

The ways to Epirus are many and varied: by ferry from Corfu to Igoumenitsa (where one of the tours in this section starts); by ferry across the Ambracian Gulf from Ag. Nikolaos in Central Greece; by road from Western Macedonia in the north east through Pendalofo and Eptahori; from the east via Kalambaka to Metsovo; and from the south, from Athens, by road through Patra, Agrinio and Amfilohia.

Thesprotia

1–2 days/235km/from Igoumenitsa (the mainland port facing Corfu)

A short ferry-boat trip from the popular holiday island of Corfu (see p. 121), and you are in another, fascinating, world. Epirus, overshadowed by the Pindos range of mountains to the east, and by Albania to the north, is a region of contrasts, and this tour experiences them in full.

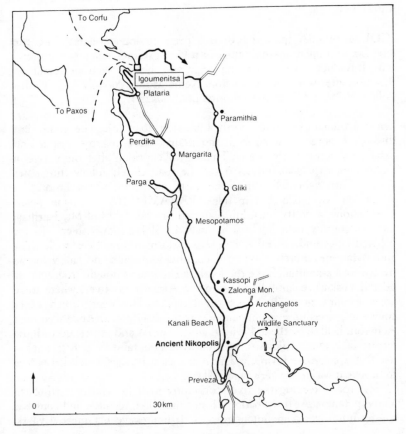

From the ferry port of Igoumenitsa, the road runs through a dramatic gorge and makes passing acquaintance with varied and isolated villages. Castle ruins, Byzantine churches, even the remains of ancient cities become almost commonplace along the way, although such a description could never be pinned on the Roman city of Nikopolis, just north of Preveza.

Along the coastal road heading northwards, the scene is like a dream holiday film — the miles and miles of sandy beaches defy description. They are beautiful. Talking of contrasts, a short detour up into the mountains, and one is face to face with ancient beliefs and Greek mythology. Here is the place where in ancient times the inhabitants gathered to commune with their dead, and from which it was but a short rowing-boat ride down-river to the gates of hell! A sanctuary and a temple remain to give substance to this chilling observation.

Detours to the westward, to the pretty little seaside town of Parga and then along the secondary road with roller-coaster views, lift the spirits considerably. And near Plataria, almost at this journey's end, the climax is a truly gasp-making cliff range, folds and folds of sheer rocks topped by an incongruously neat row of trees in silhouette and sheltering a cosy waterside village.

IGOUMENITSA (pop: 4,100) is a busy coming-and-going port, the ferry-boat terminal linking Epirus with Corfu (Greek name Kerkira) and Italy. It is a new town with a long bright and cheerful sea front, rebuilt on the ruins after war-time occupation. **Xenia Motel**, 0665/22.282. Tourist Police: 0665/22.302. Port Authority: 0665/22.235.

Leave Igoumenitsa going north (direction Ioanina). The road runs through a gorge between high mountains, rises to cross a spur and descends again into the scenic Thiamis valley. Soon after the village of Parapotamos (*potamos* means river) the road closely follows the water course. Turn right (24km from the start), direction Paramithia, on to a minor road over a mountain ridge. **PARAMITHIA** (its name means consolation), a pretty township scattered on the slopes of **Mt. Karillas**, was temporarily held by British forces in 1941. It has steep, narrow cobbled lanes and several tumble-down old mansions. See: castle ruins and Byzantine church. The road continues through the valley in the shadow of Paramithia. Take the left fork (in 4km) through Prodromio to **GLIKI** (18km), beautifully sited on the **Akherontas** river, where there are the ruins of a church of the Despots. The river, which never completely dries up even in summer, is the reality of the mythical river Acheron, held to be the link with the other world and associated with the terrors of Hades. It flows down from the mountains of Suli through a deep, steep, sombre ravine, a dark remorseless passage which led people to believe it was the waterway to hell (see below).

The road, keeping the river constantly in sight, continues through Vouvopotamos. At the junction 11km from Gliki, turn left and continue southwards, over a mountain ridge with impressive but narrow views, through Kato Despotiko to (16km from the junction) Mirsini. In just over 3km there is a track on the left, signposted Zalonga, leading (in 5.5km) to **Kassopi**. It's only a few minutes' walk along the footpath to the remote ruins of the 4C BC city, burned by the Romans 167 BC but still offering rewarding exploration. See: the Odeon, Agora, theatre, hostel, chamber tomb. The path climbs a further 500m to the **Zalonga Monastery** where Suliot mountaineers took refuge from Ali Pasha. In terror of being discovered by the Turkish invaders, 60 women and children escaped to the summit and, after performing their ritual dance, threw themselves over the precipice. A monument commemorates this act of mass suicide on the desolate peak.

Back-track to the main road which continues, through Archangelos, after which turn left. The road runs through the Louros valley to the Bay of Gomarez, where it joins a new major coastal road. Turn right. Beyond the village of **MIHALITSI**, where 4C BC tombs have been discovered, the peninsula narrows considerably. To the east it forms a marshy lagoon, a sanctuary for herons and other wildlife. It is definitely reach-for-the-binoculars time.

Another archaeological treat is soon in store. The road passes the large site of **Ancient Nikopolis**, the city built 30 BC by the Roman emperor Octavius. Park among the brambles, wander (if it's spring or summer) through carpets of rose-red herb Robert and rose-pink mallow and clouds of yellow butterflies (a scintillating colour combination). To see: ruined Roman external walls and Byzantine inner walls with towers, 2 theatres, stadium, gymnasium and the Temples of Mars and Poseidon. Also, Roman baths, 2 burial grounds, remains of 4 early-Christian basilicas (mosaics) and museum (lion, Roman portraits). In any terms, this magnificent and well-maintained site is worth a visit.

The road continues south through the isthmus to **PREVEZA** (pop: 11,400) linked by half-hourly ferry to Aktio, across the Ambracian Gulf. The town was founded 3C BC by Pyrrhus, king of Epirus, to guard the Gulf and is now a port and popular seaside resort (good bathing, camping). See: cathedral church (artistic altar screen, Venetian clock tower). Nikopoleia celebrations, traditional costumes and dancing, during July. Hotel: **Zikas**, 0682/22.258. Port Authority: 0682/22.226. Customs. Yachting facilities. Good fish tavernas.

Leave Preveza on the coastal road (direction Igoumenitsa) passing Mitikas and the Nikopolis site (now to the right), alongside some of the most beautiful sandy beaches imaginable, to **KANALI BEACH** (villas, hotels, camping). At intervals cliffs and trees tantalisingly mask the view; at others the sand-sea-sky combination is breathtaking.

At **MESOPOTAMOS** (45km from Preveza), at the junction of the Kokytos and Akherontas rivers (see above), is the ancient necromantic oracle of the dead, Greek mythology you can touch and feel. Take the track to the right, signposted **Necromanteion**, and in 7km, on a rocky hill high above the confluence, there is the sanctuary of Persephone and Hades, the only one of its kind in Greece. According to ancient belief it was here that the inhabitants of Epirus communicated with the souls of their dead, and according to mythology it was here that Charon rowed the dead across a subterranean lake to Hades. Some attempted to 'pay the ferryman' with a ritual coin. Only 2 living souls ever made it to the kingdom of the dead, Hercules and Orpheus. See: remains (partly destroyed by fire 168 BC) of Sanctuary with a labyrinth of corridors above and below ground and the Acropolis of Ephyra. Modern perceived wisdom (suggested by remains of bronze windlass) is that mechanical trickery was employed, after treatment of the believers with hallucinatory drugs.

Return to the main road, turn right (direction Igoumenitsa) and in 10km turn left, signed to **PARGA**, 10km distant. The tap, tap, tap of boat-building greets the ears just before the little seaside town comes into view, spread out on a rocky headland, backed by olive and orange groves, and crowned by a Norman castle (Lion of St Mark decoration on the keep). Looking out to sea, you seem to be within hailing distance of the island of Paxos, only 20km away. The small bay is pretty, with terracotta-red houses, clutches of fishing boats and a jollity of tavernas; the speciality is not just fish, but *saganaki*, fried *kefalotiri* cheese served with fried eggs and salad. The large bay, Chrissoyiali, 2km to the west, is rapidly attracting its fair share of tourists, and Club Mediterranée is there. **Lichnos Beach**, hotel and bungalows, 0684/31.255.

The road to Parga is a go-and-come-back one, lined with oleanders and, on a good day, with flashes of sea views as bright as a kingfisher's tail. Return to the main road and turn left. Because it makes its way inland (and one has been spoiled by such coastal scenes) this short stretch of the route, through a rice-growing plain, does not inspire. Turn up the *syrtaki* tape! If children in the party are getting restless, turn right into **MARGARITA** (9km from Parga). There are castle ruins on a rocky crag just to the right of the road — perfect race-you-to-the-top material. The village has a sad recent history; it was completely razed to the ground in 1944 by the Germans.

Back on to the main road, turn right and there is plenty to see, a huge lake on the right, a bird sanctuary brimming with wildlife. At the Karteri junction, turn left (direction Perdika), through gentle mountain scenery spattered with olives and hummocky scrub and scattered with clusters of shepherds' huts. At **PERDIKA** the coastal view warrants more than a second glance, the soft slopes of the hills and tiny islands looking like green woolly sheep in the water. Turn right in the village square and, in 1km, there are views of Paxos and now of distant Corfu. Continue for 14km to **SIVOTA** where, 1km to the left, a tiny, picturesque harbour beckons. (**Robinson Club**, 0665/31.461.) Take the right fork (direction Igoumenitsa) and, given a chance, steal a backward glance at the misty islands. Very soon the distraction is straight ahead. There, spread before you, is the most astonishing rock formation, huge cliffs rising in folds like a giant serpentine wall with the village of **PLATARIA** (straight across at a cross-roads) sprawled at their feet. It's a charming little waterside community, with quaint old houses wrapped in pine trees scrabbling up the hillside.

The road follows the coastline and the serpentine cliffs and rounds a point where (13km from Plataria) **IGOUMENITSA** is on the horizon. Continue on the road to the port.

Zagoria

1 day/180km/from Ioanina

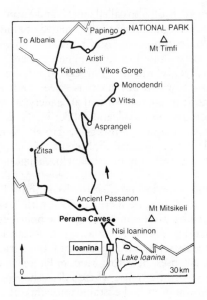

Massive, impenetrable mountains washed by sparkling, gushing streams and clad in pine and fir; fields and fields of rare and exotic wild flowers, wild lilies a speciality; friendly stone villages fortified against the winter snows and glinting in the summer sunshine along every precipitous track; a majestic national park to conserve the pride and joy of the region, the flora and the varied wildlife; and the Perama caves which some experts take to be the most spectacular and polychromatic of any in the world — that's Zagoria.

Setting out from Ioanina, the local capital, the route takes to the high-road, direction Albania, through the massive Vikos Gorge. The region is known as Zagorohoria, the villages of Zagoria. To the east and west of the road there are 46 of them, set in breathtakingly beautiful surroundings, each one with a character of its own but showing a strong family resemblance.

Houses of grey local stone with grey slate roofs; mansions which bear witness to 15C prosperity; two-storeyed churches with arched cloisters, 3 aisles, sometimes a small painted dome and always inside, intricate carved screens; single-span bridges crossing the tumbling trout streams; and, here and there, remains of Cyclopean walls and dwellings as a reminder that Zagoria has a proud, ancient past as well as an optimistic future.

Optimistic because, after a prolonged period of migration, especially of the young people, to the cities, the villages are coming to life again, and most of them have now been declared conservation areas.

The tour pays a fleeting visit to traditional settlements along the way. With time on your hands you could take in many more.

IOANINA (pop: 40,150), also called Janena and Yannina. Largest town of Epirus, capital of the region. Beautifully situated at altitude of 500m along the shores of **Lake Ioanina**, also known as **Lake Pamvotis**, where (on the 'mainland') a bazaar, mosques and minarets date from the Turkish occupation. The Lake is brimming with eels, trout, crayfish and frogs, the tasty specialities of waterside tavernas. See: archaeological museum (Classical, Byzantine and later) with an art gallery; Municipal Museum in Aslan Tzami mosque (historical and folkloric); Folkloric Museum; and exhibition halls in Ioanina University. Hotel: **Xenia**, 0651/25.087; **Palladion**, 0651/34.602. Tourist Police: 0651/25.673. **NTOG**: 0651/25.086. Epirotika Festival: traditional dancing, August.

A wooded island on the lake, **Nisi Ioaninon** (11km by 3km) is surrounded by marshy reed beds criss-crossed with backwaters, while the lake is criss-crossed by scullers in training. The hourly ferries (15 minutes, from Mavili Square) give way. The island, with its attractive paved square and narrow cobbled streets, has a medley of monasteries and mosques set in densely-wooded copses. See: 16C Mon. of Panteleimon, surrounded by huge plane trees, with the house where Ali Pasha was shot dead by the Turks in 1822 (now a print and costume museum), also 16C church with a cave; 13C Mon. of the Prodruomos (St. John the Baptist) with 18C frescoes; 13C Mon. of the Philanthropini (16C frescoes); 11C Mon. of Stratigopoulos (exceptional 16C frescoes). Gift shops glisten with silverware, brass and copper. Taverna owners invite visitors to 'pick your own' delicacy from live-fish tanks on the pavement. There is a flurry of *kafenions* and a general air of friendly hubbub. Well worth a trip.

Take the Kozani road from Ioanina, going northwards, and in 4km turn right on to the main Trikala road. Turn left in 1km, signposted **PERAMA**, which would never win a best-kept village competition. Car parking for the caves is ample and well indicated. There is a clutch of metalsmiths' and jewllers' shops like sparks from an anvil — numerous and brilliant. Bargain before buying. Hotel: **Ziakas**, 0651/28.611.

Perama Caves are spectacular, some say the richest collection in the world of jewel-bright stalactites and stalagmites. They were discovered accidentally in 1941 by inhabitants seeking shelter from the bombardment, 2km of galleries and vaulted chambers which are now easily accessible — though presenting a steep climb to the exit — and discreetly lit. Red, blue, gold and even green towers and turrets, pillars and pinnacles, flower and tree look-alikes. A high priority on any schedule. After this exciting visit, it's some 500m back to the village along a footpath above the caves. Return to the main road and turn right. The road soon leaves the messy outskirts of the town, passes the airport and runs across the marshy Lapsista plain at the foot of **Mt. Mitsikeli**. This part of the route is somewhat unremarkable, but it's a means to an end. At 14km from the Perama road, pass Asfaka and in 2km turn right, signposted Vikos Gorge and Monodendron. The road, snaked with double S-bends and climbing steeply around a mountain ridge, nevertheless has a good surface, and there are glorious mountain-peak views at every turn. In about 7km the road levels. At 9km from the main road, turn right to **ASPRANGELI** (1km), its grey stone houses with grey stone roofs looking like heavy fortifications on a domestic scale. Here, the first encounter with a church typical of this region. With its heavy overhang to the first floor, long outside gallery and curving stone staircases, it looks for all the world like a slightly run-down and friendly farmhouse (fine wooden altar screen, frescoes). Retrace the 1km, turn right and follow the signposts to Vikos Gorge.

VITSA is on the right, a village that shows the effect of population migration in the bleak, empty façades of many deserted houses ranged up the hillside, and shows the worthwhile policy of conservation and restoration in as many others. There are 2 pretty Byzantine churches, Ag. Nikolaos (1610) and Taxiarchis (1700), and a cheery *kafenion*. Continue on the road to **MONODENDRI** (at 1,100m) which is the end of the line until early April when the snow melts — and the mimosa blossoms — and opens up this route to the Gorge. The village has a year-round air of cosiness, the grey stone houses with shingle roofs furnished with wall tapestries and the semi-circular fireplaces hung with heavy fringed rugs. Churches of Ag. Panteleimon (fine frescoes), 1630, and Ag. Thanassis, 1830. Cheerful family *kafenion*. Beyond the village, through the hamlet of **OSIA** the road leads to the spectacular **Vikos Gorge** and the deserted **Monastery of Ag. Paraskevi** (1412) perched on a cliff above it. The cells and chapel (with frescoes) have been restored. Treacherous paths lead beyond, to monks' cells and hermits' caves. In the summer season there are guided tours (recommended only for the sure-footed with a good head for heights) down the cliff face to a viewing platform. And the view? The gushing confluence of the **River Voidomatis** (renowned for its trout) and a mountain stream some 1,000m below in this wild, wild territory.

Return along the mountain road through Monodendri and Vitsa. Just beyond Vitsa, take the U-turn to the flourishing village of **ANO PERDINA** which has large, elegant double-fronted houses with moulded stone eaves — one reminiscent of a Cotswold-stone vicarage — and, by contrast, neat little round houses. The pretty church is especially noteworthy, with every feature — first-floor overhang, massive stone-arched cloisters and a small cylindrical dome painted in stripes — proudly pointed out by the village priest. There is a stone bell-tower in the square, and a monastery and a large new collegiate. Return to the mountain road and at the junction (in 10km) bear right. Chicken farms and a collage of

A village priest or papas

strip-cultivated fields line the route back to the Ioanina–Kozani road. Join that road, turning right ('towards Albania', as my companion said darkly). The surrounding hillsides are well wooded with pine and fir trees and the views are friendly.

After 18km, turn right (signposted Aristi) through copses of evergreen oaks (brown in springtime, actually) and (in 4km) pass through the village of Mesovounion. After another 4km, turn left to **AG. MINAS**, where a couple of dozen houses huddled together on the hillside cower beneath the massive mountain-side. It's amazing what a face-lifting effect orange tiled roofs — and blossoming almond trees — have on grey stone dwellings. Return to the road and continue to **ARISTI**, 2km from the junction. Athenians have summer houses here, elegant ones with stone porticos and green shutters, and there is even a sales kiosk, a *periptero*, a familiar sight elsewhere but a trading oasis in this context. The church is grand, with a stone-arched walkway and an end-to-end stone seat, 'sitting cloisters', an old man told me. And what do the villagers do for a living? 'Oh, this and that. There are plenty of trees. And animals.' And an imposing old 3-bay stone drinking fountain for them.

Stand on the hill in Aristi village, look north-eastwards and see the there-and-back road to Papingo (13km each way) — multiple S-bends and climbing — and take stock! First, in 3km, signposted, there is another not-to-be-missed view of the Vikos Gorge.

MIKRA PAPINGO and **MEGA PAPINGO** are twin villages at the mouth of the Gorge; show villages in the heart of the **Vikos-Aoös National Park**, considered the most beautiful in Greece, a conservation area for the rare exotic flora — lilies especially — and the wildlife of this exceptionally lovely region. The 2 villages are traditional but not entirely typical. The houses have been restored, families resettled after working abroad, crafts revived (wood-carving, weaving and gold embroidery). There is an air of bustling prosperity, and more than a trace of an Australian accent. Some village houses have been beautifully converted as guest houses.

Return to Aristi and then to the main road. Turn left, direction Ioanina. In 5km, on the right, at **KALPAKI**, there is a Museum and Memorial to the Fallen of 1940-1. This is a strategic road junction, representing the parting of the international ways. Only 21km to the west is Ktiamata and the Albanian border. Be prepared to meet a heavy military presence.

Spinning the wool for an Epirus fabric

Continue southwards on the main road for 17km. At Asfaka turn right on to a poor road across a mountain ridge and in 7km fork left to **ZITSA**, a picturesque little town at 686m, which shows signs of former prosperity under Turkish rule. Its main claim to fame is the **Monastery of Profitis Ilias** (fine frescoes) and the sweet, sweet Zitsa wine, the product of vineyards for miles around. The splendour of the view from high-up Zitsa prompted Byron to eulogise about it in *Childe Harold*.

Continue south from the village and in 7km fork left, joining the main Igoumenitsa–Ioanina road. To the left (7km along a track) are remains of **Ancient Passanon**, which flourished until Roman times. Continue to Ioanina.

Arta
2 days/210 or 270km/from Ioanina

It would be a simple matter to drive from Ioanina to Arta, its 'twin' town to the south of Epirus, a matter of 75km along the main highway. But the most glittering prizes are rarely awarded by the major roads, and the route takes to the mountains to explore a succession of villages quite, quite different from those of Zagoria, and to make some exciting discoveries.

The first is the site of the Oracle of Zeus at Ancient Dodona (near which is the new village of Dodoni). The Oracle is believed to be the oldest in Greece, and its popularity over many hundreds of years prompted the building, close beside it, of a stadium and a theatre that bears comparison with the one at Epidavros. Such grandeur! Such a magnificent state of preservation.

The villages along the way extend a warm and friendly welcome — visitors don't come that often. Stop for a coffee or a stroll around any of them and it seems the villagers are in competition to make one feel at home; even to the extent of putting on an impromptu birthday party.

Arta, with its unusual hump-backed bridge and wealth of Byzantine churches, changes the pace of the tour — and has comprehensive shopping and banking facilities. On a 2-day tour it is the obvious place for an overnight stop.

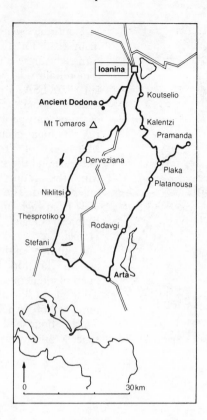

If time and the driver's stamina permit, there is an optional detour to the caves beyond Pramanda, a never-to-be-forgotten subterranean wonderland of weird shapes and rainbow colours in a beautiful mountain setting. Allow time to take the whole of the 50km return journey carefully and in daylight.

Leave **IOANINA** (see p. 64) on the Arta road, direction south, passing the large military barracks and an extensive tobacco plantation. In 6km, signposted Dodoni 13km, turn right. It's about another 4km before the conglomeration of light engineering gives way to almond trees and vines, and shortly the horizon is a mist of mountains. Old stone walls etch the roadside, the smattering of tiny stone shepherds' huts looks like dolls' houses, and magpies swoop overhead.

Ancient Dodona in a high valley and presided over by **Mt. Tomaros** (1,974m), is one of the most important archaeological sites in Epirus. Its oracle is believed to be the oldest and its theatre one of the largest and most complete in Greece. In recognition of this fact, there is expansive car-parking space. In high season, plan to arrive early in the day.

Here is the site of the Pelasgian Oracle of Zeus which flourished from the second millennium BC until 4C BC. According to Herodotus the Oracle arrived with a dove from Egyptian Thebes, and made its pronouncements in the rustling of leaves in the sacred oak trees. The word was interpreted by priests and, later, priestesses who kept in touch with god's divine messages by sleeping with their ears close to the ground. The Hellenistic theatre and environs were later developments on the site. See: remains of the 3C BC stadium; the late 3C BC theatre 13m by 22m and in an incredible state of preservation, with over 40 rows of seats intact. The theatre was converted under the Romans to an arena for gladiatorial and animal combat. The wall built for public safety and a deep, semi-circular drainage channel remain. Foundations of assembly hall and Temple to Aphrodite and, the *pièce de résistance*, the remains of the Sanctuary to Zeus Naios which contained the Oracle and the sacred oak. Traces of an Early-Christian basilica (AD 6C); in Byzantine times Dodona was a bishopric. **Dodona Festival**, presentations of ancient drama in the open-air theatre, during the summer. Hotel: **Andromachi**, 0651/91.196.

Retrace the road 1km from the site; it then takes a sharp U-bend. In 4km turn left to **DRAMESII**, an agricultural village settled among fertile fields at the foothills of the mountain. Neat new houses with vine-covered terraces alternate with old stone cottages, and a *kafenion* and general stores in the centre looks inviting. It is. A couple of cups of coffee led to a bottle of local *mavros* wine (brick red, cloudy and potent) and a bar of chocolate shared with the elderly proprietors, 4 farmworkers and the policeman; the jolliest birthday party on record! It is too high, up here, for olives and citrus fruits to flourish ('a pity,' says a new friend, 'there's money in them now'), but vines, walnuts and almonds soften the land-scape and gladden the welcome offered to visitors.

Return the 1km to the road junction, fork right and return to the main Ioanina-Arta road; turn right. The scenery is soft; rolling hills, lakes, meadows and market gardens. In 14km, turn right by a Shell petrol station on to a minor road. Shepherdesses undeterred by rain crochet under umbrellas. Small friendly hamlets mark the route. Theriakisi, Kapani, Variades and, after a twisty descent, Ahladec. A monastery on the hillside, an old convent, a large new basilica, the milestones pass until **DERVEZIANA** (30km from Dramesii) which has sustenance to offer, a *kafenion* which serves food. The road is one of contrasts now with vicious, jagged (and sometimes tumbling) rocks on one side and a green and pleasant valley on the other. At the junction, with an Assos signpost, go straight on. At **NIKLITSI**, an agricultural 'first', the first olive trees of the descent. Oh, and banks and banks of rosemary, blue-flowering and delightfully fragrant. However small the hamlet, there is a *'kalos ilthate'* sign of official welcome, and many a friendly handshake, should you decide to pause. **ELIA** is an example. The bird's-eye view into the Louros valley gets prettier all the time. **THESPROTIKO** (20km from Derveziana), a village of town proportions, comes as a surprise, with its elegant stone houses set in neat gardens, hedges clipped, lawns watered and flowers in profusion. In another 10km, at **STEFANI** (the Greek name for the May-Day celebration flower wreath) turn left on to the Preveza-Arta road where orange and lemon groves fill the horizon.

Take the right turn, after 6km, signposted to the 'ruins', to **Panayeai Castle** with open-to-the-sky remains of massive external and internal walls and tower, colonised now by wild asparagus and perambulated by sheep. Continue past the site and, turning right, rejoin the main road where, throughout the springtime, roadside fruit stalls make a zingy orange and lemon patchwork and tractors block the road. In 14km detour to the left to see the legendary **Arta Bridge**, the 17C hump-backed Turkish packhorse bridge — the largest and oldest in Greece — over the river Arahthos. The main feature of the bridge is its alternating wide and narrow curved arches to stem the flow when the river is in spate. Legendary? The story goes that the mason embedded his wife into the foundations to strengthen them. Continue on the main road to Arta.

ARTA (pop: 19,500) Second largest town of Epirus. A treasure-trove of Byzantine monuments, and excavations are gradually revealing its more distant past as Ambracia, capital of Pyrrhus. See: 13C Church of Panageia Parigoritissa with mosaic-decorated dome (now houses a museum); Ag. Theodora (decorated capitals); Ag. Vasilios (exterior ceramic decoration). On southern outskirts, by the river, Kato Panageia, a nunnery occupied by orphan girls who weave blankets and carpets for sale. Hotel: **Xenia** (in the 13C Frourion castle) 0681/27.413. Tourist Police: 0681/27.580.

Take the north-east road out of Arta, signposted Helatos, which is 7km away, with Pistiana 9km beyond. This is a 'geological' stretch of the route, with amazing rock formations and variations of colour and texture. To the east, the Arahthos, which forms a lagoon just north of Arta, narrows and points the way to the road. **RODAVGI** (10km) has mountain-chalet-style houses and a fresh and smiling appearance. There are wonderful views of minutely terraced and hummocky hills as far as the eye can see. A waterfall threatens the road, but on investigation its speed is worse than its depth. **SKOUPA** has a kaleidoscope of smart 'town' houses and tiny artisans' stone cottages. People rush out to say hello, 2 children offer a flower posy and an old woman makes coffee. This she shyly presents, with tiny plates of syrupy grapes and iced water. No need to look for a café! A picnic area (roadside tables and chairs) is designated in 6km to take advantage of the into-the-blue-yonder view along the ravine and river valley. **PLATANOUSA** and **MONOLITHIO** are pretty hamlets packaged in beech woods, and for a spell the landscape has an almost Scottish appearance.

This is a spot known as **Plaka** where there is a graceful old stone bridge. To see the caves (an optional detour from the route which adds 50km) take the right turn to **AGNANDA** (12km) and **PRAMANDA** (12km), both busy, compact head villages or townships built in the large, fertile meadow in the shadow of the tall peaks of the Southern Pindos range. A further 5km along this most minor of minor mountain roads, **Anemotripa Pramanda** cave, a subterranean river with one-after-another chambers and galleries extending for 320m and richly decorated with colourful stalactites and stalagmites, a fairyland discovery in this most remote of regions.

There's nothing for it but to turn round and go back to the Arta road. Mountain routes are like that. Turn right, direction Ioanina, and soon the road, comfortably wide and way, way above the heads of its neighbouring peaks, creeps round an awe-inspiringly steep mountain face. Vertiginous views of a maze of rivers and streams in the valley. Turn right, taking an S-bend and descending 8km after the Agnanda junction, and in 2km **KALENTZI**, known locally as the village in the valley. Neat little houses with neat little gardens look incredibly diminutive in the majestic setting. Bear left at the junction in another 8km, just before **AETORRAHI**. From a distance this is like a toy village, the stone houses all of identical size and shape and capped with steep-pitched tiled roofs. The *kafenion* is bright and airy, and as always visitors are friends. Bear left in 4km. The road runs through dark, densely-wooded hills defying the sunlight. In 7km, **KOUTSELIO** has centre-of-the-road white lines, a sure sign that civilisation is just around the corner. It is. Go straight across at the road junction, where the signpost indicates Ioanina, 10km. Continue to the town.

4 THESSALY

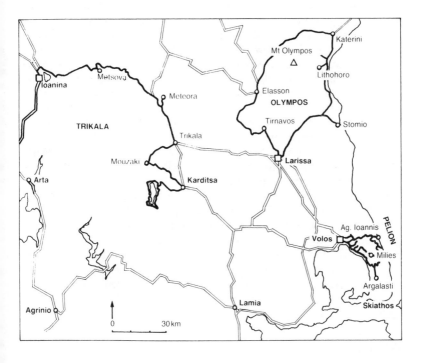

Surrounded as it is by mountains — Pindos, Olympos, Pelion and Ossa among them — the plain of Thessaly is one of the most fertile and bountiful in the whole of Greece. The river Pinios, rushing down from the western slopes of Pindos, cuts the region in two, hurtles through the Vale of Tempe — one of the most magnificent areas of natural scenic beauty — and meets the sea in the Gulf of Salonica.

The plain, which now yields cereals, rice, tobacco, vegetables, almonds and fruit, has long been seen as a valuable prize. It was originally divided into four districts with, for political expediency, one ruler. When that ruler — both Jason and his successor Alexander, both 4C BC — became intolerable the region sought and found the protection of the Thebans, and then came under, in turn, Philip of Macedon, king Pyrrhus of Epirus, and Rome. The people of Thessaly took part in the Trojan war and provided many ships, with the hero Achilles as their leader. For centuries invaders came thick and fast. In 12C Thessaly became the centre of the Bulgar–Vlach kingdom when it was known as Great Wallachia; some town and village names still have echoes of that occupation and some members of those tribes have remained as nomadic shepherds. The Turks put their stamp on the region for 500 years. The area south of the Pinios was ceded to Greece in 1881 and the remainder only in 1913.

Thessaly is a region which has strong links with the mythical past, and where legends not only abound, but were born. Pelion, the peninsula reaching out to the Sporades islands, on the east, was the magnificent natural setting chosen by the gods for their beauty contests. Olympos is the home of the 12 immortal gods and the Centaurs, and was said 'never to be struck by wind or snow'. That is no longer the case!

The 7 peaks rising above 2,750 metres — of which Mitikas is the highest — can be scaled only by experienced climbers and only in summer. The ascent takes two days, with overnight refuge in one of the mountain huts.

To the west of the region and close to its boundary with Epirus is Meteora, not a mountain but a geological wonder of the prehistoric world, when 24 vast and sheer rocks were thrust up from a gentle plain. The devotion of holy men — and remarkable architects and builders — turned them into a monastic retreat and a feast of Byzantine art.

With a history going back to the beginning of time; natural phenomena that have one gasping in amazement; recent excavations revealing important Paleolithic settlements; the remains of ancient cities strategically sited at the entrance to narrow passes and straits; with jewels of ecclesiastical and domestic architecture stretching from the Middle Ages to — on Pelion particularly — 18C, and with mountain and coastal scenery that is just beautiful, Thessaly is a valuable prize for the traveller, too.

Trikala

2 days/325km/from Ioanina to Karditsa

One runs out of superlatives to convey the luxury of the scenery on this route. From Ioanina, a town perfectly poised on the springboard to both Epirus and Thessaly, the Trikala road, cutting through the north and south Pindos range, is spectacular. Long, clear, pine-clad mountain views alternating turn and turn about with a bird's-eye perspective on fertile plains busy with vines and orchards, and then Metsova. This is a ski resort situated in a bowl in the mountains, splashed with the bright colours of the traditional village costumes and handicrafts — carpets, rugs, blankets — hanging from countless windows.

On to Meteora, one of the most outstanding natural wonders of Greece. Natural, and incredible, the 24 sheer, perpendicular rocks on

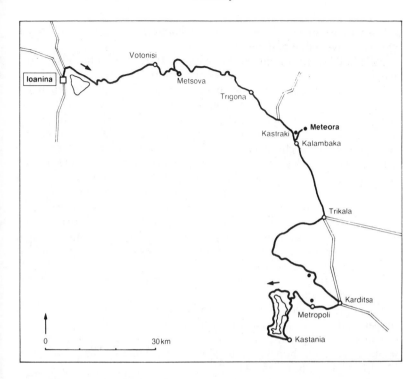

which, some 600 years ago, Byzantine monks built elaborate and beautiful places of worship and founded their skyscraper community. See the rocks from a distance and the effect is startling. Visit the monasteries — 5 of them are still inhabited and reached by a tricky drive and a steep climb — and one is in another world.

Meteora is an impossible act to follow. The route does its best, tracing the ancient Straits of Pili, through way-off-the-beaten-track farming villages set in a puff of cotton fields, and finishing with a flourish, a 48km circuit of a man-made lake high up in the mountains. Refreshingly cool in summer and 'crisp' in spring and autumn, the lake with its scattering of hospitable villages is a pretty and peaceful away-from-it-all spot.

Leave **IOANINA** (see p. 64) on the Trikala road, going eastwards and passing close to **Perama Caves** (see p. 64). There are good views across the lake to the island with its skyline of monasteries and tall trees. The route is spectacular, with a few talking points along the way. It crosses a river by Baldouma's Bridge, follows a tributary and then crosses it by a narrow single-lane bridge with wooden tracks. A shepherd shelters from the pouring rain in a novel way — he has a black bucket on his head. A reassuring sign notes that Katara Pass (crossing the gap between the north and south Pindos range) is open; good news in April. **VOTONISI** is a roadside ribbon of *kafenions*, the click, click, click of backgammon pieces like a shrill greeting call. A bread and feta-cheese breakfast is shared with a dozen or so shepherds leaning on elaborately-carved wooden crooks which are, every one of them, works of art.

METSOVA (turn right off the main road), reached after 58km from Ioanina, is a mountain and ski resort at an altitude of 915m, refreshed by icy-cold streams and refreshing in its approach. The people secured a grant to set up new industries and attract young people back, and now the local timber goes to make beehives and cheese barrels for the whole country, and there's a gleaming new factory making sheep's and goats'-milk cheeses. A delightful cameo; a woman in the traditional costume of red-and-black check skirt, red bolero and shawl passes with a huge tray of bread on her head. She had taken it to the baker's to cook and yes, it is different, she puts eggs and butter in it. A torn-off corner of the steaming brioche-like loaf proves the point, deliciously. The folklore museum is a must, half-way up the hill, up a steep stairway on the left. It is the restored mansion of the Tositsa family complete in every detail, with a tack room, gun room, kitchen and dairy with exquisite pewter, brass and wooden utensils, salons and bedrooms furnished with dark red and navy blue woollen coverings, and cupboards full of antique silverware, pottery, porcelain and antique costumes.

Shopping: wooden items of every kind (wool-winders a speciality), copper and brass, woollen and leather garments, colourful rugs and blankets, ski equipment, sheep's and goats'-milk cheeses, sheep's butter, smoked sausages, honey, Zitsa white wine. Hotels: **Diasselo**, 0656/41.719; **Alpine Club**, 0656/41.249.

Return to the main road and turn right (passing the sawmill). The scenery is grandiose, pine-covered mountains way, way into the distance, with snow measuring poles outlining the road. Water-taps in little chalet-houses at frequent intervals would take care of engine overheating problems; the gradient is wickedly steep in places. Larch forests hung with birds' nests; picnic chairs and tables under pitch-roofed shelters; crops of white clover covering the valley like thick snow; a petrol station, the first since Metsova, 35km away; donkeys ambling along, laden with kindling wood; families tending terraced vines; and then it's tiny **TRIGONA**, with its pretty whitewashed houses and a chatter of restaurants, tavernas, and *kafenions*. Down by the stream an old lady beats the wool out of a blanket with a huge stick and hangs it on a tree to dry.

Back on the road the scenery mellows until suddenly in the distance **METEORA** erupts from the apple orchards, startlingly sheer rocks with monasteries improbably perched on top. The first ones were established on these (then) all-but-inaccessible rocks 14C and a centre of Byzantine art created which reached its heyday in 15C and 16C, when there were 24 flourishing communities. To reach them, follow the signposts to **KASTRAKI**, the village at the foot of these formidable pinnacles, and turn left in the centre. A good paved (though steep and multi-zig-zagged) road now leads to each of the 5 still inhabited monasteries and ruins of others. See: on the left of the road, Doupiani Hermitage (12C chapel) and ruins of Pantocrator and Doupiani monasteries; 3km on left, Mon. of Ag. Nikolaos Anapafsas (early 16C, beautiful frescoes) and, near by, ruins

The typical costume of a villager in Meteora

of Mon. of Ag. Moni (early 14C); 6km on right, Roussaneau Mon. (late 13C, frescoes 1560); to the south, Ag. Trias Mon. (1458-76) reached by flight of 140 steps; and beyond, Nunnery (and museum) of Ag. Stephanos, on 2 pinnacles connected by a bridge (gilded wood carvings, wall paintings and fine icons); to the north Mon. of Varlaam (1517) reached by 195 steps (frescoes 1548); at the end of the road, the biggest and most important, Mon. of the Great Meteoron (exquisite church of Transfiguration, 12-sided dome, fine frescoes, museum, library). Access to this monastery used to be precarious — by jointed ladders and netted baskets on a pulley. The monasteries with their wooden galleries and corniced rooftops are a wonder of medieval architecture, their existence on these stalagmites of rock thrusting from the fertile valley a miracle of devotion and perseverance. Be sure to leave time just to stand and stare in amazement.

Continue through Kastraki (direction Trikala) to **KALAMBAKA**, a small town nestling to the south-east of Meteora (12C cathedral church with 1573 frescoes, marble pulpit and furniture). The town's main claim to fame is its weaving industry. This is the centre for *flokarti*, the thick-weave peasants' blankets and capes, so brilliantly colourful and so necessary in this mountainous area. Hotel: **Galaxy**, 0432/23.233. Tourist Police: 0432/22.813. There are big celebrations on Easter Sunday in both Kastraki and Kalambaka, with dancing in local costume. Continue on the long, straight road to Trikala, 21km that are a welcome rest, after so many twists and turns, for the steering wheel!

TRIKALA (pop: 35,000) See: south west of town, ruins of the oldest sanctuary to Asclepius, the physician-god who, it is believed, was born here; Byzantine castle (from which, fabulous view), public park and zoo. At the end of May, the Hadjipetria Festival with athletic contests, national dances and lectures. Hotel: **Achillion**, 0431/28.192.

Leave Trikala by the Pili road (direction south west), along the banks of the Portaikos, which crosses the plain and touches the foothills of Koziakas. These are the Straits of Pili, in ancient times the shortest route to Epirus and where — as can be seen by the smattering of ruins all around — there were 2 ancient cities. Turn left, 4km before Pili, sign-posted **MOUZAKI**, a large unattractive 'working' village. Just beyond the clutter of outskirts housing, fork right at a garage and in 1km, on entering **MAVROMATI**, fork right. This is another agricultural village, one with pretty stone farmhouses and sturdy cottages with outside bake-ovens and other facilities, and a large — and especially friendly — *kafenion*.

Turn left in **KAPA** and go over a narrow bridge. Hills covered with vines, fields and fields of springtime mauve and white anemones, impregnable castles, a large church with a sky-blue dome, the road runs around a hillside shelf over the plain. **KOMBELOS** must boast the smallest chapel in Greece, a perfect miniature by the roadside, and then **LOXADA**, in the cotton fields, notable for having 3 petrol stations and little more. Blue and green striped beehives and fenced off in little honey gardens all to themselves, and the roadside is a riot of flowers. The road runs straight into the western outskirts of **KARDITSA** passing the hospital on the left. (We by-pass Karditsa for the time being — but return later.)Follow the signs to Nea Plastiras Dam (do not take the road on the left, signposted to Nea Plastiras Factory).

The road goes through **METROPOLI** (9km) close to the site of ancient **Metropolis**, a civic centre formed of several towns, which was captured (191 BC) by the Romans and occupied by Caesar. In 11km the road reaches the head of the artificial lake, **Nea Plastiras**, 800m above sea level and formed by the Tavropos Barrage on the tributary of the Achelos. The lake is set amidst the spectacular Agrafa mountains and ringed with attractive and unspoiled villages just opening their eyes to the possibilities of tourism.

Take the right fork, to Filakti, **NERAIDA** (just inland), an up-and-coming summer resort, and Neohori. **KASTANIA**, at the south-eastern tip, is delightfully hospitable and well set up for renting rooms. Look out for the *domatia* sign. Continue around the lake, take the right fork through one of the 4 parks created in this serenely mountainous region, and return (in 20km) to Karditsa.

KARDITSA (pop: 25,700) Important market town trading in cereals, cotton, silk, tobacco and cattle, and with strong echoes — particularly in the town planning — of its Turkish occupation. It's a jolly place with lively tavernas, metalsmiths working practically night and day in their shop windows, and 3 busy main squares. Food specialities: sheep's and goats'-milk cheeses (several shops devoted to them) and smoked sausages. In May there are folkloric celebrations in the town, with dancing, parades and pageantry depicting the lives of the guerrillas at the time of the Ottoman rule. Hotel: **Astron**, 0441/23.552.

Olympos

2 days/265km/from Larissa

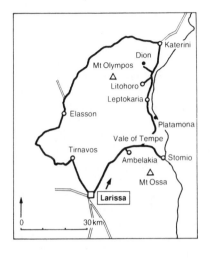

Scenery as grandiose as this, brought about by a phenomenon few people truly understand, is the stuff of which legends are made.

Starting from Larissa in Thessaly, the tour takes the only road through the massive gorge forged between the Olympos and Ossa mountains, known as the Vale of Tempe, home of the Greek gods and birthplace of many a legend. The gigantic rift in the mountains happened in the Quarternary Epoch some 2 million years ago but, according to Herodotus, the god Poseidon got the credit for it. Apollo cleansed himself in the Pinios river after he had slain the serpent Python and, flushed with success, cut a sprig of bay from the river bank and planted it by the Castalian Fountain in his sanctuary at Delphi (see p. 49). Sweet bay still flourishes along the valley.

The road, like the river which rushes joyfully through the ravine, makes straight for the coast — and at this point crosses the regional border and enters Western Macedonia. Sandy beaches stretch for miles.

Just inland, where the coastal plain broadens into the area known to the ancients as Pieria, birthplace of the Muses, are the remains of Dion, an ancient city of the gods. Under the mighty shadow of Olympos the atmosphere lingers on. A festival of games was held in the stadium; Euripides contributed plays to be performed in the theatre, and Alexander sacrificed here before invading Persia. History beneath your footsteps.

Round Olympos to Katerini in the north and the route returns through another spectacular valley, the one separating Olympos from the Pieria range.

LARISSA (pop: 72,300) Capital of Thessaly, in the middle of the Thessalian plain, a major industrial and commercial centre which manages to retain a particular charm. The Pinios river flowing through the centre, the old mansions with their well-maintained courtyards and flower-filled gardens, the Alkazar park and the large, elegant squares edged by shady limes and orange trees give a feeling of space and luxury. The town was built on a site probably inhabited since 10 millennium BC; Paleolithic remains have been excavated on the outskirts. More recently, it has been annexed by the Thessalians, Rome — Pompey passed through the (then) city after the battle of Pharsalus — the Bulgars, Franks, Byzantines and the Turks who occupied it for almost 500 years. The physician Hippocrates died there. See: remains of Byzantine castle; mosque; covered market; archaeological museum. Specialities: ouzo, halva (a honey and sesame sweetmeat), and rose-flavoured ice-cream. Hotels: **Divani Palace**, 041/252.791; **Motel Xenia**, 041/239.002. NTOG: 041/250.919. Tourist Police: 041/227.900.

Leave the town on the major road going north east (direction Katerini) which runs side-by-side with the railway through the delightful Dossian plain where, in prehistoric times, the flood waters of the Pinios formed the lake of Larissa. The lake is no more (see below) but its fertile legacy is evident in the abundant crops — cereal, sugar beet (the road passes a large refinery), potatoes and almond orchards. Lesser kestrels drift overhead. Storks nest noisily on church rooftops and, precariously, on telegraph poles. Otters live among the willows along the river banks. Binoculars are busy. The massive Olympos range towers to the north and, to the east, the huge 1,978m cone which is **Mt. Ossa** (see p. 73). After 30km, turn right to **AMBELAKIA** (5km), a summer resort (alt: 605m) beautifully situated amongst the oaks that soften the outline of **Mt. Kissavos** (1,995m). Already known for the production of cottons and silks the town became, in 1780, the first industrial co-operative set up to spin, dye and export red thread and yarn. At its height it had 6,000 members and agencies all over Europe, including one in London. Ali Pasha all but destroyed the town in 1811, but some fine houses remain. And the tradition of women's industry lives on, in a state-assisted scheme to develop rural crafts and tourism. Agrotourist Co-operative: 0495/31.495. See: 2 Schwarz mansions (rococo painted interiors, murals, wood carvings, stained glass windows); churches of Ag. Georgios, Ag. Paraskevi, Ag. Athanassios. Speciality: the dry red wine that gives the town its name (*ambelia* means grape vines).

Return to the main road and turn right. The road, running alongside the fast-flowing river Pinios, now enters the legendary **Vale of Tempe**, just **Tembi** to the Greeks, and the beginning of the toll road. The narrow gorge, some 10km long and in places only 30m wide, was formed at the time of the Ice Ages when the Olympos and Ossa mountains were torn apart, making an exit route for the pent-up waters of the lake of Larissa. They took it, and the lake became the plain. According to Herodotus (5C BC) the Thessalians attributed this upheaval to Poseidon, god of the sea and storms. The magnitude of the split, known in the Middle Ages as the Wolf's Mouth, is awe-inspiring. The contrast between the uncompromisingly sheer, almost vertical cliffs and the calm greenness of the river banks burgeoning with bay, willow, plane and pink-blossomed Judas trees is unforgettable. See: (on a hill, right of road) ruins of Castle of Oria, subject of folk song.

Turn right (8km after the Ambelakia road) for a there-and-back detour, first to **OMOLIO** (3km), where once a Temple of Poseidon was erected in recognition of his earth-shattering feat. Tombs recently excavated have yielded iron, bronze and gold objects and classical jewellery (now in Larissa museum). Continue to **STOMIO** (12km) which crouches below the steepest face of Mt. Ossa. This peaceful seaside resort has thermal springs (recommended for rheumatism), good fish tavernas and apartment blocks. **Vlassis** furnished apartments, 041/226.529. Return the 15km to the main road and turn right, crossing both the river and railway. The mouth of the river Pinios, on the right, is now extensively farmed — for fish.

Continue to **PLATAMONA** (14km) where the Crusaders (13C) built a splendid castle on a hilly knoll to guard the narrow straits. How did the castle escape destruction when the Turks overran Macedonia in 15C? It protected the invaders from both pirates and mutinous local inhabitants. And so there it stands, gazing out to sea and rising from pomegranate and oak thickets with colourful carpets of anemones, marigolds, sky-blue anchusa and wall-colonising alyssum. See: well-preserved wall, keep, some interior buildings, and a superb view. Also, left of castle, Spring of the Muses. **Xenia Motel**, 0352/41.204; **Platamon Camping**, 0352/41.301.

The sandy beaches backed by grassy tree-clad fields all along the way are on the point of being 'discovered' and there is no shortage of facilities. The toll booth is between **SKOTINA** (**Olympos Camping**, 0352/41.487) and **LEPTOKARIA** (in 11km), a village splashed by streams and lapped by waves. Hotel: **Koralli**, 0352/31.264. Turn left in 5km to **LITOHORO** (pop: 5,600) a health resort 5km from the main road. The village is at an altitude of 308m on the eastern face of Olympos, and an ascent can be made from there. Festivals: January, the Epiphany festival; February, at Platamona, Skotina and Litohoro, Carnival; July, Naval week of maritime events (the inhabitants of Litohoro have a long maritime tradition). Hotel: **Leto**, 0352/22.121. **Stavros Mountain Refuge**, 0352/81.944.

Return to the main road, turn left and in 6km turn left for **DION**, an ancient city site at the foot of Olympos and 5km inland from the Pierian coast. Here the Macedonians gathered to honour Olympian deities with offerings and sacrifices, and King Archaelaus (414-399 BC) enlivened the proceedings with contests in the nude. The city was destroyed 220 BC, rebuilt, and finally sacked by Alaric AD 4C. Excavations have revealed sanctuaries of the gods, including Dionysus and Zeus, Greek and Roman theatres, stadium, statues of Asclepius and his family, paved road network, houses, workshops, public buildings, communal baths, water and drainage system, basilicas with mosaic floors. See: remains of all this, and the museum too.

Retrace to the main road and turn left for **KATERINI** (pop: 28,800), capital of the Pieria region, which is wedged in the valley between Olympos to the south and the Pieria range to the north and has, not surprisingly, wonderful mountain views in a massive arc. Hotel: **Park**, 0351/25.103; or hotel at Katerini beach: **Aktaion**, 0351/61.215. Tourist Police: 0351/23.440.

Leave Katerini by the Elasson road (direction west), 71km of picturesque and ever-changing scenery. Mountainsides are now pinky beige and jaggedly naked, now clothed in pine, beech and fir, and always host to a galaxy of flowers — pheasant's-eye narcissus, columbine, gentians, fritillaries, red hellebores, St. Bernard's lilies, martagon lilies and more, all with an unwritten understanding: admire, but never pick. Valley life is peaceful. A goatherd having his lunch by a stream at **FOTINA** breaks off a hunk of bread and divides up a cheese hanging in a cloth to drain. This in exchange for a chat and the admission that yes, it rains in England. Further south, between Pithio and Kallithea, a shepherd dresses a lamb for Easter (a polite term for a gory, abattoir-like act) and that, too, is suspended from a tree.

ELASSON (pop: 7,200) is situated at the mouth of a gorge and surrounded by white limestone rocks. It stands on the site of Homer's 'white Olooson', a Bronze Age town which flourished until 5C BC. See: Byzantine bridge over the river, Monastery of Panageia Olimpiotissa (13C, wood carvings), riverside museum in mosque. Leave the town on the Larissa road, going south.

There's a feeling of rich, lush pastureland all around as the road snakes its way to **STEFANOVOUNO** and **GALANOVRISI**, both distinctly agricultural villages almost deserted during the day. The work is in the meadows and up in the hills. **DOMENIKO** has a fresh, bright air — they know how to make a good cup of coffee there, too — and children seem reluctant for visitors to leave. The Titarissios river describes a long, wide arc from here, and so does the road. Sensible the traveller who has time for a picnic, or at least a glass of something, beside its banks. Butterflies hover, speckled woods and painted ladies, and wood warblers start choir practice. The road eases its way through a narrow gap between 2 hills, with a ruined tower standing guard, and continues to **TIRNAVOS** (pop: 10,500) where it parts company with the river. This is the chief town of the region, its revenue coming from textiles and ouzo; so plenty of jolly *ouzarias* in the side-streets. The road turns sharply south east out of the town and makes its uneventful way for the 17km return to Larissa.

Pelion

1–2 days/250km/from Volos

Practically in the heart of Greece, Pelion is the both fertile and mountainous peninsula wrapped around the western side of the Pagassitic Gulf. Farther west lie the Sporades islands and to the south, the only-just-an-island of Evia. Pelion's only geographical link with the mainland is the massive Mt. Pelion range rising at its tallest peak, known as Pourianos Stavros, to 1,651 metres.

Scientific evidence shows that the peninsula was formed millions of years ago during the gigantic geological upheavals that shook the whole of the Aegean, forming the steep slopes, sheer precipices and deep ravines

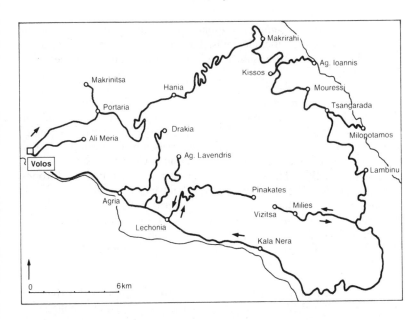

that now, on Pelion, shelter 24 beautiful and varied villages.

Myths and legends abound, and it is sometimes hard to sort fact from fiction. In his cave among Pelion's wooded hills Chiron, the wisest of the Centaurs, healed the wounds of the sick with herbs that still grow abundantly and aromatically on every hillside. The seeds of the discord that gave rise to the Trojan war were supposed to have been sown here, after Peleus' marriage to Thetis. And then there is the one about the Titans. The giants in their war with the gods tried to pile Mt. Pelion on top of Mt. Ossa to create a peak that would surpass the mighty Mt. Olympos. It was not to be!

The region was only sparsely inhabited until the Turkish occupation in 15C, when terrified inhabitants from the plains fled to the mountains for refuge and — owing to the terrain and the fact that the Turks had dug themselves in to a fortress in Golos (now Volos) — were largely left to their own cultural and commercial devices. By the time the country was liberated in 1829 the villages were prosperous and elegant, business was booming, and the much-needed international trading port of Volos was founded.

Pelion is lush and green, from its deepest valley to its craggiest peak, a fertile basket of orchard fruits, apples especially, nuts, olives and herbs — there are said to be over 2,000 species of aromatic plants to fill the air — and a forest of pines, oaks, planes and beech. It is well worth a trip!

VOLOS (pop: 70,000) The main port of Thessaly, situated between Mt. Pelion and the Pagassitic Gulf; a sophisticated and lively place. The action — jostling restaurants, tavernas and *kafenions* — is chiefly around the fishing harbour, behind which is the main square, and the quayside and Argonafton, a magnificent esplanade occupying over 1km of the waterfront. Industries include mills, tanneries, refineries, and its international trade is in cotton, silk, sheep's and goats' skins, vegetables, olive oil, sugar and soap. The port is linked (mainly during summer months) with the Sporades islands and Kimi, Evia (see p. 95). Volos has had maritime connections since the earliest times. Built on the side of the mound which housed Homeric **Iolkos**, from which Jason and his Argonauts set sail in search of the Golden Fleece, the town has yielded some important archaeological finds. See: museum (reconstituted burials from Mykinean to Classical times, Paleolithic implements, Neolithic tools (7 millennium BC), Hellenistic gold jewellery and painted tombstones, Roman statues). The 'Balkan meeting' held in Volos each year 20–30 August includes exhibition of folk arts from the Balkan countries, dances by Greek and foreign troupes, theatrical performances and concerts. Hotels: **Pallas**, 0421/23.510; **Adonis Pension**, 0421/38.015. NTOG: 0421/23.500. Tourist Police: 0421/27.094. Customs: 0421/23.376. Greek Motoring Club: 0421/25.001.

Leave the town (direction north east) on the Portaria road arriving in 5km at **ANAKASSIA** at the foothills of the mountain and bubbling with streams and rivulets. Beyond that, in 2km, is **ANO VOLOS**, a high-vantage-point village with interesting 18C houses and mansions on the sides of a hill rising to 800m. See: Kondos house with remarkable (1912) wall-paintings by folk artist Theofilus; Church of Metamorfosis on Episkopi hill (16C icon). Continue to **PORTARIA**, a popular summer resort with cobbled streets and fine 18C houses dating from its commercial heyday, when it boasted a weekly fair. Tavernas line the gracious square under the umbrella-shade of a huge plane tree. See: 1273 church (late 16C frescoes) and 1855 church of Ag. Nikolaos (frescoes and reliefs). Specialities: sheep's and goats' cheeses and red wine. The village is the starting-point for the climb to Pliasidi (1,548m) one of the highest peaks of Pelion (3½ hours) with magnificent views across the Plain of Thessaly, Mt. Olympos and a wide, blue expanse of the Aegean Sea. It is said that if the sun rises in China, then it certainly sets in Pelion. In August there are folkloric performances of a mock wedding, Pelion style. Hotel: **Xenia**, 0421/99.158.

Take the left road from the village, a 4km-each-way detour to **MAKRINITSA**, built on the slope of a hill and rising tier after tier from 300m to almost 700m above sea level. Clinging to the mountainside at a precarious-looking angle the whitewashed houses with every-colour-of-the-rainbow shutters are designed to cope. They have 3 storeys at the front and only a single storey at the back. See: tiny church of Ag. Ioannis in the square, where a massive hollow plane tree has a door in the trunk, and a marble fountain. The National Tourist Organisation has converted 3 guest houses, **Mousli Pension**, 0421/99.228, **Sissilianou Pension**, 0421/99.556, and **Xiradakis Pension**, 0421/99.250.

Return to Portaria and turn left. The road tacks its way along a high ledge to, after 12 steep kilometres, **HANIA** at the head of the pass, with an altitude of 1,170m and appropriately rewarding views. The village, rising dramatically out of a ring of beech and chestnut woods, is a flourishing ski resort. A chair lift connects it with Pliasidi (see above). Speciality: *fasolada*, bean soup. Hotel: **Manthos**, 0421/99.541. The road starts a gradual but contortionately twisty descent towards the eastern coastline and the scent of the herbs is intoxicating. At the junction in 14km, turn right to **MAKRIRAHI** (alt: 300m) a hamlet renowned for its healthy climate, its tranquillity and an abundance of orchard fruits. Face to face with the village and reached by a road across the valley, is its opposite number on the other side of the ravine. **ANILIO** (which means sunless) is a typically hospitable small village which has the misfortune to be looking northwards. Take the right turn, a detour in 2km, to **KISSOS** (alt: 500m) a pretty village almost hidden by wild, lush vegetation. See: 18C church of Ag. Marina, an aisled basilica (magnificent gilded iconostasis, wooden sculptures, and frescoes).

Back-track to the junction and take the coast road through Ag. Dimitrios to **AG. IOANNIS**, a sea-side resort which has everything going for it — pale sandy beaches, sand dunes bristling with wild thistles (magnificent for floral decoration), an incredibly calm, blue sea (it's in a sheltered spot) and a backdrop of the gentle slopes of an intensely green, densely wooded mountain. Hotel: **Maro**, 0426/31.241. Return the 6km inland, turn left and in 5km at **MOURESSI**, see Church of the Theotokos (wonderful carved wooden iconostasis). The road continues (4km) to **TSANGARADA** (alt: 477m), an elegant and stylish village surrounded by chestnuts, oaks and plane trees, with colour-washed houses, clouds of pink hydrangeas and beautifully decorated churches typical of the region. **Kentavros Pension**, 0423/49.233; **Xenia Hotel**, 0423/49.205.

A road edged with sweet-scented *rigani* (oregano) leads down (8km) to the beach at **MILOPOTAMOS** a favourite spot with water-sports enthusiasts. Sandy strands of beach, long slender silver-and-gold fingers reach out to rocky islets and shelter in shallow coves. Hard to beat for bathing and picnics. The main road, spectacular by any standards, threads its way along the mountainside through Horichtio to **LAMBINU**, and the island of Skiathos appears briefly on the horizon before the road turns sharply and steeply inland, by-passing Kalamakio on the left. Take the right turn (2km after that junction) to **MILIES** (alt: 360m) which, as its name suggests, is a delightful village in the heart of apple orchard country (*miless* means apples). See: Church of the Taxiarches (frescoes), library and private folkloric collection.

VIZITSA, 3km farther, on a geological cul-de-sac, has its own proud folk traditions and magnificent 18C mansions, some now being restored as guest houses. Return to Milies, take the left fork and in 6km fork right again, through Neohori (in 4km) and on through mountains cloaked in forests breathtaking at any time, but specially in autumn. Take the right fork 7km from Neohori, through Afetes and dropping gently down through olive groves towards the Pagassitic Gulf again. The road does not slide straight into the sea, as it seems to threaten. Turn right at the

T-junction, keeping in line with the shore, through the hamlet of Koropi to **KALA NERA** ('good waters') a peaceful village in a most favoured situation, set among rich vegetation and facing a wide-ribbon-strip of sandy beach. Hotel: **Alcyon**, 0423/22.364. In fact, it's beaches, beaches all the way for a while, plus small, jolly tavernas serving the crispest of pick-up-in-your-fingers small fish. If you don't stop at **KATO GATZEA** then 5km farther along the coast there's another chance, at **MALAKI**. Take the inland road on the right at **LECHONIA**, driving through bountiful orchards to Strofilos and then, upward ever upward, to Ag. Vlasios, Ag. Georgios to **PINAKATES**, tantalisingly close, as the map shows, to Milies, just a matter of an impregnable peak away. Stone houses with grey fishscale roofs of overlapping slate nestle amongst the lushest of forests. Hoopoes swoop overhead. The lanes are rounded with brambles, softened with bracken and at times colour-speckled with rock roses. It's beautiful.

Return the 13km to Lechonia, turn right on to the main road and in 2km turn right again for the second of 4-in-a-row cul-de-sac excursions into the mountains. The pattern will be familiar by now, fruitful low-level fields rising to dense beech and chestnut woods and tucked-away villages. At the end of the road (in 12km) is **AG. LAVENDRIS** (alt: 500m), a crisp, refreshing resort that's a good starting-point for brisk walks or gentle strolls into the green yonder. But not until one has taken in the simple beauty of this well-preserved village, a living museum to folk art. **Kentavros Pension**, 0421/92.379.

The instructions are as before. Return to the main road, turn right and right again (in 2km) to **DRAKIA** (alt: 550m) with — shades of former glories — towered mansions displaying a rare combination of wealth and simplicity. See: Triandafilos house (18C wall paintings, carved architectural features). Return to the main road, through a lane spattered in summer with sky-blue chicory and rambling, snow-white clematis, to **AGRIA**, its fish tavernas lining the sandy shoreline like so many bathing cubicles. Continue along the coast road (the gentle 'white horses' almost lapping the route) and in 7km turn right to **ALI MERIA** where, in the unlikely setting of the bakery of Velendzas (Melinis) there are fine Theofilos frescoes.

Return to the coastal road (4km) for the last time and turn right for Volos.

5 EVIA AND SKIROS

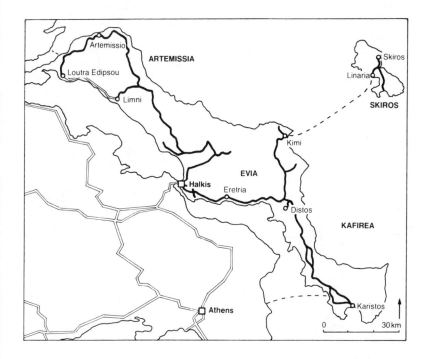

To travel to Evia, the second largest Greek island (after Crete), is to make a delightful and somewhat surprising voyage of discovery. Delightful because here is an area, 175km by up to 50km, of uninhibited scenic beauty, cloaked in the frosty greenness of olives, poplars and pines; the mellow fruitfulness of vines, figs, pomegranates, walnuts and chestnuts; dappled from one season to the next with a palette of pink Judas tree blossom, tree heather, mallow and oleander, and shimmering all summer long with butterflies.

Surprising, perhaps, because this majestic and tranquil, mountainous and fertile only-just-an-island, a mere 88km from the centre of Athens and conveniently connected to the mainland by a drawbridge, has not as yet attracted what one might consider its fair share of tourists. This is particularly noteworthy because Evia is intermittently fringed — where the massive rocks don't sweep down to the sea — by that usually most come-hither of all natural attributes, a ring of some of the sandiest beaches in the Aegean.

In common with the country as a whole, Evia had for centuries endured the political see-saw of a succession of colonisers and rulers. Wrenched from Attica and Viotia on the mainland by an earthquake, the island was first inhabited by settlers from Thessaly, then by Ionians, Aeolians and Dorians. One by one the 7 city states which were formed — Halkis, Eretria, Karistos and the others — fell in turn to the Spartans, the Athenians, the Persians, Romans, Venetians and Turks — it is a long list — until, after the War of Independence in 1830, Evia settled comfortably into Greek hands.

The island's chequered history has left it with a remarkably varied legacy, a fascinating patchwork of archaeological sites and architectural treasures. Some of Evia's most precious secrets from the past have only recently been discovered, and the interested visitor has the tantalising feeling that he or she might even now stumble across evidence of yet another chapter in its social development.

One of the most remarkable discoveries was made in 1981. At Lefkanti on the southern coast close to Vassiliko, a huge building was unearthed — its purpose as yet undefined — dating from the 9C BC and revealing, nearly 3,000 years later, female skeletons and gold jewellery. The puzzling thing is that the building, with a floor area some 54m long and 10m wide, represents a style of architecture which pre-dates by 300 years other examples common in Ancient Greece.

But perhaps the greatest conundrum that surrounds Evia is the gulf which divides it from the mainland. The dangerous waters of the Evripus Channel can reach 7 or 8 knots and change direction 6 or 7 times a day, defying all known theories of time and tide. Indeed, the phenomenon is said to have so baffled the philosopher Aristotle, when he retired to Halkis, that in 322 BC he flung himself into the fast-flowing waters in an admission of defeat.

Artemissia
2–3 days/469km/from Halkis

The scent of pine drifting down from the mountains; field after field of green-turning-to-yellow vines; the statuesque silhouettes of poplars and cypresses etched against the sea; the awe-inspiring remains of ancient cities surviving side-by-side with modern towns and villages; the sharp contrast between high rocky peaks and low fertile plains — this is the character of the northern half of Evia, more lush and fertile north of a line from Halkis to Kimi.

The tour explores the road that links Halkis, a mere 40m from the

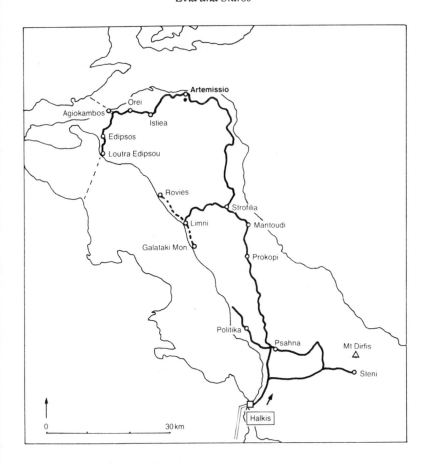

mainland, through Artemissia in the north to Lihas Gialtra, the western-most tip of the island. But we do not always keep to the straight and narrow! There are too many places of interest to divert our attention, off to one side and the other.

As with the southern route (see below), if you wish to keep your wheels firmly on the ground and travel to and from the mainland by the road bridge, you cannot avoid retracing your steps for most of the way — there is no other route over the mountains.

The alternative is to take one of the ferry routes, from Edipsos to Arkitsa on the mainland (148km from Athens on the Athens-Lamia motorway) or from Agiokambos to Glifa (56km from Lamia, joining the motorway at Pelasgia).

Leave **HALKIS** (see p. 98) by the coast road travelling north (direction Mantoudi). After 5km, at Nea Artaki, turn right. The road wanders through a patchwork of cereal and poultry farms to Katheni. Turn right at the village and, after 1km, turn left (direction Steni). The road begins to climb the foothills of Evia's pride and joy, its highest mountain, Mt. Dirfis

(1,743m). In 5km there is a sharp left-hand bend and, much steeper now, the road winds up to the cool mountain village of **STENI**, a welcome haven from the summer sun.

Icy waters gush down from a great height, and the region abounds with alpine flowers; many species are local to this region. The architecture is alpine too, the wooden chalets in marked contrast to the cubic-style houses elsewhere on the island. In good weather you can drive part of the way along a steep track towards the summit; there is a mountain refuge hut from which the climb takes about 1½ hours. Visitors who are not into serious hill-walking will find beautiful tracks (and picnic spots) leading through chestnut and conifer forests.

Follow the road back to Katheni. Continue straight on at the junction, through the hamlet of Paliura, to Makrikara. The road, which takes a very sharp left-hand turn in the village and then slides gently down from the mountain slopes to a fertile plain, leads to **PSAHNA** (pop: 4,600).

Go straight over the crossroads in this small market-garden town, and then across the main south-north road. Follow the by-road for 9km to **POLITIKA** (15C Byzantine church) and, for a lazy swim, continue along the track to Dafni, where the slopes of Mt. Kandilio sweep almost down to the sea.

Return to the main road and turn left (direction still Mantoudi). The road zig-zags through the valley between Mt. Dirfis and Mt. Kandilio with — if you feel like veering off-course — pretty villages along passable tracks on either side. In 36km you come to **PROKOPI** (pop: 1,300), the star of the Klissoura Valley. The village is the centre of a large estate which was once in the hands of Turkish landowners (pasha), when it was known as Achmet-Agha. The Turks planted their own favourite trees and flowers — palms, cypress and plane and, less familiar in the region, tulips, lilies and roses, and surrounded their mansions and villas with luxurious lawns. The estate, now owned by a British family and the centre of a charitable foundation, is run as a model farm and health centre.

Continue on the main road through the industrial outskirts of **MAN-TOUDI**. Take the left fork (the right one leads to the town) to Kirindos and then, 4km farther on, turn left through Strofilia along a scenic road, passing through several small villages, to **LIMNI** (pop: 2,400), an attractive fishing village (**Avra motel**, 0227/312.20). This is a pleasant spot to while away an hour or so. The pine forests and olive groves almost dip their feet into the water and the sea, trapped in the harbour by the rugged coastline, has the appearance of a lake. A 1-hour climb from the village to the Byzantine **Galataki monastery** is rewarding for its frescoes.

If time is not of the essence, take the small coastal track, heading north west and shaded by olives, along to **ROVIES**, another pretty fishing village with cheerful tavernas and good beaches. It is a tougher climb (8km) to the near-by monastery of Geronda (17C frescoes).

Return to Limni and then retrace the 19km road to the T-junction. Turn left on to the main road at Strofilia (direction Istiea). The road, carved on a high ridge, skirts the eastern slopes of Mt. Xiro, through Papades and on to Vasilika. All along this road there are tantalising views eastwards (but not for the driver!) of the Northern Sporades islands. At Agriovotanon, the most northerly village of Evia, the road loops inland a little to emerge close to the coast again at **ARTEMISSIO**.

The whole region of Artemissia, and this Cape in particular, has played an important role in the island's history. Scattered under olive trees close to the shore, the remains of a massive temple dedicated to the goddess Diana excite the imagination as to the scale and beauty of the monument. In 480 BC the straits below were the scene of a no-win encounter between the Greek and Persian fleets before the battle of Thermopylae. At the bottom of the sea a shipload of works of art was discovered in 1928. Among the treasure was the massive bronze statue of the god Poseidon (now in the National Museum in Athens).

The road leaves the coastline and turns inland again to the modern town of **ISTIEA** (pop: 4,000) which is sheltered by a bowl of surrounding hills and has grown up among some of the most prolific orchards and vines on the island. Six km further on, it is **OREI** that marks the site of one of the oldest cities on the island, Histaia, which was mentioned in Homer's Iliad. Guarding as it does the Evoikos Gulf, and within sight of Mt. Othris on the mainland opposite, the city was well fortified in antiquity and through to the Middle Ages. (The Venetians recycled ancient materials to build their castle.) A 4C BC marble bull, found in the narrow channel in 1965, stands impressively in the small village square. A car ferry links Agiokambos (5km to the west of Orei and 1km off to the right) with Glyfa on the mainland, in Thessaly, a 30-minute crossing (10km from Pelasgia, on the Lamia-Larissa motorway).

Running south from Agiokambos, the road leads to **EDIPSOS** and then the spa town of **LOUTRA EDIPSOU** (pop: 2,200) which could be journey's end. A ferry connects the port to Arkitsa, on the mainland. Tourist Police: 0226/22.456.

'Arcades, hostelries, shops and a theatre provide visitors with all comforts as well as entertainment.' Not a come-on for Loutra Edipsou, as it is now, but a description of its attractions in Roman times. The curative and restorative properties of the thermal springs were well chronicled. The spa was mentioned by Aristotle and Plutarch, and Augustus and Hadrian had recourse to the warm, sulphuric waters.

The present-day resort, with its neo-classical pump room, literally dozens of hotels, and with elegant parks, gardens and tree-lined avenues is a fashionable oasis in an island whose charm lies in its 'local' character.

Another resort which owes little to its surroundings — except in the matter of sun, sand and sea — is the new holiday complex at Grego-limano, on the north-western tip of the island. The road from Loutra Edipsou follows the coastline to Lihas Gialtra, and then to the holiday village.

If you are not tempted by any of the ferry-hopping ports along the route, it is 180km by road back to Halkis.

Kafirea

2 days/362km/from Halkis

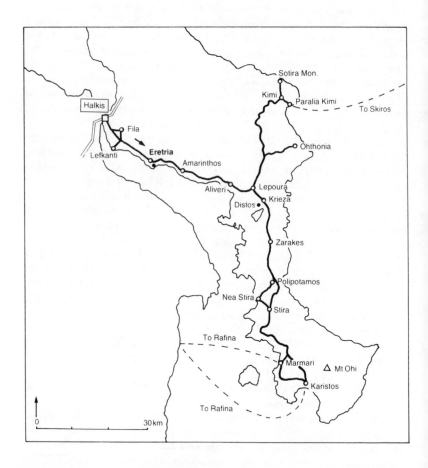

What Evia lacks in the matter of a comprehensive road network (there is but one major road running both north and south from Halkis) is compensated for in the number of tracks and footpaths with fascinating destinations, and the variety of terrain and scenery. South from the drawbridge, towards the port of Karistos, the road is bordered on one side by the Evripus Channel and on the other by the Lelantine Plain, an area so fertile and fruitful that for centuries it provoked a tug-of-war between the two neighbouring city states of Halkis and Eretria.

Visually along the way all is not quite sweetness and light, and around Aliveri and much farther south at Marmari there are stark reminders of the island's other main sources of wealth, lignite mining and green cipolin marble quarrying respectively. In addition Aliveri is scarred by a massive thermo-electric plant — not a spot on which to rest one's gaze.

Leaving industrial progress behind, the road emerges into the sunlight, so to speak, crossing the enchanting valley of Distos where you can see, idyllically situated beside a lake, the remains of an ancient town which the Venetians later fortified for their own protection. Indeed, a rewarding game of 'spot the Byzantine church, the Venetian fortress, the prehistoric remains' can be played all along the route. Approaching the southern tip of the island the road gradually falls under the dominating shadow of Mt. Ohi (1,495m) which presides over the villages to either side.

Here, at Karistos, you come up against a slight local difficulty. To reach Kimi, as one must do to visit Skiros, you have to retrace your steps northwards as far as Lepoura, where the road forks right and hastens towards your destination, the small ferry-boat harbour known as Rupert Brooke's port. There is an alternative. Instead of approaching Evia by the road bridge at Halkis, you can make the ferry crossing from Rafina, on the mainland (32km east of Athens) to Nea Stira, Marmari or, preferably, Karistos. That way, after a 2-hour crossing, you arrive on Evia with a greater sense of being on an island, and you avoid back-tracking along some 75km of the route.

HALKIS (pop: 36,300) has been connected to the mainland since the first bridge was built over the Evripus Channel in 411 BC. Its advantageous position has meant that the city — now a town — has, according to the ebb and flow of its fortunes, been in turn fortified by its invaders and itself formed colonies, notably in Italy. It is now a centre for heavy industry — cement works, food processing and textiles — and a busy trading port. Two museums provide a glimpse into its more glorious past, the archaeological museum in *leof.* Venizelou and the medieval museum, housed in a former Turkish mosque in the Kastro region. Close by is the impressive basilica of Agia Paraskevi. Tourist Police: 0221/24.662.

Take the coast road, heading south. Bear with the distinctly non-rural aspect for a while. This is the part of Evia that has been colonised anew, by weekending Athenians and by tourists; no shortage of hotels, restaurants and other tourist facilities. **ERETRIA** is a prosperous modern holiday centre overlapping a prosperous ancient city. The archaeological remains are mostly to the north west of the village beyond the museum on *leof.* Timokratou — a 4C palace complete with clay bath, the foundations of a Temple of Dionysos, and a theatre. Eastwards, at the foot of the acropolis, is the gymnasium and, still in that direction, the remains of a sanctuary to a goddess, perhaps Artemis Olympia.

The road follows the coastline, through **AMARINTHOS** where the fish tavernas may well prove irresistible and **ALIVERI**, where a mineral railway plies between the lignite mines in the hills and the small commercial port of Karavos. Turn right (direction Karistos) to Lepoura, and then right to Krieza. After 5km there is a track on the right leading to the ruins of ancient **Distos** (not to be confused with the new village) on a wild hill close to the lake. The earliest remains are terraces of 5C BC houses.

Successive civilisations have left their mark, an acropolis, a 5C city and a Venetian tower.

The road continues south through **ZARAKES** (crumbling windmills) and Almiropotamos over a rocky ridge to (taking the left fork) **POLIPOTAMOS**, with sea views on both sides. To the east of **STIRA**, on the slopes of Mt. Kliosi, is the massive Frankish castle of Larmena. The village has a peaceful little square, offering a pleasant coffee break.

Now the route becomes spectacular. This 30km stretch between Stira and Karistos is known as Eagles' Road; birds of prey hover over the craggy hillsides. It runs along a ledge up to 800m above sea level. Cameras at the ready to capture the magnificent views into the wide bays, the hilly Petali islands to the west and, on a spur to the south of the Kliosi ridge, approaching Friga, a terrace of three ancient buildings known as the dragon's houses.

The road comes to **KARISTOS** (car ferry connection with Rafina), a busy but unremarkable town (pop: 3,500) on the site of an ancient city, set among lush vineyards and dense olive groves, in the benign shadow of Mt. Ohi.

The southern end of the long esplanade is a springboard for excursions, as energetic or passive as one wishes. A secondary road heading west and then north (take the left fork at Aetos) hugs the mountain foothills just inland and leads to several away-from-it-all hamlets. Dedicated hikers can continue to explore this track as it climbs, round to Kalianos, Yanitsi and the dauntingly situated castle at Filagra.

Back in Aetos, the same track heading in the opposite direction (north west) leads to the pretty hamlet of Mili with welcome cafés (ascent of Mt. Ohi by the southern route in about 3 hours), continues to Gravia, over a stone bridge and joins the major road north of Karistos at Mekunida.

Optional sightseeing trips aside, our route leaves Karistos, returning northwards by the main road. After 2km, take the left fork towards the coast, to **MARMARI** (as the name indicates, its main claim to fame is its marble deposits). Take the left fork in the village through Friga (good beaches along this strand), then rejoining the main road. Take the left fork 1km farther on and then, after passing through Stira, the left fork to the new holiday village of **NEA STIRA**. On the tiny offshore island of the same name there are remains of a Homeric town. This coastal loop in the road rejoins the main road. Continue to **LEPOURA**, a major junction and dull little place, and take the right fork (direction Kimi).

The road is narrow and steep in parts, and ageing buses make seemingly impossible turns in workmanlike and totally non-touristy village centres — causing many a good-humoured breach in the timetable. There are typical villages (square white houses, trailing vines and flower-packed terraces) on both sides of the road, the ones to the west nestling at the foot of Mt. Dirfis and to the east, mistily coiling round pine-covered hillsides. Worth a small detour, as they say, is **OHTHONIA**, not so much for its architecture but because it is a hive of local cottage industry — especially during the walnut and grape harvests.

Turn right 11km beyond Lepoura, and in 8km you will come to the village.

Back on the main road, it is 24km to **KIMI** (pop: 2,250). The town, newish, with a concrete-like look and most mod. cons, is a disappointment, but glimpses through bamboo-lined footpaths leading down to the small port of **PARALIA KIMI** are, correctly, reassuring. The port is 4km by road, or an exhilarating scamper by goat track. (**Hotel Acteon** 0222/6.04; good waterside tavernas.) The beach is long, sandy and wild, fanned by pampas grass and protected by pretty blue-domed fishermen's chapels. And it has practical uses. Towards Platana, south east of Kimi, rows of wine barrels are stored on the sands and sheep and goats roam lazily about.

From the town, 'upstairs' as the Greeks say, you can drive (due north) along a stony road to Sotira monastery, but it is more fun to walk — if you feel strong enough to carry the bunches of grapes, bags of figs or jars of honey, not to mention samples of wine, ouzo and coffee you will surely be offered along the way.

The 17C stone-built monastery — nunnery, to be accurate — has a commanding position and an infinitely intricate tiled roofline. It is just possible you will be welcomed with the customary hospitality of chunks of sour-dough bread and crumbly goats' cheese. In the ornate chapel (only women visitors are allowed inside) dried verbascum flowers gathered in the mountains are floated on oil reservoirs to serve as lamp wicks. It is thought that the monastery, high up on the cliff ledge, is built on the site of ancient Kimi.

Paralia Kimi is the departure port for the group of 'Rupert Brooke' islands, the Northern Sporades (see page 175), the closest of which is Skiros (see below), where the poet is buried.

To return to Halkis, follow the road back to Lepoura, fork right at the junction and continue on this coastal road until, 8km after Eretria, the turning on the left to **LEFKANTI**. Make this small detour to see the coastal hamlet where continuing excavations are revealing successive ancient civilisations and, at the same time, puzzling archaeologists. Returning to the Halkis road you will see straight ahead (a staggered crossroads) the turning to **FILA** where a medieval castle dominates a high mound, and there is a 6C cemetery.

The main road continues to Halkis.

Skiros

At least 1 day and overnight/2 hrs by ferry from Paralia Kimi (on Evia)

The largest and most easterly of the Northern Sporades group of islands, Skiros has carved a place in both legend and history. It was to the court of Lykomedes, king of Skiros, that Achilles came, disguised as a girl to avoid the Trojan war — only to be lured to Troy, and his death, by Ulysses.

In ancient times Skiros was renowned for its multi-coloured marble, and magnificent marble temples were raised to Apollo and Poseidon.

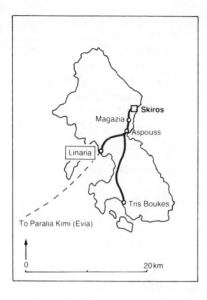

Skiros
Magazia
Aspouss
Linaria
Tris Boukes
To Paralia Kimi (Evia)
0   20 km

An isthmus accentuates the natural division between the tree-covered and fertile northern half of the island — where the capital is situated — and the more mountainous and less hospitable southern part.

Ferryboats connect Skiros to Evia, and the other islands in the group. In high season be sure to book your return passage. Skiros has been discovered.

The island is magic. At least the old town of **SKIROS**, or **HORA**, is. The ferry from Paralia Kimi — a 2-hour journey — generally arrives in the evening (check the timetable with the Kimi port authority, 0222/ 26.606), which means that you jostle into the full fairyland effect of bustling shops, cafés and tavernas — Skiros style. The boat returns to Kimi early the next morning, so you have to stay at least overnight. Have to? I know someone who hopped over 'just for the day' and stayed a fortnight!

The island port, **LINARIA** on the west coast, is clean, tidy and has a ring of bright newness — and very pleasant rooms and tavernas on the waterfront. If you think you have seen it all before, make straight for the old town, 12km away on the north-east coast. Park your motor car outside the town — it will be of no more use to you there — or leave it behind in the car park at Paralia Kimi. The maze of steeply stepped white-washed streets is for foot passengers only — and functional wheelbarrows. A bus meets the boats and rumbles off to Hora.

As for somewhere to stay — 'no problem'. (**Xenia hotel**, 0222/ 91.209.) You have only to set foot in the town and someone will come forward to offer you a room, or even a dazzling white, cluttered and cosy little terraced house with outside 'facilities', and all for a remarkably low rent. Traditional Skirian houses, unique and wonderful, have massively thick rounded walls, and at least one suitably thick step-seat outside, for the evening ritual of a chat with the neighbours. Inside, there are beehive-shaped fireplaces-cum-ovens, wood-panelled room divisions — if any at all — and raised sleeping quarters (*patari*) resembling minstrels' galleries with elaborate balustrades. The walls are hung with generations-old gleaming copper pans, blue and white china, and colourful woven blankets. As outworking is a principal source of income, many houses are 'furnished' to the exclusion of practically everything else with large traditional looms.

The foothills of the town are the hub of this island universe. The warm, sweet scent of *bougatsas* (cinnamon custard pies) drifting from the bakers, the competing attractions of spit-roasting lamb and charcoal-

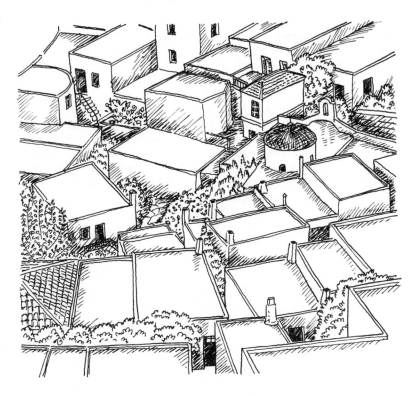

Flat-roofed houses in the old town of Hora

grilled fish, and high-quality shops of all kinds, they are all here.

Take any path leading 'upstairs', and it's another world, a maze of icing-sugar churches and chapels with intricately carved stone porticoes; flat-roofed cubist houses veiled with vines, mimosa and bougainvillea; narrow shady passages permitting the occasional long-distance view across to Mt. Olympos (403m) or down to the golden shore at **MAGAZIA** and **ASPOUSS**.

High up after the criss-cross of domesticity there is a memorial statue to Rupert Brooke, where visitors tend to place wild flower posies. Almost as far as you can climb there is a monastery (it has been closed, due to earthquake damage) apparently hanging on the steep vertical rockface known as **KASTRO** and, beyond that, a 14C castle. The hilltop was the acropolis referred to in Homer's ancient city of *Aipus*, 'steep'.

The homely museum (in the town hall) spans the history of the island from Mykinean times until the present day, with fine examples of typical folk art, furnishings (fascinating wine and oil bottles) and traditional costumes — the old ones even more elaborate than the billowing blue pantaloons, cream woollen shirts and flat black hats still worn by the men today.

From Skiros town there is many a delightful stroll to be made across the green and pleasant northern half of the island. Orange and lemon groves, vines, patches of wheat being thrashed under olive trees, it makes a truly pastoral scene. (But take provisions with you. You will find plenty of shepherds' huts and monasteries, but no means of formal sustenance.)

The southern half of the island, dominated by Mt. Kokilas (789m) is another matter and, especially in the summer, is arid going. To visit Rupert Brooke's grave and the little harbour of **TRIS BOUKES** in the south west, it is best to hire a caique from Linaria. The poet died of blood poisoning on a French hospital ship in 1915 and was buried in an olive grove 2km inland from the sheltered hamlet of **Trebuki Bay**. His grave was restored in 1961 by the Royal Navy. It is in a truly poetic setting.

*

Specialities

Not every Greek island has its local speciality, and so it is particularly pleasing to report that Evia has. Two of the most prolific crops of this fertile island come together to produce *sesfikia*. In late summer, keep a look out for long, honey-coloured strings hanging from three branches in gardens and terraces and, if you are lucky, from ropes in small general stores.

They may look like links of small sausages, but they are something much more special, shelled walnuts — *karithia* — dipped in a sweet translucent paste and traditionally hung on fine thread from V-shaped twigs. To a long-standing recipe of ingenious thriftiness, the paste is made by boiling grape skins and pips, the 'must' left over after making wine. The strings are dried in the sun and wind to preserve them — fresh, moist nuts in a chewy coating — for Christmas. The paste is also served warm, straight from the outdoor cauldron, as a dessert, sprinkled with chopped nuts.

Dried figs are a major export and in Kimi and elsewhere shops and kiosks have stacks of them, neat boxes that make good take-home presents. These figs are different; pale golden, plump and smooth and a match for any you have ever tasted. In homes around the island they are simmered in water and cinnamon and served as a *gliko*, a sweet to enjoy with coffee and iced water.

And not every Greek island, it has to be admitted, boasts a dazzling selection of fresh fish. But — yes — Evia does. Amarinthos, by no means one of the island's rural attractions, is the place for seafood connoisseurs. Fishmongers' shops line the village street, separated from the sea front by main road traffic thundering to and from the mainland. Even late into the evening you can admire artistic displays in boxes of ice, glinting and glistening under floodlights. And backstage, so to speak, in the many neighbouring fish tavernas, every *yia-yia* (family matriarch) will offer you her own speciality, pickled octopus from a huge jar on the counter, to enjoy with ouzo as a *meze* while your fish is grilling.

6 MACEDONIA AND THRACE

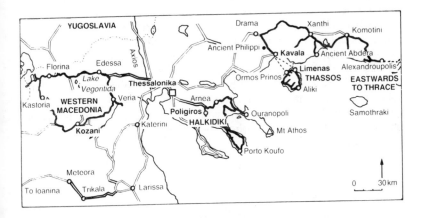

The scene is Stavropoulis, a village perched on the very brink of the river Nestos which divides Macedonia and Thrace. We are in a small café in the square, chatting to shepherds and huntsmen, farmers and labourers taking a break from the rigours of life in the towering Rodopi mountains to the north. All around the walls are the tools of their trades: crooks and rifles, sheep and cow bells, sickles and scythes, and the staring trophies of many a successful hunt. The atmosphere, heavy with the aroma of Turkish cigarettes, is partly familiar, partly not. It is Balkan. Not Greek.

This is scarcely surprising. The two most northerly provinces, Macedonia (which borders on Albania, Yugoslavia and Bulgaria) and Thrace, with Bulgaria and Turkey as its neighbours, came comparatively recently under the umbrella of Greece, and cultural ties are strong.

The first inhabitants of Macedonia, in Neolithic times, were probably tribes who came down from the Danube. By 6C BC it was under Persian rule, and after the defeat of the last Macedonian king, Philip V, became a province of Rome. That Empire has left its mark. Not only with its territory-cutting military road, the Via Egnatia — long stretches of which are still in use — but with the legend of the massive Roman battle fought (in 42 BC, see p. 117) at Ancient Philippi. To this day a Greek backing out of a hopeless argument will call up Caesar's ghost and throw out the challenge, 'I'll see you at Philippi!'

In Alexandroupolis, well on the way to Turkey, two young children are going from shop to shop selling refreshments. The boy, sturdily built and with a crew-cut, has a copper tray on a yoke round his neck, and a chilled yoghurt drink in beaten copper beakers. His sister, a pretty shawl tossed over her head, follows with sweetmeats. It could be Istanbul.

This scene is a reminder that, in a political break in the clouds, there was a massive exchange of population between Greece and Turkey after the end of the First World War. But some families stayed, and the two cultures co-exist colourfully and peacefully along this frontier.

Thassos, a small off-shore island with the twin benefits of natural mineral deposits and a strategic between-east-and-west location, inevitably led to a succession of conquering forces but — perhaps because it is an island — has retained a regional, but varied character. From the mountain village of Panagia, its lovely old timbered houses like fruit barrows laden with pomegranates and peaches, figs and plums; to Theologos, one-time capital of the island and now drawing a veil of vines over its political past; to the harbour of Limenas throbbing with tavernas doing a brisk trade in egg and lemon soup, stuffed vine leaves, *moussaka*, spit-roast baby lamb and goat, and grilled fish straight from the boats, the island — like the region as a whole — invites you to glimpse into its past and enjoy its present.

Western Macedonia

2–3 days/375km/from Kozani (140km west from Thessalonika)

Thickly wooded and ruggedly high mountains; gushing streams and waterfalls; well-stocked wildlife parks; fruitful orchards and fertile fields, this is an area of great natural beauty. Its supreme importance in former

times had less to do, however, with its green and pleasant landscape; much more to do with its strategic situation in the heart of the Balkan peninsula.

The tour spans 4 of the 7 prefectures (regions) of Western Macedonia, Kozani, Kastoria, Florina and Imathia, and glimpses a cultural inheritance which spans 3,000 years. In a single day (if time presses) you can wander among Early Iron Age burial mounds, have a guided tour of underground Macedonian royal temple tombs and see their magnificent contents in a museum, explore a string of Byzantine churches, a cluster of Turkish workshops and a parade of fine 18C mansions.

Towns and villages close to the Albanian and Yugoslav borders — and the tour comes very close to both — reveal more than a hint of their close proximity to foreign lands, and their earlier domination by invading armies.

Discover, in this ring around Western Macedonia, a part of Greece quite unrecognisable to those who may perhaps know only the sunshine islands and the holiday coastline.

KOZANI (pop: 23,000) Overshadowed by **Mt. Vermion**, and the capital of the largely mountainous region of that name. A strategic cross-roads in Northern Greece, and a centre of the textile and agricultural tool-making industries. During the 500 years of Ottoman rule it became known as a haven of Greek culture and a seat of learning. Its famous library of rare books and manuscripts, founded 16C, is second in importance in Greece only to the National Library in Athens, and in 18C the town was the home of many prominent scholars and scientists. The modern town, with its large, tree-lined square comes well and truly to life at spring carnival time. The narrow, winding, cobble-stoned streets, maze-like and intriguing, reveal a few fascinating examples of old Macedonian-style timber-framed mansions and cottages with deep first-floor overhang (they need them, in the snow), curved timber buttresses and heavily leaded windows. Don't miss the museum, recently completed and almost entirely funded by local subscription. It is of exceptional interest, the brainchild of Constantinos Siambanopoulos, a retired schoolmaster, who will take you on a journey through the ages, from the beginning of time. Below ground you are in the bowels of the earth, to study rock formations and such-like geological exhibits. Upstairs (marble stairs, at that) there are prehistoric flints and other implements, pottery, bronze, wood carvings, wonderfully elaborate costumes, stuffed animals and birds found by local hunters — red deer, jackal, wild boar, badger, wild cat, wolf and bear, cranes and eagles — an amazing collection. It deserves time. See also: Church of Ag. Nikolaos, built mainly of wood with fine carved screen, stalls and gallery, and frescoes; on banks of river Aliakmon, 15C Zavorda Monastery (fine frescoes). Hotel: **Xenia**, 0461/28.484.

Leave Kozani by the road going westwards (signposted Ioanina) which, running at a level of around 615m, affords, as they say, spectacular views.
In 25km turn right on to a minor road to **SIATISTA** (5km), a

prosperous trading centre in 18C and 19C and with some beautiful old mansions remaining to prove it. Often an enquiring glance and a friendly smile is the key to the door. Some houses have stained glass windows and interior walls and ceilings lavishly painted with panels of birds, trees, flowers, fruit and landscape scenes — murals of exquisite workmanship and design. This is one of many towns in the area whose more entrepreneurial inhabitants sought — and found — their fortunes, and often a title as well, in Central European countries after 18C and later distributed some of their new-found wealth for the benefit of those back home. One such benefactor was a merchant, John Trabandzis, who made a fortune in Romania, and built and maintained the Siatista gymnasium (high school). Nowadays, since the vineyards were destroyed (1930s) by disease, the people, like those in Kastoria, make their living from the fur trade, mostly working with fur trimmings. See: 18C church of Ag. Paraskevi (carved altar); Paleontological museum; library endowed by 19C scholar; Poulikos mansion (restored 1962). Hotel: **Arhontikon**, 0465/21.298.

Continue on the minor road to **KALONERI**, which is on a branch to the left, rejoining the major road in 8km. The village is set in a green and fertile pocket. In a couple of kilometres you see why — the road crosses the Aliakmon and several of its tributaries and dallies with the river almost to **NEAPOLI** (12km), a dairying village proud of its cheese. Shops are filled with cheese in store, windows with bags of curds draining in muslin and, if you should stop to pass the time of day, your pockets with bags of cheese given 'for your long journey'. Hotel: **Galini**, 0468/22.329. Turn right in the village, striking north (signposted Kastoria). The road recrosses the river and makes its way through steep slopes covered with evergreen oak to (in 17km) **VOGATSIKO**, perched on an epergne of hills beneath its namesake mountain. It's a refreshing place to stop for coffee. The road continues (passing a small airport on the left) down to **DISPILIO**, on the southern shore of **Lake Kastoria**. This village and, more particularly, **AG. ORESTIKO** which is 5km to the left, is noted for the design and quality of its traditional carpets, *flokarti* and *kilimia*, which for centuries have been washed in the mountain streams. Take the road to Kastoria, 7km away.

KASTORIA (pop: 15,400) A town built on a triangular peninsula, a finger pointing into the eastern shore of the lake. The central 'Turkish quarter' could aptly be named 'fur coat street' for it is here, in 17C and 18C ground-floor workshops scattered amid leafy cobbled alleyways, that the generations-old skill is carried on, of piecing together fur clippings to create luxurious fashion garments. The town has undergone a few personality changes. In ancient times it was known as Keletron; in the Byzantine era — when it was a prosperous trading centre — Justinianoupolis, and during part of its occupation by the Ottoman Turks (1385-1912) it was called Kesriye. Its present name derives from the beavers that inhabited the lakeside. We are looking here at a feast of ecclesiastical and domestic architecture, in the 50 or more Byzantine and medieval churches, mostly of basilica formation with superb frescoes, and the wealth (literally) of

Exterior of mansion house, Kastoria

18C mansions with their carved wooden ceilings, open fireplaces and, too, remarkable frescoes. See as many churches and mansions as time and interest allow, especially: 11C church of Panageia Koumbelidiki (13C–16C frescoes), Ag. Nikolaos Kasnitsis (11C frescoes of 'light and shade'), late 11C Taxiarches (external 13C and 15C and internal 14C frescoes) and early 11C Ag. Anargyri, in the pretty Kariadi quarter by the lake (with 12C and 13C internal and external frescoes). As to mansions, there are for example Nantzis, Tsiatsapas, Sapoundzis, Emmanuel and Nerandzis, which now houses a folkloric museum. Hotels: **Xenia du Lac** 0467/22.565; **Acropolis**, 0467/22.537. Tourist Police: 0467/22.696.

The road continues northwards (signposted Florina). Look back, as it twists and turns and climbs a ridge, to Kastoria, basking in its lakeside setting. The presence of military patrol vehicles is a reminder that you are advancing on a three-way international border between Albania to the west and Yugoslavia to the north. As the road glides down through a series of blink-and-you've-missed-them agricultural hamlets it closely follows the Albanian frontier only 10km away. **KOTA** (26km from Kastoria) is named for a Macedonian martyr who was burned alive by the Bulgarians. In 9km take the left turn to **Mikra Prespa**, or Mikrolimni, the lake shared between Greece and Albania. It's a haven for rare and exotic wildlife, a unique nesting ground for pelicans and home of the largest known cormorants in Europe. Train the binoculars on the dense growth around the southern (Greek) shores, since 1977 preserved as a national park, and wander among the small Byzantine chapels scattered around this refreshingly tranquil area. Follow the road around the eastern shore and you come to the tip of the much larger (as its name implies) lake, **Megali Prespa**, of which Yugoslavia has the lion's share. There's no border crossing here, so it's a case of turning back to the Kastoria-Florina road.

Turn left and in 32km of beech forests and mountain views (with some gradients to match) reach **FLORINA** (pop: 11,200) at an altitude of 666m, which successfully held out against the guerrilla rebels in the Civil War (1947 and 1949). Its name says it all — it means lush vegetation. The town is cupped in a narrow valley between high peaks spilling over with trees and flowers and, naturally, acts like a magnet to tourists all year round. In winter it is the base for mountain climbers and ski enthusiasts on their way to **VIGLA** on **Mt. Pisoderi**, where there is a refuge. Hotel: **King Alexander**, 0385/23.501.

A road from Florina, north through Ag. Kaliniki and Niki, reaches the frontier crossing in 17km and leads to the Yugoslav town of **BITOLA**, or Bitolj. This route, in the strategic Monastir plain, is known as the Monastir Gap.

The tour — not wishing to cross the border — takes the road going eastwards from Florina. It is signposted to Ptolemaida, but you don't want that. It's a cloud of heavy industry. Over the international railway line it goes, and briefly follows the route of the ancient Roman Egnatian Way, or Via Egnatia, which crossed Macedonia to link Constantinople with the shores of the Adriatic. In 12km the road turns sharp right. Fork left in 6km, through Vevi and Kella and landscape which for a while shows the grim face of mountain life. It is bleak, but improves considerably as the road is practically lapped by the northern tip of **Lake Vegoritida**. Look across the water to **ARNISSA** on the other side — the road will just by-pass the village — where there is a flourishing trout farm. Remains of a mosque on an islet in the lake are evidence, local legend has it, of a submerged Turkish village.

The road parts company with the lake and (in some 18km) reaches **EDESSA** (pop: 14,000), the capital of the region, magnificently situated on a semi-circular plateau at the foothills of Mt. Vermion. The town is criss-crossed by streams scurrying to unite in massive waterfalls which thunder down some 70 metres to irrigate the Salonican plain, and account for its fruitful harvest of nuts, grapes, figs and pomegranates. They account, too, for the sparkling, shimmering fairy-tale grotto just below the cascade and, indirectly, for the town's prosperous carpet industry. Edessa is history at a glance. The site of the flourishing ancient centre is 5km beyond the town; (see: cave shrine, colonnade, remains of marble Byzantine church); on the north side of town is the single-span bridge which carried the Roman Via Egnatia (see p. 99); there are traces of medieval encircling walls, and the 15C mosque behind the clock tower has Roman inscriptions and 5C mosaics on show. Coming closer to time present, there are fine examples (in Macedonian Road) of 18C mansions. Hotel: **Xenia**, 0381/22.995.

Leave Edessa on the Thessalonika (or Salonica) road and in 12km turn right (signposted Veria or Beroia) through Sevastiana, soon after which fork right again. In 10km, at **LEFKADIA**, 3 underground Macedonian tombs have been unearthed. Don't miss them. The 3C BC Great Tomb (clearly signposted) is the largest known temple tomb with a 2-storey façade, Doric in the lower section and Ionian in the upper, with a painting of a dead warrior being led to Hades. See also: Kinch Tomb and 2C BC Lyson Kallikles Tomb. Turn right in 4km to **NAOUSSA** (5km), a surprisingly large town (pop: 17,400) for so rural a situation, and encircled by so many streams that it is practically moated. This is the home of the well-known full-bodied, rich red wine, of succulent peaches and apricots, and silk, an industry favoured by the preponderance of cool, clear water. Naoussa has had its ups and downs, and the downs, prolonged occupation by both Turks and Bulgars, are commemorated in a masked dance of oppression — complete with scimitars — at the annual carnival. Hotel: **Hellas**, 0332/22.006.

Return to the Edessa–Veria road and continue south for the 14km to **VERIA** (pop: 29,500), the Berea of the New Testament, to which in AD 54 St Paul came from Thessalonika to preach to the Jews. The city had surrendered to Rome 168 BC, was overrun by the Bulgars (10C) and the Serbs (14C) before falling to the Turks, who established a military colony there. Look behind the characterless modern façade concealing the maze of back-streets and alleyways for fascinating Turkish houses and small timber-framed and wattle Byzantine churches. See: museum with Neolithic finds, Roman portraits and some jewellery and weapons from tombs at Lefkadia and Vergina.

To see those latter tombs, take the road going south east from the town (it's one of 2 signposted to Thessalonika), crossing the Aliakmon river over a 350m-long barrage. In 11km, **VERGINA**, on the site of the ancient capital of Macedonia which prospered from the Iron Age through to Classical times. It was both the residence and last resting-place of kings, and Philip II was assassinated there 336 BC. The tombs were pillaged by Gauls 274 BC, but are still 'see-worthy'. See: Early Iron Age cemetery (10C–7C BC); remains of 4C BC Palace of Palatitsa (pebble-mosaic floor) and theatre; 3C BC Macedonian temple tomb (Ionic façade, painted marble throne). Other royal tombs dating from 4C BC are still being excavated, and not accessible.

Return to Veria and turn left on to the Kozani road which follows the tributary of the river and gives tantalising glimpses of trout pools. As the road climbs in the Tripotamus valley, orchards give way to oak and beech forests until (in 16km) at **KASTANIA** (alt: 910m) apples and nuts take over again. Just above the village, the Monastery of Panageia Soumela, built by the refugees from Asia Minor, is the setting for an annual pilgrim-age on 15 August. Up and up the road continues, with magnificent views of now the fertile valley, next the jagged peaks of the Pieria range (rising to 2,210m) and then, to the east, of **Mt. Olympos** itself. The road reaches its own summit at **ZOODOKOS PIGI** (1,372m) where a tiny churchyard hovers over a gushing spring, and the driver will probably be in need of a spot of refreshment. Down and down the road goes, through

POLIMILOS with its attractive watermills and Kilada, returning (64km from Veria) to Kozani.

Halkidiki

2–3 days/350km/from Poligiros, 69km south-west of Thessalonika with optional excursion to islet of Amoliani

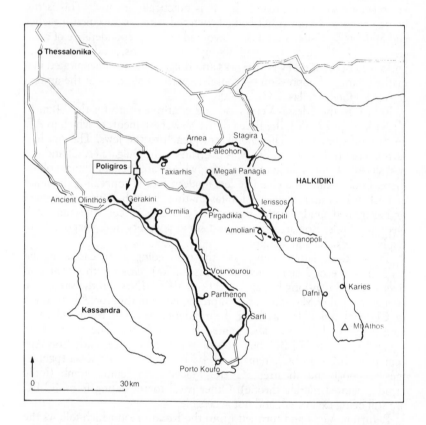

A casual glance at the holiday brochures, and it may be tempting to classify Halkidiki, the 3-pronged peninsula south of Thessalonika, as a sun-sea-and-sand holiday paradise. It certainly is that — how could it be otherwise, with all that sun, sea and sand? — and Kassandra, the most westerly of the prongs, is rapidly falling into the hands of the tour operators. But the region as a whole has so much more to offer — purple mountains cloaked in dense green forests; cool, stream-splashed valleys (a great blessing in the humidity of summer); spectacular mosaics of high-altitude wild flowers; centuries-old traditions of handicrafts — woven rugs especially — and regional architecture with a gentle charm all of its own.

Traditions of all kinds characterise Halkidiki, and lucky the visitor whose stay coincides with one of the many village festivals or fairs, exhibitions or religious ceremonies. Easter is a very special time, from the frantic spring-cleaning of Clean Monday, the first week in Lent, to *adrahtoudes*, hanging out beautiful home-made red rugs on Maundy Thursday and the festival dances of Easter Day. The first of May (*protimaiou*) is celebrated with a festival dedicated to swallows, and then there is *halvadosavato*, the Saturday of (lovely thought) eating nougat.

The tour begins in Poligiros, the modest capital of Halkidiki (no match in size for the capital of Thessalonika, less than an hour's drive to the west) and circles around the central spur, Sithonia, making here and there an excursion into an out-of-the-way mountain village. It presses its nose to the closed gateway of the isolated independent monastic state of Mt. Athos and, no previously applied-for entry permit to hand, takes a consolation trip — and an exhilarating one at that — to the lovely little off-shore island of Amoliani. Through forests and glades, vineyards and orchards, the tour reaches Arnea, a village that is so beautiful, you just have to see it for yourself, and returns to Poligiros.

POLIGIROS (pop: 4,500) is built like an amphitheatre at the foothills of **Mt. Holomon**, the second highest mountain of the peninsula. On a clear day, by climbing to the top of the Profitis Elias hill you can have a bird's-eye view of all three prongs of the Halkidiki 'trident': **Kassandra**, **Sithonia** and the almost inaccessible **Mt. Athos** to the east. In the old quarter of the town the houses have the distinctly Macedonian characteristics of carved wooden gables and first-floor overhang, often with curved (and carved) buttresses. See: Archaeological museum (0371/22.148) with exhibits from all over the region, including black-figure idols from Olinthos, head of Dionysos and other finds from near-by sanctuaries, and 3 coins taken from the hand of a skeleton at Akanthos.

Leave the town by the road travelling south (signposted Gerakini), through hummocky, scrubby hills and eye-averting quarries. **GERAKINI** village is at the T-junction in 13km. If the finds in the Poligiros Museum have excited your imagination and you want to explore the site of **Ancient Olinthos**, turn right along the coastal road for an 8km diversion. Just past the modern village of **OLINTHOS**, turn right. The track crossing the river on the right is clearly marked. You can perhaps feel rather than see the significance of the city when, in 5C and 4C BC, covering 2 vast flat-topped mounds, it supported 30,000 inhabitants and was the most influential community in the area. Its history predates that period — Neolithic dwellings have been traced on the south mound. The city was so effectively destroyed by Philip of Macedon in 348 BC that there is, sadly, little to see, just the outline of the street plan, open cisterns and scattered mosaics. Return to Gerakini (Hotel: **Gerakini Beach**, 0371/22.474) and continue around the Kassandra Gulf on a road herring-boned with tracks to the right, each one leading to a popular bathing beach. In 7km, just past **PSAKOUDIA**, turn left, diverting to

Beach on Halkidiki peninsula

the traditional inland village of **ORMILIA**, a treasury of lovely 18 and 19C houses and tiny churches. Return to the coast road and turn left.

At the fishing village of **NIKITAS** (15km) which marks the head of the Sithonia 'prong' of the peninsula, a glimpse of endless pleasures to come: a strip of golden sand heavily fringed with aromatic pine trees almost dipping their toes in the water. It is just possible, here or elsewhere, that you will meet a herd of black goats making their way purposefully along the water's edge, utterly oblivious of sun worshippers in their path. On 15 September each year the village celebrates with a folkloric festival.

From here, a new road carves an asphalt ring around Sithonia; on the west coast there is a less formal alternative, a friendly but slightly rickety road, which this tour prefers. Take the first-right road from Nikitas passing on the left a restored Early Christian (5C) church and then one by one — it's almost like sand-sailing — the hamlets of Ag. Georgios, Kastro, Elia and Tripotamos. **NEA MARMARAS** (20km) is a delightful fishing village, too inviting to pass by, and well set up for camping and water-sports. A minor road leads inland, turning its back on all the fun of the sea-shore, to the mountain hamlet of **PARTHENON**. They don't get many visitors making the 5km ascent. Perhaps that's why, on the terrace of a modest stone cottage, we were invited to share a convivial lunch of small fried fish ('caught this morning'), olives and home-made red wine.

PORTO CARRAS, 2km to the south, is an oasis of leisure activity, newly built as a holiday village for some 3,500 guests who enjoy the theatre, golf, riding, tennis, surfing, sailing, and generally having plenty to do. Hotels: **Sithonia Beach** and **Village Inn**, both 0375/71.381.

The old road continues to dip in and out of rugged and sandy coves, comes under the watchful shadow of the luxuriantly wooded **Mt. Melitonas** and in 24km reaches **TORONI**, where a spot of exploring is in order. On a narrow promontory nosing out to sea, the site of an ancient city where you can wander around what remains of 3 separate civilisations, ancient, Byzantine and Early Christian. **PORTO KOUFO**, just to the south, has a small natural harbour, hence the scene of vigorous fishing activity, with much loading and unloading of boxes, mending and rolling of nets and quay-side bargaining. It's also a perfect spot for private fishing excursions. The coast from the south-western tip of Sithonia at **Cape Drepano** around to **SARTI** on the west is specially favourable for skin diving.

Our route takes a minor, inland road from Toroni, climbing through densely wooded hills fluttering with butterflies to (in 10km) the tranquil and pretty village of **SIKIA**, held in the bowl of a hill and memorable for the combined scent of pines, basil and roasting goat. Turn right in the village and in 1km turn left, where the minor road rejoins the 'ring road'. Villages are fewer and farther between on the west coast, but, after **SARTI** (in 8km), the sun-sea-sand combination is never-ending. This is as good a place as any to stop and indulge in the test-your-powers-of-observation game of the region: count the monasteries visible along the rocky shores of Mt. Athos. The answer, a dozen or so!

Continuing around the coast; in 30km a track beckons to the little tucked-in-a-cove village of **VOURVOUROU**, a kaleidoscope of colourful fishing smacks glistening with the morning's catch. Pension: **Diaporos**, 0375/91.313. Much the same can be said of **ORMOS PANAGIAS**, 7km farther on. Fork right 2km after the village. In 3km, at **AG. NIKOLAOS**, the road surface changes from good to acceptable. **PIRGADIKIA** has all the makings — fast being realised — of a perfect holiday resort. The road bends sharply to the left and starts to climb in the incredibly green valley of Marmaras, passing through the hamlet of Ag. Ioannis Prodromos then turning sharp right in 4km, just before Plana. It's a bit of an uphill struggle to **MEGALI PANAGIA** in 11km, way off the beaten track and perched among spectacular mountain scenery. A religious fair is held annually on 15 August. Turn sharp right there, taking the minor road going south-east to (in 13km) **GOMATI**, a pretty mountain-side village where visitors are welcomed with, so to speak, open arms. Continue descending gradually to **IERISSOS** (pop: 2,400) a fishing village sprawling around the bay and built on the site of Ancient Akanthos. There isn't much evidence of the days when (5C BC) the city was founded by islanders from Andros; just a few mounds marking the isthmus, a small protective harbour and the remains of a cemetery. The finds are in the Poligiros museum.

Turn right on to a smart new road through the picturesque fishing villages of Limani and Nea Roda and then, crossing the 2km-wide top of the **Mt. Athos** peninsula, to **TRIPITI** a yacht harbour on the west coast, facing the islet of **Amoliani**. You can do more than face it. You can visit it. Small boats from here and **OURANOPOLI**, 7km around the coast, make frequent trips to the tiny, peaceful island nestling in the protective arc of the bay. It's a joy for bathing, water-sports and just lazing. **Xenia Motel** (Ouranopoli), 0377/71.202.

Ouranopoli is the gateway to the independent state of Mt. Athos, a gate that is closed, by the Chryssobul edict of Emperor Constantine Monomachos in 1060, to all women. And to men, too, unless they have a valid permit (see below). Assuming this not to be the case, what you are missing is this, some of the reputedly grandest and most rugged scenery in the Aegean and a wealth of Byzantine monasteries founded between 10 and 16C and at one time supporting 40,000. Only 20 of the 40 or so establishments are functioning now — 17 Greek, one Russian, one Bulgarian and one Serbian — and the monastic complement is around 1,700. Incidentally, if you do have a permit, access to the community is by boat from Tripiti or Ouranopoli to **DAFNI**, on the south-west coast, and then overland to **KARIES**, the state capital.

For the rest of us, it is a question of retracing the road to Ierissos. Follow it for 17 easy kilometres between forest and sea. Just before Stratoni turn left, inland, to **STRATONIKI**, at the foothills of ancient gold and silver mines, and continue to **STAGIRA**, close to ancient Stageira, the birthplace of the great philosopher, Aristotle. The honour bestowed on the area is marked by a modern statue on a wooded knoll among the ruins of a Byzantine fortress. Continue, through 8km of the calmest of mountain scenery, to **NEOHORI**, the calmest of mountain villages, though it's a busy thoroughfare for goats and a happy hunting-ground for cheese gourmets. In 4km, **PALEOHORI**, a delightful village rightly proud of its crops (vines and tree fruits), handicrafts and architecture. **Park Hotel Tassos**, 0372/41.722.

ARNEA (in 5km) is magical. Set amid an ocean of vines, the village is almost too pretty to be true, with cobbled street after street of traditional houses, some stone, some plastered, most with wooden balconies, many dripping with heavily laden vines, and more with colourful, flower-filled windowboxes. Please don't miss it. The village tradition of handicrafts goes back for centuries, and the quality and design of the hand-woven fabrics — rugs, especially — is almost legendary. The wine is good, too! There's an annual craft exhibition, festivities and dancing, in July.

The ambience that is Arnea will sustain you through the ascent (the road eventually reaches about 1,000m) along the considerable slopes of **Mt. Holomon**. After forests of beech, chestnut, fir and pine and quite a bit of low-gear work, you come to **TAXIARHIS** (just off the road, in fact) and a well-earned cup of coffee. You have been almost on top of the world. The descent is gradual. In 11km turn left at **PALEOKASTRO** (it is signposted to Poligiros) and continue the 11km to the town, where the tour ends. NTOG, Thessalonika: 031/271.888. Tourist Police, Thessalonika: 031/425.011. Permits for visits to Mt. Athos (males over 18 only): Ministry of Foreign Affairs, Directorate of Churches, 2 Zalokosta Street, Athens, 3626.894, or Ministry of Northern Greece, Directorate of Civil Affairs, Dioikitirou Square, Thessalonika, 031/270.092. Only applicants with authorised religious or scientific status are allowed to stay overnight.

Thassos

1–2 days/150km/from Limenas, the port on the north-eastern cost of the island

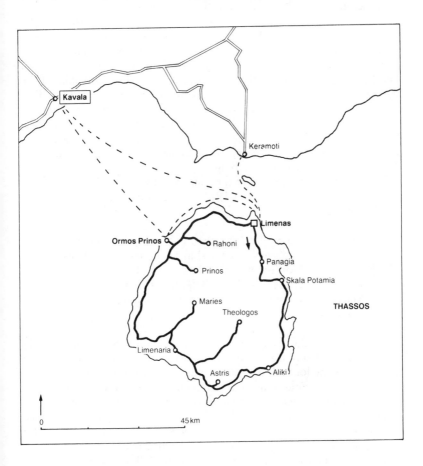

At the northernmost tip of the Aegean, and less than an hour's sailing time from the eastern Macedonian coast, Thassos (440 sq. m) rises up from the sea like a giant green cone, its mountains cloaked in forests of plane and pine, chestnut and oak, olive and walnut trees. The whole island is fringed by the sandiest of beaches and the rockiest of coves and speckled with tiny off-shore islands, heaven on earth for bathers and fishermen. Small villages tucked comfortably into the hillsides are almost untouched by time or tourism and blissfully washed by streams gushing down from the highest peak, Mt. Ipsaron (1,150m). There are people who know the Greek islands well who pronounce this emerald isle the most beautiful of them all.

Apart from its obvious scenic attributes, Thassos has been richly endowed with natural wealth. The island is covered with white and grey-green marble (which is why fields seem to be polka-dotted with stones), a principal export in ancient times. Others which kept the ports busy were oil, wine, gold and silver. The precious metals were mined in such quantities that they were minted for coins in use throughout the Mediterranean.

Herodotus maintained that Thassos was first occupied by Phœnicians, but extensive excavations have failed to prove his point. The island is known to have been colonised 7C BC by the Parians, who were also from Asia Minor, who exploited the gold mines, and it later fell victim of the Persian Wars. It had a spell of allegiance to Athens, was seized (4C BC) by Philip II of Macedonia and changed hands again when it fell to the Romans in 196 BC. Its medieval rulers were largely the Genoese and the Turks, followed in 1770 by the Russians who exploited the forests for their own ship-building industry. Then came the Greeks, the Allies (in 1916) and finally (in 1941) the Bulgars.

The island now forms part of the Macedonian region of Kavala. Silver and zinc are mined there and in 1971 another important natural deposit was discovered — an off-shore oil field.

How to get there: From **KAVALA** (see p. 115) car ferries sail once a day to **LIMENAS** (also called simply Thassos) in 1½ hours, and 7 times a day to **ORMOS PRINOS**, on the north-western coast of the island, in 1 hour. Port Authority: 051/224.472. From **KERAMOTI**, just across the Strait on the Macedonian/Thrace border, there are 6 sailings daily to Limenas, taking about 45 minutes.

LIMENAS (pop: 2,000) is the bright and cheerful modern capital of the island, neat and tidy houses and jostling cafés and tavernas set among leafy lanes at the foothills of a mountain. The town takes its connections with the ancient world so much for granted — it is built on the site of the ancient city of Thassos — that pieces of marble and chunks of stone are lying all around, apparently undisturbed for centuries. Excavations have been going on (by the French) more or less non-stop since 1910 within the boundaries of the imposing 5C BC encircling marble wall; some of its gates are still adorned with bas-relief carvings. Follow the path inside the ramparts (reached behind a fine old Turkish building overlooking the harbour). Traces of the ancient naval and commercial ports are there for all to see beneath the shallow water. See: remains of AD 5C Early Christian basilica church on a promontory; Hellenistic theatre which the Romans converted to an arena; the acropolis (from which, magnificent view of islands of Thassopoula and, in the distance, Samothrace) on 3 peaks. One had a sanctuary to Pythian Apollo; one shows foundations of Temple to Athena; the other, a small rock sanctuary to Pan, with bas-relief of the god piping his goats. Also: the agora, with traces of Roman porticoes and an altar, and museum (bronzes, ivories, other sculptures, Roman portraits, coins). During July and August performances of ancient drama are given in the open-air theatre. Hotels: **Xenia**, 0593/22.105; **Timoleon**, 0593/22.177; **Angelika**, 0593/22.387. Tourist Police, summer only: 0593/22.500.

Leave Limenas by the southern road, passing the yellow-ribbon beach of **MAKRIAMMOS** near the Xenia hotel (*ammos* means sand), the most spectacular and in summer most crowded beach on the island. You can reach it down a minor road to the left. More fun, if you have time, is to go by caique from the port. The boat sails under the ancient walls and the acropolis. The round-the-island road — a new, asphalt one — climbs gently, giving time for many an admiring glance at the sea views, disappears into a charred silhouette of pine forests devastated by fire in 1985 and, in 9km, emerges into the sunlight at **PANAGIA**, a mountain village refreshed by gushing streams. This is a good introduction to the traditional architecture of the island. The whitewashed houses, some actually astride the narrow streams, have slate roofs, covered wooden balconies and corridors and unusually high fences enclosing the gardens. Centuries of mis-rule led the islanders to look inwards, and protect their property. *Kafenions* in the square come under the protectorate of huge, shady plane trees: irresistible. On Easter Monday the young people of the village, in island costume, carry an effigy of Judas around the village and gleefully re-enact his hanging. Hotel: **Chryssafis**, 0593/61.451.

Continue for 2km to **POTAMIA** a larger village with high-rise stone streets and a pot-pourri of old Turkish houses, some almost obscured by their fragrant flower gardens. In fact, the whole village is almost obscured by the dense green forests thrown like a cloak down the hillsides all around. In 3km, **SKALA POTAMIA**, a superb beach with jolly tavernas and, a stone's throw from the sand, dense, leafy copses, the prettiest of natural parasols. Pension: **Kamelia**, 0593/61.463. The road hugs the coast to (in 8km) **KINIRA** and then **LOUTRA**, small fishing hamlets facing the temptingly close off-shore islet of Kinira. A swimmer's paradise it is, all along here.

The next port of call is **ALIKI** in 9km where, apart from sun, sea and sand, there are remains of former glories — an Archaic double sanctuary and traces of 2 Early Christian basilica churches. Not only that, the massive ancient marble quarries, impressive at this distance in time, are evidence that white marble was one of the island's main exports, 7C to 5C BC. See also, preferably from the terrace of a fish taverna, and with a glass of *retsina* in hand, the purple-robed sunset over **Mt. Athos**, in Halkidiki, to the south west.

Plane, oak, cedar, pine and olive trees paint the landscape all shades of green as the road continues for 11km past flowery meadows to **ASTRIS**. What's this we see? A heavy concentration of fortified towers, built to fend off invasions by pirates. And for just that reason, the medieval capital was hastily removed to **THEOLOGOS** (now returned to the status of a typical mountain village), hidden below the southern slopes of **Mt. Ipsarion**. To reach it, follow the rugged coast road for 7km and turn right at **POTOS** (good camping facilities). See: remains of castle; house where Mehmet Ali lived as a boy.

Return to the coast road, which brushes the fabulous sandy beach at **PEFKARI** (Hotel: **Thassos**, 0593/51.596) to **LIMENARIA** (pop: 1,500), the second largest village on the island. Fishing boats put out to sea at night-time, their lamps bouncing on the water like so many balloons. You can sometimes join the crew, or hire a small boat to fish or swim off the tiny islet of Panagia. If you are lucky enough to catch a crayfish, any local taverna will gladly do the honours. On the Tuesday after Easter the elders and young men of the village, in traditional costume, perform the *vari* dance.

From the village take the inland road, the right fork, through olive and nut groves, mulberry and myrtle trees and turn right, climbing deep into the mountains to **MARIES**, almost at the heart of the island. This, only 10km from the beach, is another world. Some of the villagers still wear their traditional costume, the men in black baggy trousers and two-pointed caps, and hospitality is at its height. Allow time for a friendly coffee on a terrace or in a garden, offered with a tiny plate of preserved fruits ('spoon sweets'), ice-cold water and the warmest of welcomes. Return to the inland road, turn right and in 4km, you come to Maries' own beach, etched deep into an idyllic bay, **SKALA MARION**, the most westerly point of the island.

Stop where you will around the coast, at Klisma, Skala Kalirahis or Skala Sotira — it's beaches, beaches all the way — and at **KALIVES** (in 13km) turn right to **PRINOS**, a village 5 steep kilometres from the coast. It's a true mountain refuge from the heat of summer, splashed by streams and sparklingly cool. Return to the 'circular' road, turn right and soon come to **ORMOS PRINOS**, the port with ferries to Limenas and Kavala. Off into the hinterland once more, turn right again to **RAHONI** (3km). Children making posies of cowslips, violas and Pasque flowers thrust them shyly into the hands of visitors, almost as if that was their purpose. (A tiny jar to fill with water is almost a 'must' in the car, if you can't bear to let such gifts just wither and die.) Back-track through the chestnut glades, turn right and in 13km (past **SKALA RANONIOU**, where there's organised camping) return to Limenas.

Specialities: *retsina*, honey, nuts and sea-food of all kinds, especially crayfish.

Eastwards to Thrace

2–3 days/470km/from Kavala, 182km east of Thessalonika

Eastern Macedonia and Thrace comprise a long, narrow stretch of land bordered on the north by the largely uninhabited and inhospitable mountain ranges across the Bulgarian border; to the south by a wide gulf in the Aegean Sea and to the east by the massive landmass that is Turkey. Such a situation has long made the territory a strategic bridge between north and south, east and west; a thoroughfare for wandering nomads, advancing armies — the Romans particularly — and, on a lighter note, for migratory bird-life.

The region has its own share of mountain peaks. Kavala, where the tour begins, is arranged on the friendly slopes of Mt. Simvolo; Komotini

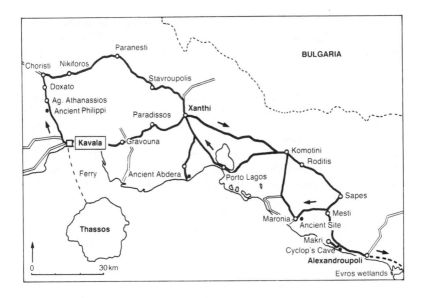

stands in the shadow of the Rodopi range behind it, and Maronia crouches at the feet of Mt. Ismaros; ancient Maronia, Homer's Ismaros, where Odysseus obtained the fragrant, ruby-red wine with which he tricked Cyclops Polyphemus into a state of drunkenness. And at near-by Makri, the tour even takes in Cyclops' cave.

Mountains and myths! Legends and lakes! Lakes such as Vistonis, mid-way between Xanthi and Komotini and watered by a network of silver streams, which changes the pace of the tour. You just *have* to stop and stare at the comings and goings of the whooping and whirling water-birds.

Prosperity past and present is evident in towns and villages along the way, notably in the visually delightful Thracian houses, their curved, flowing, icing-sugar-plastered lines contrasting sharply with geometrically severe iron balconies. Much of the wealth derives from the incredibly lush and fertile valleys, principally from wheat and — sorry, non-smokers — tobacco. The aroma of 'Turkish' cigarettes hangs heavily in the air.

KAVALA (pop: 46,200) Rises gently on the rocky foothills of **Mt. Simvolo** at the head of the Gulf of Thrace, rows and rows of whitewashed houses, their coloured shutters dazzling in the sun. The town has risen from the site — inhabited since Neolithic times — of ancient Neapolis, the port for the ancient city of Philippi some 15km inland, where travellers disembarked from Levant, where Brutus stationed his fleet and St Paul landed with Silas; the town was later renamed Christoupolis in his honour. Burned by the Normans on the march to Constantinople (1185) the town arose, was to come under Turkish rule until 1912, and then to fall 3 times to the Bulgarians who were finally ousted only in 1944. It is now a major trading centre for the Macedonian tobacco industry, and the car-ferry terminus linking the Gulf with other ports on the mainland and with Thassos, Limnos and other Eastern Aegean islands. The west end of town, with its spacious squares and modern office blocks, is the business quarter. The east end offers a glimpse into the medieval past, with its narrow, cobbled streets, traditional old houses with stained-glass windows and courtyards full of flowers. In the Panageia quarter above the town (see: 15C Panageia church, old city walls and Venetian fortress) the house where Mohammed Ali, founder of the Egyptian dynasty, was born is a museum to the Eastern way of life, complete with harem. See also the Archaeological Museum with centuries of local finds from Neapolis, Philippi and Amphipolis, and the 16C Kamares aqueduct built by Suleiman the Magnificent to carry water from springs in the facing hills.

The port is flanked by a trio of small fishing harbours: Keramoti, Nea Iraklitsa and Nea Peramos. There's a lot to be said for sitting with a pre-dinner ouzo, watching the caiques leave on their nocturnal expeditions, their lanterns flickering across the bay. There are specially good sandy beaches, organised water-sports, and a treasure-trove of small but spectacular caves speckling the coastline. Hotels: **Galaxy**. 051/224.521; **Vournelis** Pension (at Nea Iraklitsa), 0592/71.353. NTOG: 051/228.762. NTOG Camping: 051/227.151. Tourist Police: 051/222.905.

Ancient Philippi, scene of a famous Roman battle

Leave Kavala on the Thessalonika road and take the right fork (signposted Drama), passing the airport on the left. The road runs straight through a tobacco plain, almost as straight as the course of the Roman military road, the Via Egnatia, to the east, where pottery contemporary with the foundation of Troy has been unearthed. The old and new roads converge on the outskirts of the deserted city. **Ancient Philippi**, originally Krenides (it means fountain), was (6C BC) a colony of the small offshore island of Thassos. The city fell to local tribes, was taken (356 BC) by Philip II of Macedon who gave it his name, and was well and truly put on the map when in 42 BC the Battle of Philippi was fought there. The combined forces of Brutus (who had overpowered Macedonia) and Cassius (who had taken Syria) were strategically no match for the advancing army of Antony and Octavian, and both vanquished leaders committed suicide. St Paul preached at Philippi (his first such venture in Europe) AD 49 and, with Silas, was put in prison. He returned AD 55. Christianity became firmly established, 2 large basilicas built 5C and 6C. The city was abandoned 10C. See: foundations of Roman forum, theatre (modernised in Roman times), Greek acropolis with medieval towers (from which fine views), rock sanctuaries, and museum with Neolithic, Early Christian and Roman sections. An annual drama festival is held, July and August, in the open-air theatre.

Continue northwards, the road busy with the cultivation, harvesting and transport of cereal and tobacco crops; the villages of Krinides, Ag. Athanassios and Doxato likewise. Take the right turn (5km before Drama) at **CHORISTI**, the road and the railway making use of the same ridge, to **NIKIFOROS** where there are the remains of an aqueduct. The road chugs, heavy-footed, across the Lekanis range. The compensations: wild, uninhibited mountain scenery, swooping, swirling birds of prey and a decent asphalt road surface. At **PARANESTI** (in 21km) 3 ways meet, the road, the railway and the **Nestos river** which rises in the inhospitable Bulgarian mountains and for much of its course forms the natural boundary between Macedonia and Thrace. The 3 arteries run side by side for 21km of magnificent landscape until, at **STAVROUPOLIS** a bustling, going-about-its-business village, the road strikes out for independence, and turns eastwards. See: churches of Evangelistra and Taxiarhon (both with good icons). A few hardy hamlets shelter in the mountainside to the north of the road, and sheep and goats tinkle-tankle a warning around each bend.

In 19km, just after crossing the **Kossinthos river**, fork right to Xanthi, 8km south.

XANTHI (pop: 25,000) A city with star rating. The Byzantine settlement assembled beneath the umbrella-like protection of a fortress (Bulgaria is only 39km away). The Turks, when they came, relegated it to the role of a summer resort. It makes a delightful one. The city is bisected by the river, a ribbon of plane trees linking its banks. The old quarter is set on a plateau on the hillside, its cobbled streets a visual feast of pink, blue, white, green and golden wedding-cake-plastered houses with voluptuous,

A street in Xanthi

overhanging bow windows, stern iron railings and bright palettes of geraniums and carnations. Women sit on the doorsteps, sewing. An admiring glance at the makings of an embroidered bedspread leads to many an invitation to step inside. Do. The furnishings are exquisite. The open-air market is fun, an East-meets-West affair, and beyond that, a reminder of the source of the obvious prosperity, the picturesque old tobacco warehouses alongside the mansions of their erstwhile owners. The pace quickens in the new part of the town, positively throbbing with tavernas, cafés and pastry-shops. Specialities: cheeses and roasted chick-peas, eaten as a hot snack, like chestnuts. Hotels: **Xenia**, 0541/24.136, **Motel Natassa**, 0541/21.521.

There are 2 roads linking Xanthi to Komotini. We go by one and return by the other. Take the minor, more northerly road, the one the Romans took, striking due east alongside the railway track and through a valley brown, green or golden, as the season changes, with wheat. Neat little villages flash by. In 36km join the main road to (in 5km) Komotini.

KOMOTINI (pop: 29,000) A cosmopolitan centre for tobacco, cattle and hides. Lucky you if it's Tuesday, market day, a riot of fruit and vegetables, pottery and poultry, copper and brass, silver and gold, arts and crafts, leather and laughter. In the old Turkish quarter the cobblestones echo to the tring of tinsmiths working in open doorways. A small copper *briki*, a coffee pot hammered while you wait, is a suitable souvenir. The air is heady with the mingled aromas of freshly ground coffee, chick-peas roasting on roadside braziers, and flowers. The traditional houses with their brightly painted walls, intricately tiled roofs and carved wooden eaves all look like folkloric museums. Only one is. See: archaeological museum with centuries-spanning Thracian finds; Church of Virgin Mary, built 1800 during Turkish occupation (icons).

The road continues eastwards and we pass a bus rumbling on its way to Istanbul. Even now, the villages have an increasingly Turkish flavour. In **RODITIS** children run to greet visitors, offering trays of pink and nutty, well, the Greek translation of Turkish delight is *loukoumi*. **ARATOS** announces its presence on the horizon with a sharply pointed minaret. At **ARISVI** the road crosses the river, and so does the remains of the bridge that carried the Roman Way. At **SAPES**, where the road takes a sharp turn, the musical strains from a café are distinctly Eastern, and so is the owner. The scenery, somewhat wild and scrubby of late, suddenly mellows and vines lead the way to **MAKRI**, a fishing village idling on the golden sands. You can see the cave, filled with stalactites and stalagmites, where, legend has it, the one-eyed Cyclops Polyphemus lived. Spooky!

Meander, if you like, westwards from Makri, along the coast to **DIKELA** where there is a frizzle of fish tavernas and then to **MESSEMBRIA**, where the choice is yours. Golden sands and blue sea, or a spot of exploring. You can see traces (little more, to be honest) of an ancient port and a Roman town — streets, shops, houses and workshops — within what were 4C BC walls.

Return the 10km to Makri and continue eastwards to **ALEXAND-ROUPOLI** (pop: 23,000) a modern town with all the things modern towns usually have. And a good archaeological exhibition in the town. **Egnatia Motel**, 0551/28.661. This is the last major conurbation before Turkey, and the ferry port for the charming island of **Samothrace**, a couple of hours over the water, with its comfortingly hot springs, daringly precipitous slopes (**Mt. Fengari** at 1,600m is the highest peak in the Aegean), out-of-this-world sunsets and surprisingly bland *anthotiro* cheese.

The tour turns back at Alexandroupoli, but not before mentioning the **Evros wetlands** some 30km to the south-east. Here you can see birds of passage, migratory birds *en route* between Europe and Africa; birds resting, birds nesting. Herons, wild swan, storks, white pelicans, black-crested gulls, white-winged black terns, sea-eagles, avocets — 263 species have been catalogued. Roads lined with tamarisk and reeds criss-cross the channels, and there is cover for observed and observers alike. Need I say more?

Back-track westwards along the Komotini road to **MESTI** (30km) where turn left on to a very minor road to **MARONIA** (17km) where the mountains of Thrace sweep (almost) down to the sea and an ancient theatre nestles among olive and poplar trees. There are pretty houses and a cool *kafenion* around the square shaded by spreading plane trees. Take the road going north-west, signposted Komotini, which is reached in 19km of mountain ridges and splashing streams.

Take the main Xanthi road out of the town and in 26km the shores of **Lake Vistonis**. If you didn't have time to see the Evros wetlands, never mind. Here's the next best thing. The road runs along a narrow causeway separating the lake from salt marshes and the sea, a veritable cross-roads for wildlife on the wing. **PORTO LAGOS** a delightful fishing village poised precariously between fresh water and salt water, is a commercial breeding ground for eels, exported live in tanks. Cross the old wooden bridge amidst the reeds, past countless swans a-swimming, to see Monastery of Ag. Nikolaos on a reef in the lagoon. Continue through tobacco plantations and Koutso in 10km, to **VAFEIKA** (7km) where turn sharp left to the village of **ABDERA** in 20km, a maze of 18C mansions and tiny churches. Turn left to the site of **Ancient Abdera**, founded 6C BC and famous for its school of philosophy. See: Hellenistic walled compounds, terracotta workshops, 3C BC storerooms, Roman baths, villa, theatre, shrine. And a marvellously relaxing stretch of coastline.

Return to Vafeika, turn left to Xanthi (9km) and there take the main, southerly, road to Kavala. The villages in the foothills of the mountains display a cheerful pot-pourri of Greek and Turkish features, of minarets and churches, Eastern and Western styles of dress. **TOXOTES** (15km) is an example, it has a pretty minaret. **PARADISSOS** (5km), tidily terraced, peers over the banks of the Nestos. **KRINI** (10km) has a strong medieval fortress. **GRAVOUNA** is wreathed in flower-filled gardens. **NEA KARVALI** (11km) has a cluster of cafés swooning with the scent of Turkish cigarettes. The road passes a huge stadium and returns to Kavala. A good road follows the coastline, then crosses north of Halkidiki to Thessalonika.

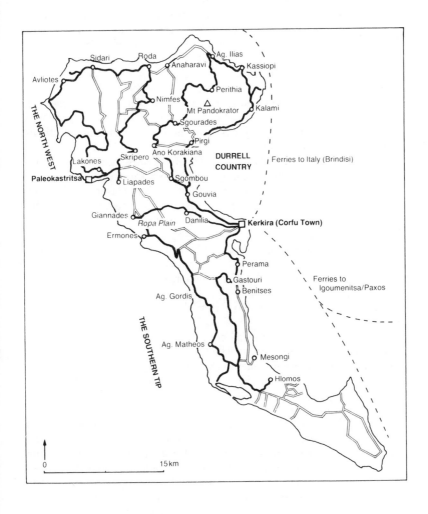

Crescent-shaped Corfu (pop: 93,000), the most northerly of the Ionian island group, lies close to the Greek mainland, though Albania — only 5km away at one point — is its nearest neighbour. The capital and port, Kerkira (an alternative name for both the island and the town), is well connected, with regular car-ferry routes to Igoumenitsa in Epirus (where one of our tours starts), Paxos, the pretty, flower-covered island to the south, and several southern-European ports, Brindisi, Venice and Dubrovnik among them.

Corfu is not a year-round paradise. It feels the brunt of lashing gales and heavy rains in winter, causing many a hardy sea-farer to retreat to the protection of the hills. Spring comes early, usually in mid-March and always in time for Easter, which is celebrated on the island with a particularly inspired combination of religious fervour and carnival fun. To join in the open-air celebration in the town square at midnight on Holy Saturday and carry a lighted candle (a symbol of hope) to the first, early-hours-of-the-morning meat meal for 40 days — *magiritsa* (an offal stew) — enjoyed with ear-splitting merriment is an experience in depth.

Corfu has that driving rain to thank for its being such a green and pleasant land, for the profusion of fig and citrus trees, cypress and olives, pink-blossomed almond and Judas trees, and a botanist's dream of wild flowers, many of them rare.

One estimate has put Corfu's complement of olive trees at 4 million — but who's counting? During the winter harvest the ground beneath the trees is covered with catch-every-last-olive black plastic netting. The timing is perfect. It is removed just in time for anemones, cranesbill, doronicum and other brilliants to show their faces.

In common with Greece as a whole, Corfu has changed hands politically many times since the Corinthians first planted a colony on the island in 8C BC; but in significant contrast to the fate of her neighbouring states, 'Corcyra' did not experience the 500 years of Turkish domination.

By 3C BC the rich and highly fertile island was an important colony of Rome, and Cato, Cicero and Nero — who danced and sang at the Temple of Zeus in Kassiopi — all put in an appearance.

It was seized by Guiscard in AD 11C during his encounters with the Eastern Empire and subsequently by one after another of the Italian states. The Venetians made the island their principal arsenal and fortified it accordingly — so effectively that it was able to withstand three Ottoman advances in 16C and 17C.

When Venice fell in 1797 Corfu, together with the other Ionian islands, was transferred to France, whose garrison was driven out a year later by a combined Turkish and Russian force. A treaty in 1807 returned the islands to France, until with the fall of Napoleon, they were declared an independent state under British protection; for a short time in 1858 Gladstone took up residence as Lord High Commissioner.

Great Britain voluntarily renounced all rights in the islands in 1864 and their Greek nationality was restored.

Durrell Country

1–2 days/195km from Kerkira, Corfu town

I favour a route with a low-key start. The surprises when they come are all the more surprising. Leaving Kerkira by the northern coastal road, passing the commercial port and then keeping pace with the wide, uneventful curve of the shoreline and a line of hotels, one may be forgiven for wondering what all the fuss is about. Why has a writer as sensitive as Lawrence Durrell spent a lifetime singing the island's praises? Where is that special magic? Has it all been bulldozed away by the not-so-sensitive demands of tourism?

This route soon answers these questions, zig-zagging off into first the hills, shimmering with olive groves and dazzling with wild flowers, and then the mountains, where villages only a couple of kilometres apart seem totally remote and peasants live very close to the land indeed. It is impossible to believe that these poeple, these villages, are but a meta-phorical stone's throw from some of the most popular beaches in Greece.

Emerging — somewhat breathlessly — from a circumnavigation of Mt. Pandokrator the route discovers the coves, the caves, the inlets and bays of the north-eastern coast, the cherished childhood home of the Durrell family, of *My Family and Other Animals* and *Prospero's Cell*. You are there, where 'the sea has become a deep throbbing emerald; the sand is freckled by long roaming silver lines . . . A white butterfly wavers in across the blue spaces.'

It is a different world from the bathing beaches just to the south, which we take in for effective comparison, and then leave for a short but pretty 'hillside revisited' excursion. After that Corfu town is only a few minutes away.

KERKIRA (pop: 29,000) Corfu town has style; several of them in fact, Byzantine, Venetian, Neapolitan, British, and of course Greek, each reflecting a period of cultural and architectural influence. The town, on the east coast of the island, has grown up along the sides of a promontory. A jagged rock divides it naturally into 2 sections, Garitsa to the south and Ag. Nikolaos. At the tip of the northern region stands a Venetian fortress cut off by an artificial moat, the *contra-fossa*, which historians identify with the Heraion mentioned by Thucydides. Kerkira is elegant shopping streets with wide, arched colonnades; it is the buzzingly busy narrow precincts glinting with jewellery and packed with boutiques; the vibrant, noisy, fascinating open-air market, and the old *cantounia*, the tiny, cobbled Neapolitan alley-ways ringing to the sound of children playing and festooned from side to side with washing lines. From end to end the town throbs with life, vitality and music — and there isn't a high-rise hotel in sight. The main square, as gracious as any in Greece, sets the scene for the Easter celebration unique to the island, the pot-throwing ceremony on Holy Saturday. The filigree-iron balconies of the Venetian mansions and tenements are packed with visiting dignitaries and residents, the Spaniada, or esplanade, is packed with the population of the island and many more besides and on the stroke of 11am, when a fire cracker signifies the first Resurrection, earthenware pots are dropped from the balconies on to the streets below. Cue for a procession of comic-opera-style brass bands (a speciality of Corfu) and drum majorettes, and a convivial drink or two. See: cathedral, close to the ferry-port; Monastery of Platytera (rare post-Byzantine icons), church of Ag. Spiridon, the island's patron saint (reliquary); archaeological museum. Don't miss: cricket on the green in front of the Royal Palace, built in 1823, both legacies from the British. On offer: a ride around town on a clip-clopping horse-drawn carriage; Son et Lumière performances in the citadel in summer; a good selection of restaurants, tavernas and — on the outskirts — discos. Ferry link: Igoumenitsa (see p. 60), Patra (see p. 38) on the mainland, the island of Paxos, and several Italian ports. Port Authority: 0661/32.655. NTOG: 0661/30.520. Tourist Police: 0661/29.503. Automobile and Touring Club: 0661/29.054. Hotels: **Olympic**, 0661/30.532; **Arkadion**, 0661/37.671; at Kanoni, **Salvos**, 0661/30.427.

Take the coast road going north, a good, wide road following the sweep of the bay. In 4km take the left fork, which leads slightly inland. After another 2km you will pass a sign to **GOUVIA** on the right. Turn there if you wish. It is a long, flat strip of a sailing village fringed by reeds and with good fish tavernas lining the muddy shoreline. Hotel: **Gouvia**, 0661/91.233. 1km beyond that junction, bear left. The road turns its back on the coast and wanders off into the olive groves. In 2km, at **SGOMBOU**, fork right. Pass through (if you even notice it) the hamlet of **GASATIKA**. Pretty little bell-towers peep through curtains of tamarisk and Judas trees, and 'garden escape' flowers tumble over crumbly stone walls. Bear left in 3km — the road on the right is signposted to Kato Korakiana — to its high-level counterpart, **ANO KORAKIANA**, a workmanlike village making no concessions to tourism.

Take the left road out of the village, going north. The road simultaneously twists and climbs for 5km in a deep cleft in the hills to **SOKRAKI**. The next 3km, a minor road to **SIGOS**, are bumpy and stony. Go slowly, admire the scenery and count the wildlife species you see. Daphne Du Maurier's *Birds* could have been conceived here. The tyres breathe a brief sigh of relief at the T-junction. Turn right to **SGOURADES**. The presumed profits of tourism have completely passed it by; as has the modern Greek language. The older people in these remote mountain villages speak a patois all their own. Back-packing has a different meaning, too. An elderly couple pause to shift the loads that bend them double: huge faggots of olive wood for the fire on their cottage floor.

(If you are travelling in winter or very early spring, look before you leap on to the minor road the route takes next. It describes a high arc around **Mt. Pandokrator** (906m) and can be subject to subsidence and the odd rock-fall. The alternative is to return to the T-junction, turn right and follow the road through **EPISKEPSIS**. Turn right at **ANAHARAVI**. You link up with the tour route at **AG. ILIAS**.)

To continue the 8-months-of-the-year route: Turn left, 1km beyond Sgourades on to an exhilarating, wind-rushing-through-your-hair kind of very minor mountain road. Goats pay scant attention to the rules of the highway. Tiny cottages — few and far between — are lost in a cloud of almond blossom. In 6km, climbing ever higher and with Mt. Pandokrator disappearing into the clouds on your right, you reach **STRINILAS**, a celebration of a village set among vineyards. It has been a toughish climb, the road isn't brilliant, and you've made it! Tavernas and *kafenions* in the friendly elm-tree-shaded square make a glass of something refreshing seem like a good idea. Continue through the village (direction north east). In about 1km there's a track leading to the mountain summit and the monastery perched thereon. I make it a strenuous optional extra for experienced walkers, rewarded by awe-inspiring views of snow-capped Albania and the hands-on map of Corfu at your feet, for all the world like a green tapestry rug.

On to **PETALIA** which rejoices in being the highest village on the island — pretty, too — and then 7km of thickly wooded, craggy hillsides spattered with wild flowers — saxifrage, fritillaries, borage — to **LAFKI**. An old lady sitting on her doorstep whipping egg whites in a tin plate — an arm-aching job — smilingly accepts assistance. In return, she points out the views, 'from the highest to the lowest', from the mountain peak, now behind us, to the river valley running — as the road will too — into the northern coastline. In 4km of orchards, cypress spires and holly oaks, you come to the almost deserted village of **PERITHIA** nestling in folds of misty hillsides covered with wild pear trees. 'Is this really the Corfu of the travel brochures?' someone asks. Greece was never more rural!

Take the road going north east — there's a distinct improvement in the surface quality — through **LOUTSES**, which tumbles down a ridge, and Nea Perithia to (in 8km) **AG. ILIAS** and a sudden breath of sea (as opposed to mountain) air.

Turn right on to the coast road. **KASSIOPI** is 7km away. The remains of a 13C Angevin castle are in danger of being obscured by development. The road becomes a switchback through dense green hillsides lighted by the brilliant yellow touches of massive Jerusalem sage flowers. Peer through a break in the vertical cypress-tree curtain and you see **AG. STEPHANOS**, a tiny fishing hamlet sheltered in the crook of a cove and reached by a windy track on the left. You could spend all day there in a waterside taverna, sipping this and that. People do. Return — when you're ready — to the coast road and in 2km turn off left again into the heart of Lawrence Durrell country. The corniche road leads to **KALAMI** so evocatively described in his *Prospero's Cell*. Local people old enough to remember him as a neighbour (in the 1930s) will want to reminisce, and willingly show you the large, friendly overgrown house where he lived. Scramble around the cove and you come to another of his favourite haunts, the even smaller hamlet of **KOULOURA**. Judge for yourself whether this rocky coastline pitted with caves and shimmering with little lagoons is or is not heaven on earth.

There is no passable way forward, so return to the main road and turn left. In 6km, you come to **NISSAKI**, one more fishing village fanned by silvery olives and settled around a cluster of tiny coves. One, **Kaminaki**, has a large, drip-drip-dripping limestone cave housing — be prepared — a colony of bats. Hotel: **Nissaki Beach**, 0663/91.232. Continue around the near-deserted coastline for 6km to **PIRGI** where the scene changes. All along this stretch of sandy beach, running due north-south on the wide bay, more and more hotels, bars, clubs, discos, souvenir shops and villas house the ever-increasing colony of summer visitors. **IPSOS** for example, in 2km, features in many a come-hither travel ad. Hotel: **Mega**, 0661/93.208.

Turn left in just over 1km on to a woodsy lane where secluded villas hide their wooden shutters and iron balconies behind exuberant orchards and gardens. In 2km **KATO KORAKIANA** is an unspoiled, pleasant-stop-for-coffee village. Continue to the T-junction and turn left. The road will seem familiar. It is. Follow it back to Kerkira.

The North West
1 day/115km/from Paleokastritsa

Fishing boats bobbing in the harbour, trees dappling the sand with shade and almost paddling in the shallow water, rocky coves and invigorating

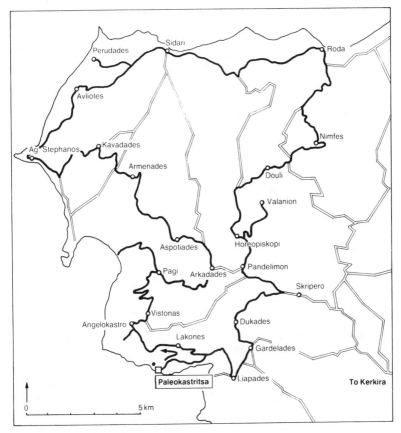

(euphemism for exerting) walks up into the hillsides — Paleokastritsa is both a pleasant resort and a good touring base.

Northwards around the coast minor roads cast their lines into one after another of the small fishing villages. Tour operators do much the same, but as yet have missed quite a few.

The countryside is soft, pretty and for the most part gentle — the highest peak and the stiffest climb is in the north east. Each hillside village appears first as a dazzling white or mellow stone blob on the green landscape — a beckoning landmark offering an unassuming welcome.

Archaeological sites and important architecture is sparse. The 'culture' on this route is in the hands of the people.

PALEOKASTRITSA is a small holiday village which has grown up around and because of a natural, horseshoe-shaped harbour on the north-west coast of the island. The 5-fingered bay, backed by cypress and olive-cloaked hills and with almond trees showering pink petals over the sand, is frankly pretty; out of high season, it is idyllic in fact. But in July and August when pedal-boats in the shallow waters are more numerous than olives covering the hillsides, well, you have to like the human race! Even so, it is easy to get away from it all. There are villas and apartments wrapped in swathes of pine and fruit trees only a couple of minutes' walk from the coast. The tavernas, of the impromptu-sirtaki-dancing kind, are good, specialising in fish and salt-water crayfish (kept live, in tanks). Taverna: **Faros**, 0663/41.305. For hotels, villas and apartments: Michalas Travel, 0663/41.298. See: delightful 13C and 18C monastery, a wedding-cake of a design, with an original vintners' cellar, on a rocky promontory from which there are bracing views. *The* view is from the Bella Vista taverna on a natural balcony high above the village where, it is said, kings of Greece have dined.

Take the coast road (direction Kerkira — it's the only one). Turn left in 3km to **LAKONES** a long, narrow strip of a village with serviceable shops and a few *kafenions*. It has hidden charms — a cob-web of cobbled alley-ways and steep stone stairways leading to clusters of pink-washed cottages, farmyards, a crisp new church and everywhere a friendly reception. A steep mule track leads precipitously down — waist-deep in flowers — to Paleokastritsa, another to the 13C fort, **Angelokastro**. Come before Easter, and you may come across the butcher's garden hanging with rows of — are they kites? — goatskins pegged out to dry. Not a pretty sight, but a fact of life. If it's May Day, *protimaiou*, in this traditional village above all, every door will be decked with a ring of spring flowers, a joyous celebration *stefani*.

The road wanders off westwards to **MAKRADES** (3km) where you can buy bottles of potent and murky home-made wine, chunky baskets, and bunches of dried mountain herbs by the roadside. At **VISTONAS** (3km) turn left on to a minor road to neat and tidy **PAGI** in a bowl of almond trees. Turn left there for **AG. GEORGIOS**, a newish little resort in a sheltered bay with a bustle of waterside tavernas and a good line in beaches. Return to Pagi and bear right through Vatonies to **ARKADADES**, strung across an olive-covered ridge. Turn left and in 1km fork left to **ASPOTIADES**, a far-from-the-madding-crowd hamlet in a gorgeous setting, and then **DAFNI**, on the rise of a hill. **Cape Aritas** appears through a veil of trees to the west. In 3km, **ARMENADES**, a pretty farming village with a lived-in look, and then **KAVADADES**, a sporadic hillside settlement wrapped in vegetation. Bear left there and in 3km, at the T-junction on the cliffs — looking out to Gravia island — turn right, following the coastline. Keep straight on at **ARILAS** (Hotel: **Arilas Beach**, 0663/31.401) in 2km, declining to turn inland with the major road. The minor one continues around the shore, the sea on one side and vineyards the other, to **AG. STEPHANOS** on a wide, sandy bay with steep white cliffs and hotels as a dramatic backdrop. I have to admit I didn't stop. Hotel: **Nausica**, 0663/31.254. The road trundles on in 4km to **AVLIOTES**, with its peeling-paint houses, an olive-oil processing plant, a proper sense of pride in festive occasions and — to that end — an almost tuneful community marching band.

Turn left in 3km to **PERUDADES** 2km off the beaten track and an energetic scamper from the cliffs down to the beach, where there's a taverna. In search of solitude, wander along the beach to the point, **Cape Drastis** with its toy-sized off-shore islet. Return to the main road which passes **SIDARI**, a popular resort. Hotel: **Mimosa**, 0663/31.361. Take the minor, coast road just beyond (where the asphalt road turns sharply inland). Persevere for 4km to **KARUSADES** where you join a loop in another 'asphaltos' road going north east. With luck, there will still be a rickety signpost saying **RODA**. Hotel: **Roda Inn**, 0663/31.358. You want that — it's another 'discovered' resort — if only to turn inland at 180° from the coast, ignoring the left turn just inland of the resort. The road you want is marked Sfakira.

The last 12 or so kilometres have been a means to an end. Now you turn into the mountain reaches. Turn left in 3km to **NIMFES** where there is cool, clear water — a fountain with 9 gurgling spouts — and the deserted but dignified Monastery of Pandokrator named for the mountain reaching for the skyline to the east. Continue for 2km to the junction and turn left on to a more major road which you join just before **DOULI**; 2km beyond the village there's a junction where 2 roads and 3 rivers cross. Turn left and in 3km, just beyond **HOREOPISKOPI**, turn left again, along an unmarked track alluring in its rural potential. 'Is this the *dromaki* to Valanion?' I asked at a smart new house near the turning. 'Yes, but you'll get the best view of Albania from my balcony', came the reply. Two cups of coffee and iced water later, who was to disagree?

The by-road is picturesque. Trees meeting overhead form a sun-dappling guard of honour. Meadows of flowers, orchards, chicken farms, herds of goats, picture-postcard cottages, misty-mountain glimpses — it has them all. **VALANION** when it comes (in around 3km) is pure nostalgia with its moss-covered walls, two corner shops, and grandmothers in traditional dress. One *kafenion*, panelled throughout in maroon and eau-de-nil, looks set for a film. Come to that, the whole village does, for its *panigeri*, the saint's-day festival on the Sunday after Easter. Half-a-dozen sheep and goats are spit-roasted in the large school playground, drinks flow freely from sales stalls along the street, a 3-piece band tunes up on a rostrum and everyone joins hands to dance. It's a hard act to follow.

Return to what we termed 'Albania junction' and turn left. In 4km you come to **PANDELIMON**. Bear left and just before **SKRIPERO** turn right (the road goes due west and is signed to Paleokastritsa) to **DUKADES** deep-set in a velvety-green hillside. Turn left and in 1km at the main road turn left to **GARELADES**. Go through the village, cross the junction in 1km and you come to **LIAPADES**. A striped awning lifts the *kafenion* a notch or two up the usual social scale, there's a *periptero*, a yellow kiosk outside it and the irresistible smell of cheese pies and custard pies from the baker's on the corner. Crumbling stone mansions cling to the last vestiges of grandeur and tiny shepherds' cottages boast massive white-starred marguerite trees and well endowed vine-covered terraces. But no facilities. You need luck (or inside information) to be on hand when the 3 musicians strut off down the hill to lead first the bride-groom's procession and then the bride's entourage, under a white organdie canopy, from their homes to the church. Flower petals are strewn in the streets, in and on the bridal car and over visitors, sugared almonds are handed around and eventually everyone goes off to Paleokastritsa for the wedding feast of *yiouvetsi*, roast lamb with pasta, and fruit salad glittering with lighted sparklers.

We take that road, too. Turn right and in 2km at the main road T-junction, turn left. The signpost tells you that you are back to base in 4km.

The Southern Tip

1 day/140km/from Kerkira, Corfu town

There are people — not travel agents, but others — who say that the whole south of the island, below the line from Kerkira across to Giannades, has been submerged by a wave of tourism — destroyed by its own popularity, in other words.

This route sets out to prove otherwise, dipping into lush mountain valleys, exploring flower-strewn by-ways that even the locals have not traversed, and putting a toe into the clear azure water of many a tucked-away rocky cove on the western coast.

There is just one short stretch, on the way to that best-known of all Corfiot landmarks, Mouse Island, that, in block after block of comfortable hotels, shows you what you have been missing.

KERKIRA (see p. 124) Leave the town by the Potamos road, direction north east. At 1km beyond **POTAMOS** you will see (and ignore) a left turn to Evroupoli. In 2km **DANILIA**, known locally as 'the village' (*to horio*) is a glimpse into the island's Venetian past, a folkloric reconstruc-

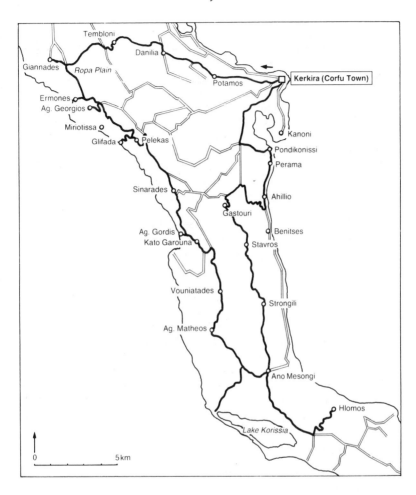

tion of a whole community, with furnished houses, workshops, arts and crafts, a museum and summer festivals. And a restaurant. Less than 1km farther on, turn left to **TEMBLONI**, set amid olive groves and fruit farms. Turn right at the T-junction and then left, following the signs to (in 4km) **GIANNADES**. The road crosses the flat-as-a-pancake **Ropa Plain**, almost refreshing in its totally uninterrupted views, a herbaceous carpet spread at the feet of distant mountains. The village, a gentle hotch-potch of slightly crumbling mellow stone half-way up the Marmara Hills, metamorphoses in springtime under a shower of bougainvillea.

Return 1km along the road to Tembloni and take the right turn, a minor road across the Plain to **ERMONES**, which had Neolithic and Bronze Age communities. Turn right for the well-organised beach complex — complete with thatched straw shelters, bar and restaurant. According to Homer, this is where Odysseus was washed ashore. Hotel: **Hermones Beach**, 0661/94.241. Return inland, passing on your left the road from Giannades. In 1km a parallel left turn leads to the pride and joy of the island, the Corfu golf course, 0661/94.220. The road bears sharp right. In 1km turn right to **VATOS**. The densely wooded slopes of **Ag. Georgios** (390m) come between the pleasant cluster of sparkling white houses and the rocky coastline. Halfway back to the 'main' road and just past a stone house a wide, pebbly track (direction due south and not marked) leads through a sparse olive grove scampering with goats and, until midsummer, dazzling with wild flowers, to **Miriotissa**. I know that now. I asked an old lady, bent on minding her goats, if this was the way to the Convent. 'They say it is, dear,' she replied, 'but I've never been down there myself.' Perhaps it's as well. In about 1.5km where the track peters out for all but the most intrepid of drivers, you come to the island's only official (albeit illegal) nudist beach. A path to the right, high above the pebbly shore, leads (15 mins) to the pretty whitewashed monastic church nestling among olives and pines, its shutters an exact match for the peacock green of the Ionian Sea below.

Meander back to the road, turn right and in 3km turn right along a road which snakes its way to the cove-scalloped beach at **GLIFADA**, good for fishing and snorkelling. Hotel: **Glifada Beach**, 0661/94.222.

That was a turn-round-and-go-back road — by reason of the craggy coastline. Turn right at the main road, to **PELEKAS** (less than 1km), a 17C village with a magnificent belvedere known as Kaiser's Throne, a favourite spot of Wilhelm II. The view has to be seen to be believed, especially at sunset. Follow the road to the T-junction. Turn right and after 5km of vineyards, fork right to **SINARADES**, a pretty country village with lovely views. In 3km a right turn leads to **AG. GORDIS**, where there is another beautiful, sheltered sandy beach fringed by a fertile plain of olive and fruit trees. There is now also a large hotel. Pension: **Alonakia**, 0661/30.407.

The main road climbs lazily up the olive-cloaked slopes of **Mt. Garouna** almost to **KATO GAROUNA**. Park at the junction and wander around this unassuming little hamlet; not many people do, and visitors are friends from the first '*kalimera*'. Turn left at the next junction and, almost immediately, right on to a minor road to **VOUNIATADES** (3km) which overlooks the Strongili Valley, and **AG. MATHEOS**, sprawling across a hillside basin almost filled in with pines, olives and cypress. Turn right in 4km, just past the remains of a Byzantine castle at Gardiki, on to a minor road heading straight for the shores of **Lake Korissia** cut off from the sea by a ridge of hummocky dunes awash with such hardies as sea rocket, sea stock and sea holly. Time for a walk perhaps? Take binoculars if you have them. The reeds and rushes are rustling with wildlife and the lagoon shimmers with swooping birds. Mallard and teal, pintails and wigeon, avocets, heron, cormorants and tern — the migratory calendar dictates what you will see. The beach, stretching without interruption in both directions, is shallow and sandy.

There is no round-the-lagoon road, so turn round and go back. Turn right into the main road, and in a little over 2km turn right at the T-junction at Ano Mesongi. In 6km turn left to **HLOMOS** an agricultural village crowded with sun-baked stone cottages in a drape of the hill-sides. Every twist and turn gives a fresh blue or purple or deep, deep green perspective on the island, on Paxos to the south, the coast of mainland Epirus to the east, and the world in general.

Return to the Ano Mesongi junction and keep straight on. The strip of beach to the east is fast being gobbled up by relentless development. This road, first running along the lush Mesongi Valley and then climbing around the foothills (waistline, actually) of **Ag. Deka** (576m) gives it the cold shoulder. **STRONGILI**, scattered along the roadside, comes up in 4km of isolated farm shacks, some of the smallest incongruously moated with wild flowers. Then (2km and climbing) Kornata and (3km and still climbing) **STAVROS**, a wild garden of a village glaring down on the sun-spots of **BENITSES**. The road wends its twisty way to Pondi. Turn right at the junction and then right at the T-junction to the village of **GASTOURI**. On a tree-covered knoll commanding a magnificent view over the bay is the **Ahillio**, or Achilleon, the Italianate villa built in 1890 for the empress Elisabeth of Austria which she named after the mythical hero Achilles. It is now a museum and casino. See: royal portraits and mementoes, landscape garden with marble statues, and the view.

Continue for 3km until the road meets the coast road, and turn left. **PERAMA** (in 7km) is lavishly furnished with hotels and luxury villas. Park at the signpost for **KANONI**, across a narrow causeway. You can walk to the gleaming white **Monastery of Vlaherna** and from there take a small boat to off-shore **Pondikonissi**, or Mouse Island, which has room for no more than a small monastery chapel encircled by trees. Its silhouette prompted the legend — beloved by the Corfiots — that this minuscule islet is the Ship of Odysseus turned to stone by Poseidon.

Turn inland and in 3km turn right. Continue on the road, passing the airport on the right, and return to Kerkira.

*

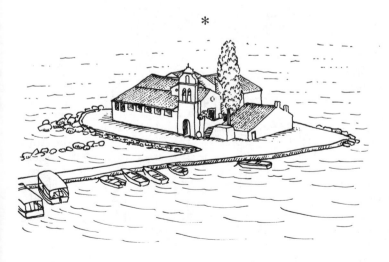

Pondikonissi, Mouse Island, just off-shore from Kanoni

Specialities

The shimmering silvery-green landscape indicates at a glance that olives are the principal crop of the island. Hooked poles like elongated shepherds' crooks are used to shake the fruit to the ground, and barrels of green and black olives in brine are as numerous as tubs of geraniums in cottage doorways. Most villages have their own oil-pressing plant, many in the heart of the olive groves.

Citrus fruits are another important source of revenue, oranges, lemons and especially kumquats — miniature Japanese oranges, which are preserved in syrup, candied and made into the golden and sticky *kumkwat* liqueur.

Both red and white wines are produced on the island. The red wine, brick-coloured and potent, may not travel well but its exceptionally long shelf life is a source of fierce pride, and a bottle of 'my 20-year-old' is considered a fitting toast for any family occasion. The white wine is dry and unresinated.

Festivals

The Corfiots love a procession. And a party. Four times a year a litany procession in honour of the island's patron saint, St Spiridon, is accompanied around Corfu town by a succession of marching bands. Dates: Greek Orthodox Palm Sunday, Holy Saturday, 11 August and 1st Saturday in November. On 14-15 August, in honour of the Assumption, there is a religious festival in the suburb of Mandouki. Most villages celebrate a *panageri*, church festival with folk dancing, around Easter time.

The wide, arched colonnades of Corfu Town

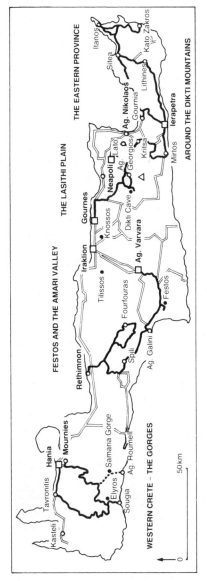

Crete (Kriti), the largest of the Greek islands at some 250 kilometres long by 55 kilometres wide, is scenery in a nutshell, from snow-capped mountain peaks and deep, deep gorges to silvery beaches fanned by date palms and the 'African wind'. Dominated by the White Mountains in the west, the Ida group in the centre and the Dikti range to the east, the island is naturally divided — and sharply, too — into lush plains and valleys, which have always been favourable centres of population, and virtually impassable masses. With the north coast of Africa only 320 kilometres across the Libyan sea, the island enjoys a mild climate the year around. And with abundant crops of olives — still being planted in droves — citrus fruits, loquats, pomegranates, walnuts, chestnuts, peaches, apples, melons, watermelons, grapes — used for both wine and raisin production — tomatoes and even bananas, it is no wonder Crete has been called the fruit basket of the Aegean.

Crete *is* history. History of an almost unimaginable intensity, but history that is there for all to see. Fossil remains have indicated that the island was once joined to mainland Europe and Asia, and it was first inhabited in Neolithic times. A large population explosion — not apparently an invasion — brought together the various peoples who formed, around 2600 BC, what Sir Arthur Evans, the British archaeologist, defined as the Minoan Civilisation. Their scripts, used mainly for administrative and commercial purposes, give some clue as to their origins. What is known as Linear A, dating from c 1700 BC, has been likened to various Indo-European and Semitic languages, whilst Linear B, a derivation dating from around 1500 BC, has been shown to have similarities with ancient Greek.

The first Minoan palaces, built for the ruling families on prime, fertile sites close to the sea at Knossos, Phaestos and Malia around 2000 BC were destroyed by earthquake and soon rebuilt, only to be razed to the ground again, and so the sites that attract visitors today show development in two or three stages.

To understand what day-to-day life was like in the great palaces and the many Minoan towns and villages around the island, it is really necessary to visit the archaeological museums, notably the one in Iraklion, to see the burial finds — the incredibly beautiful goldwork, jewellery, clay models, pottery and 'eggshell ware'; the items of cult worship to the Mother goddess, and the artisans' tools.

Experts differ on the reason for the collapse of the great civilisation in c 1370 BC — whether it was caused by yet another natural disaster or by a massive invasionary force which at last penetrated the efficient Minoan maritime defences. The next known inhabitants, who partially restored some of the palaces, were the Archaens. Then, with Crete a vital part of their Aegean campaign, came the Dorians, who reduced the native population to subserviency and established (at Gortyns) a Code of Laws.

The Romans came and saw and conquered Crete — and made Gortyns the provincial capital — in 67 BC, and held it until the division of the Empire in AD 395. Then the island came under Byzantine rule which lasted (with only a brief period of Arabic occupation, AD 824-61), until the Venetians took power in 1204. Both Hania and Rethimnon have superb examples of later Venetian architecture at its elegant best.

The turbulent Turkish occupation of the island — from which many fine mosques survive — extended for over 200 years, until 1898 when the Ottomans were finally driven out by Allied powers, and in 1913 Crete was formally united with Greece.

The more recent history of the island, the landing of British and Commonwealth troops in 1941, the German invasion and subsequent occupation, the active Resistance movement in so many of the towns and villages, and the desperate shortage of food — those dark days are still relived in conversation with the older Cretans as if they were only yesterday.

To travel around the island and meet the people in their homes carries a delightful responsibility, for Cretan hospitality, of a heart-warming, almost overwhelming kind, is legendary. 'You are not a foreigner, not just a visitor, you are a friend,' is a familiar and very touching first-time greeting, accompanied usually by home-made *raki* or wine, cheese and olives, fruit and nuts — a feast of genuine kindness.

Crete, it has been said, is now a much-discovered holiday-makers' paradise, and parts of the coastline close to the main towns have fallen by the wayside of hotel and villa development. So much so that people are inclined to talk of the 'real' Crete and the true Cretan characteristics — of the remote, obscure, wild countryside too — as if, all over the island, they were things of the past. Just don't listen to them.

The Lasithi Plain

1 day/105km/from Gournes to Neapoli

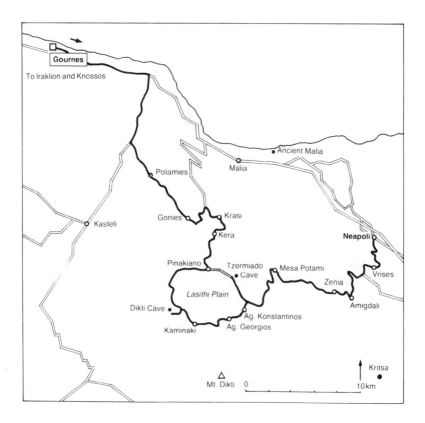

The Lasithi Plain, an intensely fertile area surrounded by mountains and irrigated, once the snow has melted, by wind power, is a familiar picture postcard subject. Windmills are particularly evocative of the Cretan landscape.

The tour begins after, perhaps, a visit to the important Minoan Palaces of Knossos and Malia, with a circular tour of the plain, making acquaintance with several of the farming villages it supports. Fruit and nuts, flowers and vegetables — it is an area of colourful and mellow fruitfulness.

By way of contrast, there are two cave visits: Dikti cave, close to the village of Psihro, where, it is believed, Zeus was born, and Tzermiado cave just outside the jostling, bustling village which cheerfully declares itself a democracy.

Kalo taxidi — have a good trip!

GOURNES is a coastal resort within easy reach (17km east) of **IRAKLION** — and therefore of the **Minoan Palace of Knossos** — and of **MALIA**, equidistant to the east. There, too, are the considerable remains of a Minoan Palace. At Gournes, Hotel: **America**, 081/761.231. NTOG, Iraklion, 081/222.487. Tourist Police, Iraklion, 081/283.190.

From Gournes, take the coast road going eastwards. Turn right in 11km (signposted Kasteli) through olive groves and lush market gardens. A hint of things to come. A truck passes with a jumble of seemingly age-old amphorae strapped on in a casual and shaky way. Minoan Crete lives on. Bear left in 7km (signed Gonies). Villages blink past, Potamies, Sfendili, then **ANDOU** draped in purple and red shawls of bougainvillea, hibiscus and geraniums.

Turn right 3km beyond **GONIES** (signed to Kera) where you start gaining height on the plain. At 3km, **KRASI**, a village round a circle. The reputedly largest plane tree on the island spans the centuries, casting shade on both a taverna terrace and the village laundry fountain. In 1km, **KERA**, a hilltop village just made for tavernas with competing and compelling views. Below the village the **Monastery of Kardiotissa** (12C frescoes). And then, on a waft of wild herbs, a row of old windmills. Camera clicking time. Turn right in 6km at **PINAKIANO** at the head of **Lasithi Plain**, a whirl of iron-framed windmills serving the fruit and cereal crops. Turn right to begin the circular tour of this abundant agricultural patchwork.

Iraklion harbour

Fork right at Kato Metohi. In 2km, **PLATI** has a triangle of busy tavernas. Fork left there, to **PSIHRO** a cheerful village with a traffic jam of sheep and goats and plenty of atmosphere. The village celebrates a religious feastday on 31 August with traditional dancing in local costumes, when hundreds of people converge on the plain on donkeys or mules. Turn left, following the sign to **Dikti Cave**. It's a case of footing it up the steep ancient pavement or taking the soft option and hiring a mule. A guide (not essential; not expensive either) lights the way with candles to show you the 2,200 sq.m cave where, according to the Hymn of the Kouretes, Zeus was born, and even the hole-in-the-wall cradle.

The plain of Lasithi with its windmills

Neolithic, Minoan, Classical, Hellenistic and Roman finds show the cave to have been in constant use. Many Minoan finds are in Iraklion Museum and a stone tablet inscribed with Linear A script in Oxford. At a more geological level, 64m below the ground, see a wonderland of stalactites and stalagmites. On foot, the return trip needs 1–1¼ hrs, and the going is steep, though perfumed by a pot-pourri of herbs. Most cave visitors feel they've earned a drink — 2 good cafés near the car park.

Return to Psihro and turn right on to the road signed to Ag. Nikolaos. **KAMINAKI** in 3km, a centre of Cretan weaving, looks pretty in its walnut and cherry grove setting. **KOUDOUMALIA**, resting on the bottom step of a hillside terrace, almost merges with **AG. GEORGIOS**, a kitchen garden of a village with a folkloric appearance. See: arts and crafts museum. Turn left at Ag. Konstantinos (signed to Heraklion) and fork left in 1km, beside a basilica-shaped shrine, to **TZERMIADO** (pop: 1,500) the main village of the region which announces itself as 'democratic'. Even the tree trunks are painted in broad blue and white stripes, the national colours. Wisteria-covered houses cling one above the other to a sheer rock face and the streets are lined with pollarded elder trees. The locals cheerfully call out to visitors, and it's all very jolly. Follow the signs in the village to the cave. Old ladies tending the vines will lead you up the steep path. Take a torch. Pension: **Kourites**, 0844/22.194.

The cave is conveniently on the Ag. Nikolaos road, which we take through the hamlet of **MARMEKATO**. Turn left at **MESA LASITHI** with its smart new basilica in the midst of a tropic of fruit and flowers. With the plain in the background, the road starts climbing and the scene changes. Spires of mullein and yucca spike the rugged hills and soon it becomes mountain-goat country. At **MESA POTAMI**, baskets of nuts for sale by the roadside. **ROUSATIANA** smells of honey — it's the broom — and **EXO POTAMI** is a leafy tunnel of plane trees, with donkeys strolling along the street.

An old man in the Cretan dress, black breeches and long black leather boots, carves wooden spoons by the roadside at **ZENIA** and 2km farther on, **AMIGDALI** means almonds — it speaks for itself. Fire has scorched the hills beyond Kato Amigdali — a desolate sight. Keep straight on to (in 7km) **VRISES**, a gem of a hillside village whose steep narrow lanes yield a notebook of impressions. Pumpkins drying on walls, rope lines draped with hay and camomile to feed the animals, a silver stream of woolly-leafed ballota trickling down the hillside, lizards scurrying underfoot, and above all, a flame of brilliant, sun-loving flowers.

Continue on the road to **NEAPOLI**, where this tour ends and the next begins.

Cretan embroidery

Festivities
At the village of **Mohos**, 6km north of Krasi, the Greek Touring Club organise a festival on 15 August, with local dances in Cretan costumes, exhibitions of hand-woven embroidered goods, Cretan food and fireworks.

Around the Dikti Mountains
1 day/90km/from Neapoli to Ierapetra

The Dikti mountain range, rising to 2,141m at its highest peak, lies to the south of the Lasithi Plain and runs almost down to the south coast.

Wherever there are towering peaks there are likely to be fertile valleys and, in spring and summer, every imaginable shade of leafy green. This tour revels in that flat collar of fruit and vegetable production, meandering around the foothills of the mountains, calling on prosperous farming villages and more remote ones; discovers the remains of the remarkably

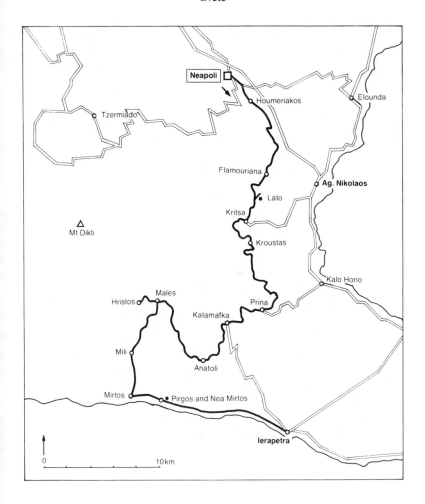

well-preserved yet little-known town of Lato which flourished over 2,500 years ago, and winds down to the coast where, in each case, a short walk is rewarded by the exploration of 2 little-documented Minoan sites.

The tour continues along the coast, fringed with oleander and bamboo and lined with miles and miles of market gardens — it's known locally as 'glasshouse street' — to Ierapetra where another route begins.

NEAPOLI (pop: 3,500), 15km north west of Agios Nikolaos, is a smart market town with a large square shaded by pine trees, and all the necessities of present-day travel — banks, post office and good shops. It appears the more exotic for rows of date palms lining the main street. See: museum with Minoan finds and a Linear A inscribed tablet. Local speciality: *soumadha*, a milk-like drink made from pressed almonds and served cool in summer, hot in winter. A 3-day festival (14-16 August) has local dances, sports events and religious processions.

Turn right on to the old road (it is marked as such) leading to Ag. Nikolaos and in 1km turn right, signed **HOUMERIAKOS** which you reach, after 3km, on a drift of aniseed-scented fennel. The village, dressed overall in bougainvillea and roses, reclines in a valley of almonds and olives. Fork right out of the village and then, in 1km, left. Turn right 1km farther on, signed to Lasithi, and turn left in 1km, signed to Lakonia. Pass through Karterides, in 3km, and Panagia (formerly Lakonia). Continue to **FLAMOURIANA** and take a track on the right, signposted to **LATO**. It's an unmade road through a valley, which climbs gently to the site of a town founded 7C BC on a spectacular hillside. Wander from room to room still furnished with stone water carriers and mortars; picnic under the plane trees; sweep grandly up (or down) the broad staircase; evoke millennia of agriculture in the just-as-it-was threshing ring, and of crafts-manship in the carpenter's shop, where saws were found, the pottery and the smithy.

Fork right at Lato, beside a plaster shrine with frescoes. Descend to the junction and turn right into **KRITSA**, which in summer is submerged in a gigantic wave of tourism. Arts and crafts of all kinds, including plastic-moulded traditional wedding breads, and tavernas galore. However, just before the village, the church of Pan. Kera, dating from the Venetian occupation, has fine frescoes. Every year (the date varies) a mock wedding is held in traditional Cretan costume and according to old customs.

Turn left in the centre of the village. The signpost reads Kroustas in Greek. Beside it, a large yellow and blue 'Post' sign in English points to the right. **KROUSTAS**, only 4km away, is as different as chalk from cheese. Pollarded mulberry trees line the street. There's only one (very friendly) taverna and tour-ists are a novelty. The village festival, with music and dancing, is on 24 June. Go through the village, on to an unmetalled road. The views to Kalo Horio on the bay compen-sate for the stony surface. In 9km, to the scent of pines and with pale blue beehives as ground cover, **PRINA**. Someone muttered 'Garden of Eden'. It must have been the bal-conies showering the road with rose petals; the stone houses in a froth of painstakingly cultivated flowers and fruit; the hum of the bees, and the heat you can hear. Ladies, with needles busy, sit on the steps of the

Church of Panageia Kera at Kritsa   pretty church with 2 rose windows.

The narrow street is all but closed, the men sitting along both sides, their fingers busy with worry beads.

Return through the village and turn sharp right. At the main road turn right to **KALAMAFKA**, in 8km, with a picturesque chapel on the hill. Almonds and mulberries, blue alkanet and mallow line the route. Turn right where loquats, small apricot-like fruits, are the thing to offer visitors — by the bag-full. Turn right to **MALES**, the road climbing steeply and scenically for 10km. The village, recumbent along the foothills of the **Dikti** range, is workmanlike and, literally, fruitful. Go straight on (it's an unmade road) for 2km to **HRISTOS**, a handful of tiny cottages untouched by modern transport; the roads are too steep and stepped for wheels. There's a small *kafenion* and a not surprising aura of remoteness among the mulberries.

Return to Males and turn right in front of the olive oil factory on to the minor road to **MILI**. It's a joggly 12km but not difficult, and affords, as they say, gloriously misty views of the south coast and, on a good day, the island of **HRISI**. Fork left in the hamlet — on to a good road now — dropping south in 4km to the coastal resort of **MIRTOS**, a still-pleasant place to stay. Hotels: **Esperides**, 0842/51.298; **Mirtos**, 0842/51.226.

Turn left along the coast road, where there are 2 little-known Minoan sites to visit. Each is clearly marked and involves a 300m walk up a track. The first, at **PIRGOS**, is dominated now, as it was then, by a large country house — with floors of variegated stone — facing the sea. The other, 4km farther on at Nea Mirtos has the remains of about 90 rooms to explore. Pottery and textile finds date this extensive site to c2500-2170 BC.

Continue, along the road lined with market gardens and plastic glass-houses, to **IERAPETRA** where this tour ends and another begins.

The Eastern Province

2 days/225km/from Ierapetra on the south-eastern coast

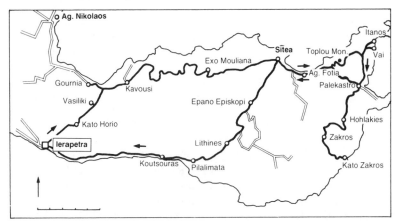

Setting off from the pleasant modern resort town of Ierapetra (not forgetting its glorious ancient past); attempting to unravel the archaeological remains at Vasiliki and then walking boldly around the Minoan town of Gournia; on to the busy and sophisticated port of Sitea, the tour begins in a typically Cretan way.

Then almost without warning it's like taking a leap into the tropics. Banana trees and date palms — a large natural grove of them, underplanted with zingy pink oleanders — paint a completely different and utterly exotic picture. No wonder the locals in this extreme north-eastern tip of the island refer to it as the African peninsula, and to their climate as African weather.

Coming due south, there is another, extensive and easily comprehensible Minoan site — stairs to climb, rooms and workshops to enter; some rooms around the perimeter are flooded, giving the site a strangely algae-coloured, moated appearance. And for non-culture-vultures, the Kato Zakros site just happens to be within a few steps of a fabulous beach.

With exploring in mind, one rarely likes to retrace one's steps. It's always more fun to break new ground and come back a different way. Not easy in this most easterly region of the island. Many a nail-biting hour was spent in pursuit of alternative routes, and many a disappointing dead end (landslide, surface eruption, or massive subsidence) encountered in the course of duty. If you do decide to go off the beaten track and take to the unmarked roads, make a note of the turnings you take (the tracks begin to look remarkably similar in the mountains, miles from anywhere) and allow plenty of time to reverse mistakes, and in daylight.

IERAPETRA (pop: 7,000) the most southerly town in Europe, on the Libyan-sea coast of the island, flourished during both Roman and Venetian times. With its mild winter climate it enjoys now, as then, a rich harvest of market-garden crops, notably tomatoes and cucumbers grown under glass. The port, dominated by a 13C Venetian fortress, displays a wealth of holiday yachts beside the fishing fleet. The long golden-sandy beaches, seemingly endless, are like a magnet to tourists, and the promenade, lined with tamarisk trees, is packed with loudly competing waterside tavernas and bars. A good choice: taverna **Napoleon**, at the extreme western end of the waterfront (0842/22.410), patronised mainly by Greeks. Specialities of the house: *kakavia*, fish soup served with 3 kinds of poached fish and boiled potatoes; *crochettas*, crisp prawn and herb fritters heavily laced with garlic; *tiropittas*, tiny cheese pies with the minimum of filo pastry, maximum of *mezithra* and herbs, and fresh fish and seafood of all kinds. Hotels: **El Greco**, 0842/28.471; **Creta**, 0842/22.316.

Leave the town by the road going north east (signposted Ag. Nikolaos) and in 7km turn right into **KATO HORIO** to see the Turkish fountain. Do the loop round to the main road, turn right and in 4km turn off left to **VASILIKI** where recent excavations have revealed Early Minoan, Mykinean and Roman dwellings. The type of mottled red and black pottery (in Iraklion Museum) found in tombs here is now known as 'Vasiliki flameware'.

Return to the major road and turn left. At the T-junction turn left towards Ag. Nikolaos. In 3km at **GOURNIA** a sign on the left points to the 'antiquities', the remains of a Minoan town sprawled across a limestone ridge. Stroll along the narrow streets, walk from room to room in the tiny houses and workshops, climb up to the governor's palace, and see the site of the shrine where cult objects of worship were found. Workmen's tools and domestic implements which brought the site even more to life are in Iraklion Museum.

Turn back to the road junction and carry straight on. After **KAVOUSI** (3 Byzantine churches) the road climbs around a mountain ridge. Villages appear to hang from the slopes and the terraced hillsides — crammed with orchards and olive trees — are known as the 'Cretan riviera'. **EXO MOULIANA** is famous for its red wine and the discovery of beehive tombs (swords and bronze objects unearthed). At 49km from the T-junction **SITEA** (pop: 6,500) attractively ranged up the cliff edge around the bay with a picturesque small harbour. Ferries link the port with Ag. Nikolaos, Piraeus (eventually) and Rhodes and there is the usual bustling air of comings and goings. Vines in the region are cultivated principally for the raisin crop, a major export, and there is a 5-day 'sultanina' festival in August. Little remains of the Venetian occupation. Hotels: **Alice**, 0843/28.450; **Crystal**, 0843/22.284.

The route hugs the **Bay of Sitea** with windmills on wide, scrub-tufted sand dunes and wig-wams of drying bamboo canes looking like a primitive encampment. **AG. FOTIA** (in 5km) has an earthy-brown pottery (good

Europe's only palm-fringed beach at Vai

plain, traditional shapes). Hotel: **Mare Sol**, 0843/28.950. In 7km turn left to **Toplou Monastery** (reconstructed 1612), of Venetian fortress proportions. See: 2C BC plaque commemorating a treaty, icons. Continue for 6km. There are lovely coastal and island views on each side of the promontory, shaggy wild goats over 'hedgehogs' of spiny spurge, and semi-circles of beehives look like toy-town villages. Turn left (signposted **VAI**) and in 1km turn right. Suddenly it's a tropical paradise, the only natural wild date-palm grove in Europe leading to and then colonising a wide, silver-sandy beach. There's a tourist pavilion and taverna and every possible scenic incentive to tarry.

Return the 1km to the major road and turn right to **ITANOS**, passing more huge, frondy date palms and now bananas under glass. Here on a wide headland is 'the deserted city', a Minoan settlement that flourished through Roman and into Byzantine times. High-walled rooms still give shelter from the warm African wind, and it's a case of 'spot (and identify) the shards'. There are pottery fragments everywhere.

Return, passing the turning to Vai, and continue south to the large old-and-new village of **PALEKASTRO** where (close by, at the coast) a Minoan harbour-town has been discovered. Pension: **Hellas**, 0843/61.240. Hotel: **Marina Village**, 0843/61.284.

Follow the road signs south to Zakros, through ribbons of olives on terraced hills. **HOHLAKIES** has pretty white cubic houses, **AZOKERAMOS** a model of a blue and white chapel, and **KELARIA** a stream of pink oleander through the river bed. Go straight on at **ADRAVASTI** and in 3km, come to **ZAKROS** the largest village which serves its beach-side neighbours. Hotel: **Zakros**, 0843/28.479. Turn right (the road is signed 'Minoan village') and in 8km of fabulous views — first a deep gorge and then soft drapes of green hills forming stage curtains for sandy coves and bays — **KATO ZAKROS** with fields of raisin-cropping vines, shady tamarisk trees and a chorus of waterside tavernas. Once again, the Minoans chose their spot. This area is known locally as the Valley of the Dead, because cave burials dating back to c2600 BC were found nearby. The palace ruins date from c1600 and c1500 BC after, it is thought, a natural disaster necessitated rebuilding. Another one, probably an earthquake, destroyed the buildings around 1450 BC when the inhabitants, given some warning, dropped everything and ran. See: remains of entrance stairway, courtyards, royal rooms and bathroom, treasury, kitchen, storerooms, workshops, cistern, fountain well. Again, the major finds (and they were many) are in Iraklion Museum.

There's no way forward from here. Return to Palekastro, turn left and in 6km turn left on to the Sitea road. Turn left at the cross-road in the town on to the Ierapetra road. **MARONIA** has elegant houses with stone balustrades and abundant loquat trees. **EPANO EPISKOPI** flashes by, a bunch of tree marguerites and wild geraniums. **LITHINES**, on a long, straight stretch of road, is a handshakes-all-round village. *Before* you get out of the car. **PILALIMATA** has its head buried in raisin vines. And then it's a straight run along the coast — some of it heavily developed — back to Ierapetra.

Festos and the Amari Valley

2–3 days/205km/from Agia Varvara (30km south west of Iraklion) to Rethimnon

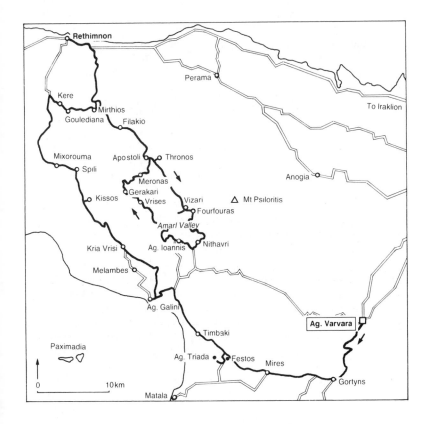

Ancient Gortyns, which flourished under the Dorians, was advanced enough to write its own code of laws and, after falling to Rome, was created capital of Crete; Festos, Ancient Phaistos, closely linked with the neighbouring Minoan Palace of Knossos and built on a spectacular amphitheatrical site; and Agia Triada, thought to be a summer palace or royal annexe for the Phaistos rulers: this tour begins with its roots deep in Cretan history.

After a brief visit to the pretty little fishing village of Agia Galini, it takes to the hills and calls on a tight circlet of hamlets and farming villages, some of them blissfully unaware of the passage of time, and each offering a characteristic welcome to visitors.

The tour ends at Rethimnon, a medieval town with fine old Venetian and Ottoman buildings, between Hania and Iraklion on the north coast.

AGIA VARVARA is a convenient, though unattractive, small town from which to start the tour. Take the south-west road, signed to **AG. DEKA**. In 13km turn right, go through that village and in 1km, in a pastoral setting — olive groves, fields of barley and of rye, and patches of scarlet poppies — **Gortina**, once the capital of the Roman province of Crete. Signs on each side of the road indicate the direction and extent of the site. The acropolis was inhabited in both Neolithic and Minoan times and Homer referred to Gortyns as the walled city. The famous tablet bearing the Code of Laws, 500 BC in a Dorian dialect, was found here. The most outstanding remains date from 2C AD. The city maintained its importance into the Christian era, when St Paul installed Titus as the first bishop to convert the island, and on into Byzantine times, until it was conquered by the Saracens, cAD 825. See: 8C BC temple; Temple of Pythian Apollo, the main sanctuary of the ancient city; sanctuary to Egyptian deities; Praetorium (AD 2C), seat of Roman governor; Nymphaion (AD 2C) where nymphs were worshipped; Odeon; AD 7C basilica of Ag. Titos, one of the most important Christian monuments on the island (frescoes).

Continue on the road, through Kaparaina and Mires, through citrus groves and curtains of bamboo, to **FESTOS**, the second most important (after Knossos) centre of Minoan civilisation. **Ancient Phaistos**, high up on a mound in a deeply beautiful setting, with the snow-tipped **Mt. Ida** to the north and the richly fertile Messara Plain to the east, is unforgettable. This site, too, was inhabited in Neolithic and Early Minoan times. The Palace — as the whole complex is known — was built in 3 phases and, with Knossos, destroyed by earthquake c 1700 BC. One needs a floor plan to appreciate the layout and determine the domestic quarters and workshops, the religious and cult areas, around the central court and hallways. Most of the finds — clay offerings, tablets, cult objects, vases — are in Iraklion Museum.

From the car park, take the Matala road, direction south, to **Ag. Triada** where the royal 'pleasure palace' (or was it a summer villa) is one of the gems of Minoan times. See: Late Minoan stairs and agora; colonnaded men's hall; queen's hall; series of storage magazines; Mykinean megaron; traces of road to Phaistos; drainage system and (down a short path) cemetery. In Iraklion Museum see: finds including harvester's vase, chieftain's cup and the Rhyton of the Athletes, Linear A tablets and 29-kilo 'talents' from the Treasury. The sound of a shepherd's pipe echoes across the fields and the air is heavy with pine and mountain herbs: it's a truly royal setting.

Return 2km to the Festos cross-roads and turn left to (in 5km) **TIMBAKI**. Hotel: **San Georgio**, 0892/56.613. Fork right (signed to Ag. Galini) and in 8km turn left. **AG. GALINI** in 4km is a neat, smart, bright little harbour-side resort with restrained holiday development, elegant *kafenions*, tavernas and pastry-shops, fishing boats bobbing in the tiny bay and sheltered coves. Hotels: **Acropolis**, 0832/91.234; **Festos**, 0832/91.223.

Take the inland road going due north (to the right of the one signed to Melambes), which rapidly gains height on the river while following its course. Views switch from side to side, Paximadia island to the west, almost permanently snow-capped mountains and a string of hillside villages to the east.

Turn left at the junction (after 10km), joining the main Rethimnon road, and soon pass Kria Vrisi. In 10km turn right to **KISSOS**, climbing sharply through olives. Just before the hamlet, a left turn to the tiny chapel (14C frescoes over the entire surface). Local women queue noisily as sacks of wool are handed out. Spinning is an important source of income. There's no taverna but, asked nicely, the *kafenion* owner fetches home-made bread and cheese from home.

Return to the main road, turn right and in 5km **SPILI**, a straggle of cobbled streets, with courtyards of flowers flattering stone houses. Hotel: **Green**, 0832/22.225; and a variety of tavernas. **MIXOROUMA** in 3km shows traces of a former elegance — grandeur, even. In 12km turn sharp right, leaving the Rethimnon road, to (in 4km) **KERE** rising from fields of marguerites and banks of lavender. **GOULEDIANA** follows hotly on its heels, a vision of tiny chapels and crumbly stone houses among cherry and walnut trees. The road bypasses Oros, goes through Selli and then, at eye level with the facing mountains, **MIRTHIOS**. Substantial stone houses, some verging on fortification level; tiny cottages with turret chimneys and hand-made lace curtains scalloping the windows; a deserved pride in their local *mezithra* cheese and distinctive red wine (which has walnuts steeped in it) — that's Mirthios for you.

In 3km, with a massive ravine straight ahead, turn right and in 3km, **FILAKIO** is a mist of fan-trained mulberries and peaches. The mountain-sides are poured out in soft folds and **APOSTOLI** (in 10km), like a house of cards, is stacked on one of them. Vines smother the gleaming white houses, and there are 2 lively *kafenions*.

Fork left and in 1km turn left to **THRONOS**, now a dreamy village, once a great city. The tiny Church of the Transfiguration with 14C frescoes, is built on the site of a Roman temple, beside a mosaic floor. High on a hill, up a steep stone track, is **Ancient Sybrita**, or what remains of it. Don't be too self-critical if you can't make out the city plan. See: recently excavated main stairway, with inscriptions; walling and a gateway. If you're into collecting wild mountain herbs, take a paper bag and scissors. The thyme is thick on the ground. Taverna rooms: **Papoutsaki**, 0833/22.760.

Return to the main road, turn left and you pass Asomati agricultural school, in a clutch of date palms. Turn right in 1km and soon it's a prickly world. In 6km, **AFRATES**, but a couple of houses guarded by the fiercest of yuccas, and fields and fields of globe artichokes.

Rounded hummocky hills soften the silhouette of jagged rocks on the way to **VIZARI** with its tiny, rounded chapels and stone cottages with elaborately moulded doorways. A track (signposted to 'archaeological site Ellinika') on the west of the village leads through olive groves to (in 2km) the remains of a Roman town. See: mosaic floor, AD 250, foundations of Early Christian basilica. Arab coins were excavated there.

Back in the village, continue on the main road. In 2km fork right to

FOURFOURAS where whole families — sheep, goats and donkeys too — take it easy under the plane trees. In 6km, **KOUROUTES** in a shower of wild roses, and in 3km **NITHAVRI**, a sleepy hamlet dissected by a rivulet of pink oleander. Fork right just beyond (direction north west) and in 3km **AG. IOANNIS**, a cheerful, hospitable village where a tiny chapel (down a track to the left, at the east end) has good 14C frescoes. Just beyond the village, turn right (signed Rethimnon). The road, high on a ridge, looks across the valley to Thronos, seen through a curtain of yellow broom. Hordaki, Ano Miros, Drigies and then **VRISES**, with guinea fowl clucking along the street. **KERLAKI** is one of the 'chestnut' villges in the area and **GERAKARI** is famous for its cherries. **MERONAS**, in 7km, has a tiny 12C church with stone rose windows and elegant stone houses wrapped in honeysuckle.

At **AG. FOTINI**, turn left (Thronos is 1km to the right) and follow the main road to **RETHIMNON**, where the tour ends. Hotels: **Idaeon**, 0831/28.667; **Olympic**, 0831/24.761; **Xenia**, 0831/29.111. Tourist Police: 0831/28.156.

Western Crete — The Gorges

2 days/190km/from Mournies (6km south of Hania, at the end of the new motorway from Rethimnon)

The geography of western Crete, which is almost entirely covered by mountains, makes circular tours somewhat erratic. There is a good road right along the northern coastline and from this, like long charms dangling from a bracelet, 'asphaltos' roads run through the valleys and high passes, some reaching the southern coast. The 'join-up' roads, linking the north-south ones, are of variable quality, some little more than stony tracks. Those included in this tour were all explored in an ordinary small, low-powered motor car without problems. Just take care, and be sure you have enough petrol before setting off.

The route begins as it means to go on, through a deep gorge between Perivolia and Theriso, blissfully cool in summer and spectacular in autumn when the plane and sweet chestnut trees turn fiery golden, and makes its way to the entrance to the legendary Samaria Gorge, excelled in length (I can say nothing of its beauty) by only one natural ravine in the world.

After a dip down to Sougia on the south coast and a chance to explore Ancient Lissos, the route wends its way northwards again, through intensively cultivated valleys and hillsides — the smell of olive oil pervades the air — and with middle-distant views of one after another of the deep clefts which split the mountain range.

The last destination is Hania, with its elegant Venetian quarter, Turkish mosques, smart neo-classical buildings and leafy squares.

Villages in the Hania region celebrate a Chestnut Festival in October, in fine style.

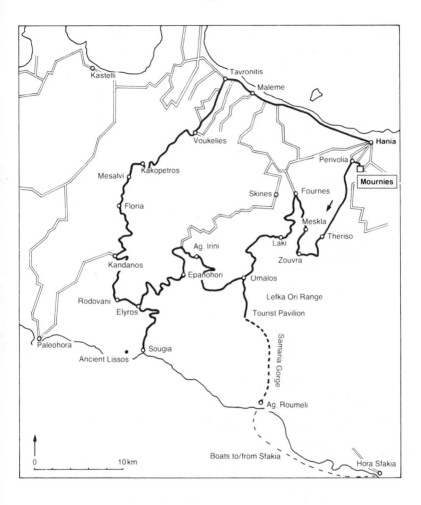

MOURNIES is a large agricultural village situated conveniently — for the traveller — where the new north coastal highway ends. NTOG, Hania: 0821/26.426. Tourist Police, Hania: 0821/24.477. Hotels: **Doma**, 0821/21.772; **Xenia**, 0821/24.561. Turn right at the very end of Mournies village (no signpost) to **PERIVOLIA**, a long, rustic village with a large, snow-flake-white church and a prosperity of orange groves. Deep breath! The road runs through a deep, deep gorge along the course of a river, through shady glades of plane and chestnut trees, to emerge in 10km at **THERISO**. Tumble-down houses peer round cascades of roses, geraniums spill out of huge amphorae on many a terrace, and the prettiest *kafenion* is across a footbridge over the river.

We need to get to Meskla next and the direct road shown on some maps no longer exists. The one that does is steep in parts and unmetalled, but passable in an ordinary car. It just needs care. Turn right at the end of the village (there's a small church on the left). In 2km turn right and in

1km bear right. The road is stony and rising. And closed by 2 sheep gates. 1km farther on (where there's a rusty notice in Greek) bear right. Soon you come to **ZOUVRA**, a way-back-of-beyond hamlet. The cottages have rounded outside beehive ovens stoked up with thyme branches and smelling of baking, and the *kafenion* patrons seem pleased to see a new face. Continue — the road gets no better and no worse — to **MESKLA** and turn right (after 13km) on to a metalled road; civilisation. Streams gush noisily through the village, there's a busy orange market and 2 interesting churches to visit. At the south end of the village, the chapel next to the large church is built over mosaics from an ancient Temple of Venus. At the other end, the church of the Metamorphosis (turn right by a disused warehouse) has early 14C frescoes.

Head north for 6km to **FOURNES**. Saints' days are celebrated in the village with processions, dancing and feasting, on 26 and 27 July. Turn left over the bridge (signed to Omalos). Bear left after 5km and in 4km, **LAKI**, announced by a pretty plaster shrine silhouetted against the stark, distant hills. It's a bright, jolly village which forms a horseshoe around the head of a valley. Pergolas and mulberries and strings of lights frame the cafés and tavernas, the houses step down steep terraces, and sheep and shepherds amble through the main street. Taverna rooms: **Kri-Kri**, 0821/67.316.

The road continues climbing through a pass in the Lefka range, on the legendary 'Road to Moussouri', identified in Cretan folklore as the road to freedom. The scenery becomes grand and almost overwhelming, and suddenly you feel *part* of the mountains. At 12km there is a spectacular subterranean water escape.

OMALOS village is disappointing — unless one has walked, and then it must be an oasis — just a few houses and a couple of cafés. The road continues for 4 flat but high-altitude kilometres to the entrance to the **Samaria Gorge**, at 18km the longest natural ravine in Europe, in the heart of the **Lefka Ori**, or White Mountains. The cleft, worn away by thousands of years of torrents (which make the gorge impassable between October and March) varies from 3m to 40m in width and from 300 to 600 light-blocking metres in height. A wooden staircase, *xyloskala*, facilitates the descent, and then it's anything up to 6 hrs of rocky walking, along the river bed or banks, through pine and cypress groves, to **AG. ROUMELI** on the south coast. To drive to the Samaria entrance, park a vehicle and walk through the gorge creates a logistics problem — it's a long walk back. Boats ferry passengers from Ag. Roumeli to **HORA SFAKIA** 1½ hrs to the east, and buses do the round trip through Hania; an overnight stop is essential. See: Byzantine churches, tiny chapels and deserted villages, caves, an abundance of rare wild flowers and, if you are lucky, wildlife. Tourist Pavilion, Samaria. **Xenia**: 0821/93.237. Pensions at Ag. Roumeli: **Ag. Roumeli**, 0825/91.293, at Hora Sfakia: **Xenia**, 0825/91.202.

Not everyone has the time or energy for the end-to-end walk, but even ½ hr spent just taking in the awesome beauty from the 1,225m-altitude entrance is good for the soul!

Return to the village of Omalos and take the unmade road to the left.

The Samaria Gorge

It's a reasonable track if taken with care, and only about 2km are really jolty. The surface improves encouragingly as it nears the Hania–Sougia road, 12km from Omalos.

Turn left and soon the scenery becomes softer and gentler, chestnuts alternating with olives, and tiny houses scattered across the hillsides. In 5km Ag. Irini and then **EPANO-HORI** with friendly shepherds outside a café-shop drinking *malotiri*, herbal tea, 'for their chests'. Prines, Tsiskiana — veiled in black olive netting — Kambanos and Maralia, and then **AGRILES** where there's a petrol pump. 2km beyond, beside an olive oil factory, turn left (signed to Sougia) and — this turn is optional — left up a track and left beside a tiny church to see what little remains of **Elyros**, once the most important (Roman and then Byzantine) city of Western Crete, destroyed 9C by Saracens, now a superb Libyan-sea-facing picnic spot. See: traces of walls, theatre and aqueduct.

Continue to the fishing village of **SOUGIA**, where there's an endless sand-and-shingle beach and a handful of fish tavernas. To see the site of **Ancient Lissos** (3C BC), with remains of Asklepion, baths, water system and temple with mosaics, involves about 1 hr walk. Turn right at beach to minute harbour, from which the zig-zag dirt track, going westwards, is obvious. **Pension Pikilassos**, 0823/51.242.

Return the 11km to 'olive oil junction' and turn left to **RODOVANI**, a frenzy of olive packing and processing. Fork left in the village and in 2km **MAZA**, strip farming (on vertiginous terracing) at a high level. Bear right in 2km and keep straight on at **TEMENIA**, a chirp of chicken farms. After Kavallariana, the minor road meets the north-south main road at **KANDANOS**, a Resistance stronghold in the Second World War, until the village was destroyed by the Germans. Turn right in this rejuvenated and rebuilt village towards a patchwork panorama down in the valley. High stone turret chimneys characterise the olive-farm cottages in **BAMBAKARDOS**, and wide breeches and boots are the workaday gear.

KAFALATOS, like so many of these hamlets, has lost many of the younger generation to the bright lights of America and Canada, leaving the village picturesque and fruitful but not very hopeful. **FLORIA**, in a valley of chestnuts; **MESAVLI**, where almost vertical hillsides are wheat-cropped and **KAKOPETROS** ('Bad Peter'), the road continues northwards, with now and then wide views of a spectacularly narrow gorge to the west, through rolling hillsides enclosing a flat-as-a-bedspread plain — it's a pleasant drive.

VOUKELIES, with a petrol pump, banks, shops and market, indicates that a population explosion is nigh. In 7km at **TAVRONITIS**, the road joins the north-coast road. Turn right, direction Hania. At **MALEME** in 3km there's a German military cemetery. Continue along this good, straight road, gradually developing the heavy industry of tourism, through **PLATANIES** (Hotels: **Adele Beach**, 0831/71.081; **Orion**, 0831/71.471) to **HANIA**, where the tour ends.

9 RHODES AND KARPATHOS

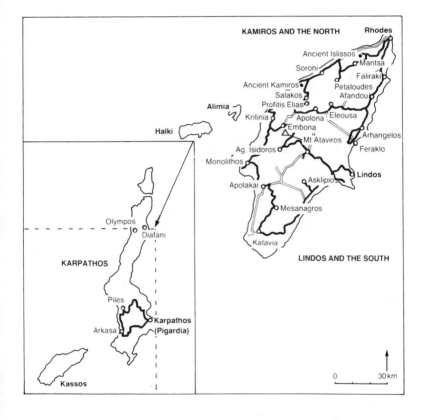

KAMIROS AND THE NORTH

Rhodes

Ancient Islissos

Maritsa

Soroni

Faliraki

Ancient Kamiros

Petaloudes

Salakos

Afandou

Profitis Elias

Alimia

Eleousa

Kritinia

Apolona

Halki

Embona

Mt Ataviros

Arhangelos

Ag. Isidoros

Feraklo

Monolithos

Lindos

Apolakai

Asklipio

Mesanagros

Olympos

Diafani

Katavia

LINDOS AND THE SOUTH

KARPATHOS

Piles

Arkasa

Karpathos
(Pigardia)

Kassos

0   30km

Greek mythology says it all. In the guise of the nymph Rhodia, the island of Rhodes emerged from the sea and was given to Helios the sun-god, whose descendants founded the 3 ancient cities of Ialissos, Lindos and Kamiros. It is easy enough to believe it, too, among the heady scents and vibrant colours of semi-tropical shrubs and the profusion of vines, figs, citrus fruits and cereal crops that bask in the mild climate; that Helios still smiles down on this green and fruitful island in gratitude.

Whether they were founded by divine intervention or not, the 3 Doric

155

cities were powerful international trading forces with well-established contacts with Asia Minor and European ports, and their people highly skilled and articulate artists and artisans. A school of sculpture, founded 3C BC, produced masterpieces for foreign commissions, and the gigantic statue of the Colossus of Rhodes was designed there (265 BC) by Charles of Lindos.

Between them, in 408 BC, the 3 powers founded the city of Rhodes and endowed it with all their resources — so successfully that it soon rose to supremacy. For the next 200 years Rhodes built up a formidable fleet and was the major commercial and maritime presence in the Aegean. The city founded colonies, minted coins and was the first to introduce maritime law. Sports and the theatre flourished and the School of Rhetoric, where Greek and Roman orators studied, was founded.

Rome turned out to be a false friend, at first taking the role of an ally, then gradually undermining the island's power until it was easily annexed to become a valuable province of the Roman Empire. The Apostle Paul brought the teaching of Christianity to the island, and the religion continued to flourish for nearly 1,000 years after Rhodes came under the Byzantine yoke (AD 395).

In 1306 the island gave refuge to the Knights of St John of Jerusalem, who fortified it as a bastion against religious and piratical invasions. Eventually the island fell to the Turks who occupied it until the citizens' uprising in 1912, when the Italians intervened and brought the region — in the matter of roads and public buildings and services — into the twentieth century. Along with the other Dodecanese islands, Rhodes was united with Greece in 1948.

Situated to the north and east of Crete — and with Karpathos almost equidistant between them — Rhodes (Rhodos) is a long, narrow island, around 75 by 35km, with a high mountain ridge, Mt. Ataviros, rising to 1,215m in the centre. A good road running almost all around the coastline and others criss-crossing the terrain in the north, makes travel easy and pleasant. As always in Greece, the minor roads, particularly those around the mountain ridges, need extra care, but can be especially rewarding.

Regular ferry services connect the island with Piraeus on the mainland, with Sitea and Ag. Nikolaos on Crete, with Karpathos and many other Greek islands beyond the Dodecanese chain. An air service between Rhodes and Karpathos makes a short stay on the neighbouring island (where motor bicycles can be hired) an intriguing possibility.

Kamiros and the North

1–2 days/170km/from Rhodes town

Rhodes town, or Rhodos (as both the island and its capital are called), is in 2 distinct parts, the medieval city built by the Knights of St John and a new town developed since the Italian occupation of 1912. Perhaps one

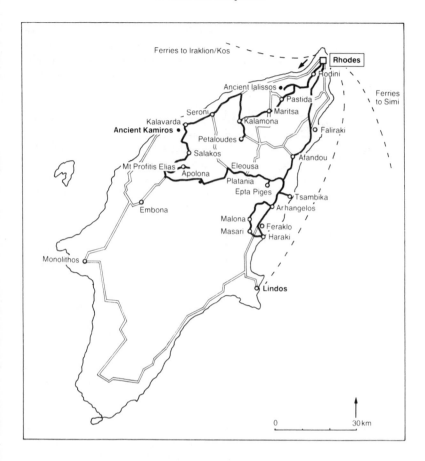

should include a third more recent development, the cavalcade of luxury hotels lining the beaches almost all the way around the northern promontary, from Trianda to Faliraki.

If, when you arrive, it crosses your mind that this is not the rural Greece you set out to explore, take heart! This tour offers you some of the most steam-heat tropical and some of the most remote and rugged countryside imaginable — and all, if you wish, in a single day.

It takes in 2 of the island's 3 ancient cities: Ialissos on an isolated wooded hill and Kamiros, history you can almost experience on a tree-fringed site on the north western sea-shore. It takes you to the sun-dappled, stream-washed Valley of the Butterflies where a rare species in an amber and black livery turns the 1km gorge into fairyland; and to Epta Piges (7 Springs), almost equally exotic in its verdant setting.

The topography of the island, with mountain ranges running from north east to south west, makes any central crossing an uphill affair. The scattered hamlets, the magnificent views, the wild terrain — they are all a far cry though only a short drive from one of the most popular resorts Greece has to offer.

The old town, Rhodes

RHODES TOWN (Rhodos) (pop: 38,000) A visual incongruity of massive fortifications — the Knights of St John left no stone unturned in erecting a fortress, encircling wall, palace and hospital — and vibrant, aromatic, exotic flowers. No wonder this is called the island of roses. Gardens of hibiscus, bougainvillea and oleander are playgrounds for the town's large and friendly feline population and offer cool, aromatic respite from the sometimes relentless sun. Relatively little remains of the ancient city. The acropolis, on the east of Smith's Square (Monte Smith) has, besides a fine view from the summit, traces of the Temple of Pythian Apollo, an unusual ancient theatre — it is square — and restored stadium. Stroll around the medieval Chora region — the open-fronted workshops are intriguing and irresistible; gaze up at the massive inns of the various Orders of the Street of the Knights; see medieval exhibits and finds from Mykinean graves at Ialissos in the Archaeological Museum; Museum of Decorative Arts in the Palace of Armeria, and Byzantine Museum in 13C church-cum-mosque. Admire the yachts and watch the ferry-boats come and go in one of the 3 harbours. Notice the bronze deer flanking the entrance to Mandraki harbour, on the spot once bridged by the Colossus of Rhodes, one of the 7 wonders of the ancient world, destroyed 225 BC by earthquake. Seek out the least sophisticated of tavernas in the back streets of the town, to have any hope of a 'local' meal. The international menu rules! NTOG: 0241/23.655. Tourist Police: 0241/27.423 for all information on hotels and other accommodation in Rhodes. There are one-day cruises to the just-across-the-water island of Simi, which has an unrivalled reputation for the quality and diversity of its fish tavernas (crayfish a speciality), and half-day excursions to Lindos.

Festivities
Greek folk dances are performed in the theatre in the old town of Rhodes May-October. Sound and light shows (Son et Lumière) are given in the municipal gardens, April-October.

To avoid the hotels and sun-bathing strip along the Kritika-Trianda-Ixia coast, take the Rodini road, from the junction near St Mary's tower in the city wall. **Rodini Park** in 2km is an old physic (herb) garden with a small zoo. Wine tastings and festivals are held, July to September. It is said to be

The gate on the west side of Rhodes old town

the site of the School of Rhetoric of Aeshines. See: remains of Roman aqueduct, and 4C BC rock tomb with decorated façade, the Tomb of Ptolemies. Continue for 3km to Sgourou and in 2km turn right. Ignore the left turn in 2km to Pastida. Turn left 1km farther on — the road is signposted, and takes a sharp left turn to **Ancient Ialissos**, one of the 3 ancient cities (with Lindos and Kamiros) of the island. A terraced footpath through cypress groves leads up to the city site, on the flat summit of Mt. Filerimos, whose strategic importance was recognised in Phoenician times. See: ruined castle of the Knights, and Knights' church with Catholic and Orthodox altars; remains of Byzantine fortifications and monastery; foundations of 3C BC Temple of Athena and (down 134 steps) reconstructed Doric (4C BC) fountain; Early Christian basilica (cAD 5C) with surviving cruciform font; minute chapel with c14C frescoes. And superb landscape views.

With Mt. Filerimos blocking the path, so to speak, return 3km to the junction and fork right. In 3km turn right, and in 1km bear right. This time you do take the right-hand road to **PASTIDA** which is 3 cool kilometres across a lush, green valley. Carry straight on to **MARITSA**, in 3km, a pretty village in this oasis of dense vegetation, and there turn right (direction due west) to **EPANO KALAMONA** (in 6km) on a rocky hillside.

Turn left to a natural beauty spot, **Petaloudes**, the fairy-tale world better known as Valley of the Butterflies. Waterfalls tumble over craggy ravines and crash into a gushing stream. Trees meet overhead in a dense green arbour to create the feeling of a tropical paradise. Tip-toe over the wooden bridges and up the steep pathways and that's all you might see. Clap your hands and it's like switching on the lights as thousands of rare orange and black butterflies, attracted (between June and September) by the aroma of the styrax trees, rise from the bushes in clouds. Allow at least 1 hr to come under their spell.

Return to Epano Kalamona and continue for 5km to Kato Kalamona, its low-level sister village. Bear left and in 1km turn left on to the coast road. The island's airport is on the right. **SERONI** in 6km is a busy little village well set up with fish tavernas. Continue along the coastal plain for 10km to **MINAS** straggling by the sea-shore, and turn left to **Ancient**

Kamiros just inland which, legend has it, was founded by Althaimenes, Minos' grandson, and was destroyed by earthquake 2C BC. The site, surrounded by olive and fig groves and dappled with pink oleander, which had, unusually, neither a castle nor an acropolis, was excavated mid 19C but is complete enough to give one a feeling of personal discovery, even now. Wander from room to room among the Hellenistic houses, several with re-erected columns. See: 5C BC Temple of Athena; 3C BC sanctuary with Doric temple, semi-circular seat and site of sacrificial altar; agora with AD 3C portico over 6C BC cistern. Impressive.

Back on the coast road, turn right and in 4km turn right at **KALAVARDA**. There are good views back to Kamiros by the sea. In 7km, just before **SALAKOS**, the road gets snaky and starts to climb. It passes through **KAPI**, in 3km, a tiny hamlet blinking in the shadow of **Mt. Profitis Elias** (Mount Elijah). Continue for 2km and bear sharp left towards the foothills, where a cool summer resort has grown up at 900m amidst the cedars and pines. The blue sea, way, way in the distance, is like a shimmering mirage. Hotel: **Elafos**. 0246/22.222.

Return the 5km to the junction on the Kapi-Apollona road and turn left. Keep straight on at the next junction (in 1km) and follow the eastern slopes of Elijah's mountain for 7km, on the 'outer ring road', to **APOLONA**. (A more adventurous one crosses on a higher ridge.) The village is a folkloric collection of 19C houses, with a popular art museum and library. Continue round to **PLATANIA** (6km), a hamlet with a top-of-the-world feeling, and then (in 2km) **ELEOUSA** with the pretty little Byzantine Church of Ag. Nikolaos.

Turn right there, starting the descent towards the coastal plain. **ARHIPOLI** (in 4km) is a meeting of cool mountain waterways. Fork right just past the hamlet to **Epta Piges**, where 7 springs tumble down to form an idyllic shallow lake in a pine copse, said to be a secret meeting place of nymphs. Take the right sweep at Kolimbia and in just over 1km bear right on to the minor road, a slightly switch-back affair, to **ARHANGELOS** (pop: 3,500) dominated by a castle. The ochre and white cubic houses have carved 'icing-sugar' chimneys, melons dry on the thick stone walls, dates hang in heavy clusters in the gardens and the locals weave carpets and decorate pottery in their open doorways. This is one of several villages in the region evocative of the Saharan settlements. See: the near-by 14C Church of Ag. Theodori (frescoes).

Take the right fork out of the village, which climbs only to descend steeply into a valley of nut and orange groves to Malona (in 6km) and **MASARI** (3km). Take the minor road (direction south east), crossing the main coastal road, to the fishing hamlet of **HARAKI**. Go through the hamlet and for a spot of exercise, climb to the remains of **Feraklo Castle**, one of the largest and strongest ever built by the Knights of St John. The views are wonderful, with the Lindos acropolis silhouetted on the southern skyline.

To join the main road, take the right fork from Haraki and in 4km turn right. Go through Arhangelos (it's well worth a second look, anyway) and in 2km turn right to Tsambika Monastery with a huge ancient tree in the courtyard. See: carved screen in the church. Return to the main road, after a swim perhaps, and turn right. The road threads a gap in the mountains. In 8km, **AFANOU** a village with a proud tradition of carpet making and a distinctly North African appearance. Hotels: **Xenia Golf**, 0241/51.121; **Oasis**, 0241/51.359.

In 5km, at **FALIRAKI**, a much-developed beach resort, a parting of the ways. (Hotel: **Muses**, 0241/85.303.) Fork right for the beach road and left for the inland road. Each leads to Rhodes town in around 20km.

Lindos and the South

1 day/180km/from Lindos

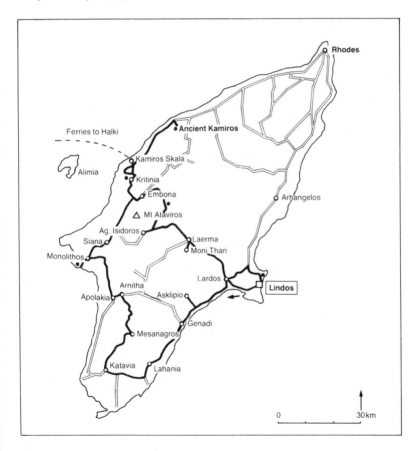

Lindos has too much to offer to be dismissed in a passing glance — or even in an afternoon's excursion by boat or road from Rhodes town. Visitors committed to accommodation in the island's capital would do well to make an overnight trip — rented rooms are plentiful and not expensive — to soak up the quite different atmosphere of this ancient city.

In high season, though, be prepared to share it with the world and his companion — or arise early, to appreciate the serenity of the marble temple on the very pinnacle of the acropolis.

The tour makes off around the coast, surprises several way-off-the-beaten-track villages, climbs up to two more castles, at Monolithos and Kritinia, and then turns inland for a breath of mountain air, exploring some 35km of second-class roads deserted but for the shepherds and their flocks.

Check your petrol level before setting out. There are no supplies in the mountains.

LINDOS is special. There are other azure bays with wide sandy beaches. Other ancient city sites with a hilltop temple. Other medieval fortresses looming over a string of higgledy-piggledy village houses. But few, if any, come together with the magic that makes Lindos a 'must' on any schedule. The hilltop site, overlooking the twin harbours where St Paul landed, has been inhabited since prehistoric times and in 10C BC it was crowned by a Temple to Athena. Colonists from Lindos founded a city in Sicily (Gela) and in Italy (now Naples). In 6C BC the Lindos community was ruled by one of the Seven Sages of Greece. The ancient port sent merchant ships throughout the Middle East and the people established a reputation — which they still enjoy — for fine jewellery and faience ceramics decorated with distinctive Oriental-style motifs. The Knights Hospitallers (15C) fortified the town and defended it with 12 knights and a Greek garrison.

Wander around the steep and narrow streets of flat-roofed houses, take in the detail of the decorative doorways, with views of courtyard gardens beyond, with the occasional curvy dome of a Byzantine church as an expression of architectural exuberance. Run the gauntlet through fashion garments, embroidery, pottery and copper spread out for sale on the steps. Or take the easy way up, and hire a donkey. See: Fortress, reached by massive stone stairway, with vaulted passage and medieval governor's palace; remains of Byzantine church of St John. From the doorway, an impressive ancient staircase leads to 5C BC entrance to sanctuary of the Lindian Athena, to whom 4C BC temple (built on the very edge of the precipitous rock, above the seer's cave) is dedicated. Miracles were performed there. Hotels: **Lindos Bay**, 0244/31.212; **Steps of Lindos**, 0244/42.249. Most of the village houses have rooms to rent, and there are many holiday villas near by.

Leave the village, perhaps reluctantly, by the minor road going south west. It crosses the tip of the peninsula along the foothills of the Marmari group. Look back in wonder at Lindos castle which, from a distance, seems carved from its rocky plateau. The road passes, in 4km, the hamlet of Ag. Ioannis. In 4km at (or just before — there are twin junctions)

Lindos: a village street

LARDOS, refreshingly cool in the valley, where donkeys shelter under trees by the café, turn left. The road toys in and out of the coastline for 10km to Metamorphosis. Turn right to the mountain village of **AS-KLIPIO**, watched over by a medieval castle and with some fine old stone houses. There are perspective views of terraced hillsides stepping down to the coast. The Byzantine church — a wall plate dates it at 1060 — has fine frescoes. Return to the coast road and turn right to (in 3km) **GENADI**, fishing and amateur fishermen's village, bright as a button with its cluster of *kafenions* and tavernas.

After 2km take the right fork to **LAHANIA** a sun-baked village in a wide valley. Turn left at the end of the village, across 4km of criss-crossing donkey tracks (a dream for motorcyclists) to Holokas. Turn right, direction due west, to **KATAVIA** (8km) the most southerly village of the island. The tavernas specialise in small crispy-fried fish served with the local inexpensive white wine.

Take the minor road to the right. The golden beach and blue sea views improve in ratio to the gradient — and the road climbs all the way. For the sake of the photograph album caption, the tiny off-shore islet is Ktenia. At 13km is **MESANAGROS**. Avoid the evening rush-hour if you wish, when shepherds, donkeys, sheep and goats trudge back from the mountains; all mule-tracks converge on the centre. A signpost to Apolakia will help sort the route from the tracks; it goes due north. In 2km a peak rises to 563m and soon gives way to another haven of sea views. 2km after Arnitha, turn left to **APOLAKIA** down in the Kourkourtahi valley, and correspondingly cool. A patchwork of small fields separates it from the sand dunes.

You want the left-hand road, which takes 10km to climb, somewhat puffily, to **MONOLITHOS**, a mountain community not quite monarch of all it surveys. The Knights of Rhodes built a castle on a seemingly impregnable rock 200m above the shore and towering protectively over the village. You have to climb a steep path to reach it. See: 2 cisterns and restored church and, on a clear day, the dim and distant outlines of the island of **Halki**.

The road from Monolithos follows the eastern slopes of **Mt. Akramitis** for 4km to **SIANA**, where the old stone houses are built on a succession of terraces. Stop a couple of kilometres beyond for an x-marks-the-spot photograph view of an island quartet, Tragoussa, Alimia, Makri and Strongili. Take the left fork, which skirts the western flank of the **Ataviros** range, and in 7km fork left again to **KRITINIA** (4km). The village is built amphitheatrically, the dazzlingly white houses spread out to bake in the sun on a natural arena.

Fork left in 3km to another legacy of the Knights, an imposing castle, c1480, built on 3 levels — one for each grand master — on a vertiginous, 130m-high rock.

If castles are a dizzying experience, **KAMIROS SKALA**, 2km round the coast, will come as a breath of sea-level air. This small port — which once served the ancient city of Kamiros — has several connections a week with Halki (1½ hours by caique).

If your itinerary allows time for the north of the island tour, which includes **Ancient Kamiros**, turn back here. If not — and the ancient site intrigues you — it is only 17 low-level kilometres along the coast. (See p. 160 for description.)

Otherwise, return through Kritinia and, 4km beyond the village, fork left to **EMBONA**, famous for the quality of its wines and ceramics. Women sit on doorsteps spinning and the hum of looms can be heard from within. Many of the garments sold at Lindos are made here. The village is a starting point for the ascent of **Mt. Ataviros**, at 1,225m the highest mountain on the island. Remains of a temple to Zeus and coast-to-coast aerial view reward a stiff 2-hr climb — even for the experts.

Fork right in 2km, sweeping in a wide arc around a mountain ridge. The Monastery of Artamiti (at an altitude of 383m) is the first building for 7km. Continue for 8km to the elevated and isolated hamlet of **AG. ISIDOROS**, and no doubt a stop for refreshment.

Back-track 1km and fork right, heading eastwards. Keep on that road for 11km to **LAERMA** a compass-point for mule-tracks going off in all directions. One of them leads (in 2km, south west) to **MONI THARI**, a convent with the charming little Byzantine chapel of the Taxiarche. If you are tempted to see it, you will need to return to Laerma, then take the south-east road out of the village. It is a gradual — some may say welcome — descent to Lardos, 13km away. The improvement to the road surface comes at the half-way mark.

Turn left in Lardos, and in 5km turn right. The romantic view of Lindos is only minutes (well, 5km away), its collar of diamond-white houses above the orange grove sparkling beneath the rocky fortress.

Karpathos

1 day/40km/from Pigadia, the southern ferry port, around the south of the island, plus excursion to Olympos, in the north

Karpathos, one of the Dodecanese group of 12 islands, almost midway between Crete and Rhodes, isn't on the tip of every Grecophile's tongue, and it isn't yet on many tour operators' brochures. The mountain range which splits it virtually from end to end, rising with Mt. Profitis Elias to 1,023m, makes distances deceptive. Although the island extends to only 48km north to south and a maximum of 12km across, the steep gradients

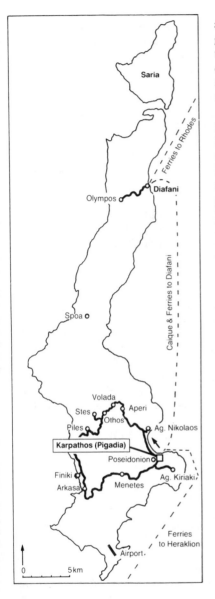

and second-class roads make the going in places, well, interesting. It is a tour to take at a leisurely pace, confident that there is a fascinating village, a glorious view or a friendly encounter just around the next bend.

The mountain effectively divides the island into 2 separate communities. The south, which has the commercial port, a ribbon of golden beaches, well-watered valleys mellow with fruit and cereal crops, and a crown of pretty villages, is known as 'European' Karpathos, and has an altogether more prosperous portent. The north, connected by a few mule paths, a treacherous dirt track and a ferry service, is locked in its intriguing medieval past; the people still use Doric terms, wear their traditional costumes every day of the week and live in a picturesque, if arduous, world of their own.

Karpathos escaped much of the early political cut and thrust that beset its neighbouring islands. Homer knew it as Karpathos, and its medieval name of Scarpanto was also adopted by the Italians. The Romans gave the island to the Genoese; it passed to a Venetian family who (in 1538) surrendered it to the Turks from whom it came to enjoy financial and other privileges.

PIGADIA (pop: 1,800) also known as Karpathos and now the island's capital, is a wide, natural port in a dramatic setting, the scarlet, blue, yellow and green of the fishing boats vibrant against the jagged sepia-mountain backdrop. The architecture, for the most part flat-faced, white and modern, is fairly run-of-the-mill and gives no hint of the beauty of the old houses in the villages around, or of the town's great and glorious past. To see traces of the classical site, of ancient Poseidonion claimed to be the sea-god's home town, climb a rocky citadel, to the east. There was a Mykinean settlement nearby. See: traces of defensive walls; 6C and 5C BC tombs (vases, coins and inscribed stone slabs in museum, below).

There was a temple to Athena and a school for priests and priestesses. See also Early Christian church, marble font, and Mykinean finds in park museum.

The port has a cheerful complement of tavernas serving not only the morning's catch but spit-roast lamb and goat and a good selection of casseroles and stuffed vegetables. There are ferry-boat connections to the small neighbouring island of Kassos to the south; with the otherwise virtually inaccessible northern port of Diafani, and thence on the Dodecanese route to Halki, Rhodes and beyond. It isn't always easy to make it to Diafani. A caique in Pigadia harbour has a board announcing, 'to rent for a day excursions to Diafani it's pleasant'. When I was there, the sea-farer was on his honeymoon and the boat lay at anchor. The only driver willing to take a 4-wheel-drive vehicle over the mountain dirt track had broken a leg and the intrepid truck stood idle. And the inter-island ferries were storm-bound for 5 days. Patience helps! Hotels: **Romantica Pension**, 0245/22.461; **Porfyris**, 0245/22.294; **Seven Stars**, 0245/22.101.

To visit some of the villages in the south, take the road going north (sorry for such confusion!) around the wide, semi-circular sandy bay. Turn left, inland at the barely noticeable Ag. Nikolaos. The road climbs sharply to (in 7km) **APERI**, the former (until 1892) capital, known in medieval times as Korakia. The village is bisected by a stream and has a noughts-and-crosses layout of steep, narrow streets. It's a jolly place, with the nose-tingling aroma of cheese pies solving the 'what to take for a picnic' problem. Locals maintain there was a Byzantine dead city where the cathedral now stands, and coins contemporary with Emperor Justinian were unearthed.

Take the left-hand road, steep and still rising, to **VOLADA**, only 2km away, at an altitude of 453m and with only 350 inhabitants to welcome you. The village is surrounded by mountains, orchards and vegetable gardens. A hesitant query, deep into the afternoon about the possibility of lunch brought forth golden courgette flowers filled with herby rice, their prows rising from creamy egg and lemon sauce. Ancient inhabitants of the Pini district of the village spread their roots far and wide — they sent a cypress tree to be planted at the Temple of Athena on the Acropolis in Athens.

The road wiggles round the mountainside for 3km to **OTHOS** (at 507m) whose inhabitants claim descendancy from the mythical ancient city of Thaeto, close to Afiartis where the island's airport is situated. See: beautiful old houses with carved wooden screens, balconies and pillars and gold-embroidered furnishings, and folkloric museum featuring textiles and pottery. Turn right for a short detour to **STES**, almost hidden in the mountains and succulent with prickly pear groves. More lovely old houses. Return to the road junction, turn right and continue descending gradually through fruit-laden orchards to **PILES** (in 4km). Vines and cherry trees trail over apricot-coloured houses, there are pretty round-domed churches and deep sea views. The main activity takes place around the water pump and the communal laundry trough.

Turn left in the village — glorious sea views — and follow the coastline for some 8km to **FINIKI**, a truly picturesque fishing hamlet of the sky-blue walls, deep-green shutters type. There are rocky coves and craggy caves all around and everyone either catches fish or cooks it for your lunch.

Continue — if you can tear yourself away — for 3km around the bay to **ARKASA**, a veritable fruit garden by the sea. 'We have a past, you know', one of the locals said darkly. He was referring to ancient Arkesia, on the summit of Paleokastro, which still yields fragments of marble slabs and mosaics. See: remains of c AD 5C church, with mosaic floor.

Take the left fork (direction south east) and in 3km fork left to **MENETES**, 350m up the slopes of **Mt. Profitis Elias**, a village clinging tenaciously to both the mountainside and its customs. See: archaeological and folkloric museum, and a rich tapestry of colourful old houses and pretty gardens.

Continue for 2km to the T-junction and turn left towards Pigadia. In about 2km take a track to the right, signposted to **AG. KIRIAKI** which, it is said, was a place of worship 7C BC dedicated to the goddess Demeter. There are tombs hewn in the rocks along the road and locals love to tell of a small gold statue recently found in one. Return to the road and turn right, into the port.

If the caique captain has returned from honeymoon and the inter-island ferries find conditions favourable, choose from a day trip or a stop-over at the north eastern port of **DIAFANI**. A road crosses the island to **OLYMPOS** (where there are rooms to rent, but no hotels) in 9km transporting you into an unbelievably beautiful medieval mountain world. Stone houses rise up the steep hillsides, the double-headed Byzantium eagle adorning the balconies and vineyard and sea-faring images decorating balustrades and cornices. And a row of more than 40 windmills twirls along a high ridge. But it is the intricate and colourful costumes worn by the women in their work-a-day lives that is most captivating, flowing white dresses sometimes worn with Turkish-style pantaloons and high leather boots, richly embroidered bodices, shawls, cassocks and head-dresses. In this incredibly photogenic and impractical garb they hoe the furrows, sow the seed, pick the fruit, drive the donkeys and work the looms. It is the custom for girls from the age of 10 to begin weaving their dowries; the wedding feast lasts round the clock for several days. See: the 3-section houses with elaborately carved interiors, and wooden locks and keys said to date back to Homeric times; Byzantine church (frescoes); remains of ancient temple. Caique trips from Diafani to the off-shore islet of **Saria**, with remains of ancient city of Nissiros.

The main island festivities take place between July and September.

*

Specialities
Good local wines, such as Lindos, Embonas and Chevaliers de Rhodes. Sweetmeat patriotically known as Rhodian delight, a delicious but weighty take-home present. Leather footwear, especially gold-painted sandals, gold, silver and costume jewellery, embroidered and hand-woven garments and furnishings, inexpensive cotton fashion goods and furs.

10 THE ISLAND GROUPS

The sophisticated mansions-over-the-hillside waterfront of Hydra; sparkling white houses sauntering across the parched terraced landscape of Sifnos; laden mules trundling past the stone windmills of Mykonos; the frenzied harbourside activity — all the weeping and wailing — when the Kalymnos sponge-divers return; the wild, rugged, desolate beauty of Ikaria; the wave-splitting watersports that draw enthusiasts to Skiathos; the pretty, flower-filled meadows of Paxos — which image comes closest to that of a 'typical' Greek island?

The answer, of course, is that none of them does. Every one of the 2,000 and more islands in the blue Aegean has a personality to call its own; though naturally, by virtue of both geography and history, the islands of each group have common bonds.

The main groups are those of the Saronic Gulf, just off-shore of Attica and the south-eastern Peloponnese; the Cyclades, the circlet of close on 40 'jewels' strung out to the south of Attica and Evia; the Dodecanese, some of which come very close indeed to the western Turkish coast and with Crete, close by, which has no grouping. East of Pelion and Evia are the 4 main Sporades islands, and further north and east, those known simply as the North-Eastern Aegean group. Lastly, off the west coasts of Epirus and the Peloponnese, the Ionian group which includes Corfu and Lefkas. NTOG, Piraeus: 01/413.5716. Port Authority, Piraeus: 01/451.1311.

The Saronic Gulf Islands

A frequent steamer and hydrofoil service connects these islands with Piraeus, making them — since they are so close to the mainland — popular holiday and weekend resorts for Athenians. **Salamis**, the largest and closest to the mainland, can also be reached by car ferry from Megara and Perama; **Aegina** and **Poros** by car ferry from Methana, and Poros also by passenger ferry from Galata; and **Hydra** and **Spetses** by passenger ferry from Ermioni.

All the islands have a noble maritime history, and Salamis is immortalised as the site of the famous battle (480 BC) between the Greek and Persian fleets. Aegina was renowned in antiquity as an art centre and, on a pine-covered hill, is crowned by the beautiful Temple of Aphaia Athena. The pistachio orchards are an attractive — and ultimately delicious — feature of the island.

Poros, facing a thick band of lemon groves across the narrow strait, is itself thickly wooded, and good walking country. Coming into harbour in

The elegant water-front houses, Hydra

Hydra one is greeted by a colourful canvas of tall, elegant town mansions — shades of wealthy sea-faring days — and a cluster of cosmopolitan boutiques. Spetses specialises in fashionable pastry shops along the Dappia Square waterfront, and resounds to the clop of horse-drawn 'garries'.

Hotel on Salamis: **Gabriel**, 01/ 4662.275. Tourist Police: **Aegina**, 0279/22.391. **Poros**, 0298/22.462. **Hydra**, 0298/522.05. **Spetses**, 0298/73.100

Festivities: the religious ceremonies on **Hydra** on Good Friday are combined with folkloric dances, and the festival of the Virgin Mary (15 August) is celebrated with special pomp and circumstance. **Spetses** celebrates the defeat of the Turkish armada (1822) with a naval festival, 8-9 September.

The Cyclades

The 39 islands — 24 of them inhabited — stand out as a ring of mainly brown, rocky outcrops highlighted by dazzling white chapels and cubic houses and topped by working windmills. The group — and Santorini in particular — boasts some of the most attractive and photogenic architecture in Greece. Island-hopping from one to another is easy and fun and may be decided on a whim: 'Where's that boat going? Let's go there,' is a familiar thought process.

Kithnos (86 sq.km) is lightly sprinkled with vines and fig trees and offers good fishing and quail and partridge shooting. **Serifos** (70 sq.km) topped by a Venetian fortress and medieval monastery and shrouded in myths, has specially good beaches. **Sifnos** (82 sq.km) maintains 360 churches and chapels and a tradition for pottery making. Specialities: chick-pea soup, goat casserole and melt-in-the-mouth cheese pies in the hilltop town of Apollonia. **Kimolos** (36 sq.km) inhabited since pre-Mykinean times, has on-going excavations on off-shore Ag. Andreas. **Milos** (160 sq.km) inhabited for over 5,000 years, where the 4C BC Statue of Venus was found, has oyster beds at Ahivadolimni, which bode well for taverna meals. **Andros** (373 sq.km), an island of orchards and lush meadows, streams and mineral springs, owes much of its prosperity to

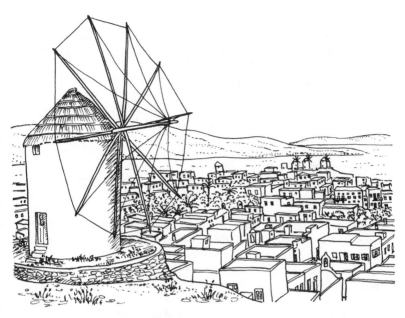

Windmills tower over Mykonos harbour

shipowners retiring there. A charming local custom: farmers carve a flute from oleander branches and pipe the family work-force home from the fields each evening. Specialities: dried octopus, and mulberries.

Pilgrims from all over Greece congregate on **Tinos** (195 sq.km) for the 15 August festival. The island has 1,200 chapels and 600 elaborately carved stone dovecots, delightful silhouettes against the wooded hillsides. See: museum with finds from ancient temples of Poseidon and Amphitrite, and Byzantine museum.

The Avenue of the Lions, Delos

Siros (86 sq.km) the capital of the Cyclades, has suitably impressive old mansions, marble squares and medieval churches; its fleet once ruled the local waves. Most sophisticated of the group, **Mykonos** (85 sq.km) has a round-the clock social life, smart clubs, fashionable shops and cute little cubist houses. A local motor boat ferries visitors across the straits to the sacred island of **Delos**, legendary birthplace of Apollo and Artemis. See: terrace of marble lions, 3 temples to Apollo.

171

A jostle of summer visitors hops between **Paros** (209 sq.km) and **Naxos**, the largest and most fertile of the island group (448 sq.km). Paros has a specially pretty fishing village, Naoussa, a reputation for fine pottery (at Lefkes) and a Valley of the Butterflies, Petaloudes. On Naxos, see: remains of Temple of Apollo (on off-shore islet), Mykinean tombs, and a Mykinean settlement at Grotsa. **Ios** (105 sq.km), one-time home of the hippies, covered with vines and olive groves, dotted with tiny chapels and fringed by sandy strands, attracts great numbers of holidaymakers. **Amorgos** (134 sq.km) has extensive Roman remains (stadium, gymnasium, Temple to Apollo) and a sparkling white Byzantine monastery, the Hosoviotissa, clinging to a sheer rock face.

Santorini, or Thira (96 sq.km, and 127 nautical miles from Piraeus) is incredible. Vast geological upheavals made it what it is — a massive rock formation with 2 black volcanic islets in the bay. Its architecture, blue-domed churches and sparkling white houses, is legendary, its atmosphere unique. Pack mules, donkeys and a funicular railway take passengers from Skala harbour to rock-top Fira, the capital. See: Minoan site of Akrotiri, abandoned in the disaster; Monastery of Profitis Ilias (religious ceremony, 20 July), and Archaic, Classical and Early Christian remains.

Regular steamer and car ferry services connect the islands to the mainland, to each other and to other island groups, and several now have airports.

Ferries: Kithnos, and also Kea, are served by Lavrio (north west of Sounio) Port Authority, 0292/25.249; Andros, Tinos, Siros, Mykonos, Paros and Naxos can be reached from the port of Rafina (east of Athens), Port Authority, 0294/23.200. Serifos, Sifnos, Kimolos, Milos, Tinos, Siros, Mykonos, Paros, Naxos, Ios, Amorgos, Santorini (Thira) and others of the smaller islands are on the ferry-run from Piraeus. As an example, the trip to Naxos takes about 8 hrs. Siros Port Authority: 0281/22.690.

Air Links: Milos, Mykonos, Paros and Santorini have internal flights to Athens and other Greek destinations, and some have direct flights from the UK. Olympic Airways, Athens, 01/961.6161.

Hydrofoil services connect Tinos, Siros, Mykonos, Paros, Naxos and Ios. Information: Zea Marina, Piraeus, 01/452.7101.

Tourist Police: **Kythnos**, 0281/31.201; **Tinos**, 0283/22.255; **Mykonos**, 0289/22.482; **Paros**, 0248/21.673.

The Dodecanese

Rhodes and Karpathos, with tours beginning on p. 156, have given us more than a glimpse into the *poliprasino* (lush green) characteristics of the (officially) 12 islands in the Dodecanese chain between Crete and Asia Minor. These islands — there are actually 14, plus a few inhabited off-shore islets — have independent local government status, and a total population of around 120,000.

The history of the islands is closely allied to that of Rhodes, and 2 of them — Kos and Kastellorizo — also have 'Knights' castles'. All the major islands are on the car-ferry run from Piraeus, although it is a long haul. Kos, for example is 200 nautical miles, a 14-hour journey. Since Rhodes, Karpathos, Kos and Leros have airports, many people now do part of their island-hopping this way.

Kos off the Turkish coast close to Bodrum, has been inhabited since Neolithic times and by 4C BC its famous red wine was flowing and its silks exported throughout the trading world. Its main claim to fame is that the father of medicine, Hippocrates ('him very clever guy', as a Greek schoolboy explained), was born there, 460 BC. The Asklepion, infirmary and school of medicine, was founded to carry on his teaching. See: The Sanctuary of Asklepios (4km from Kos town) and considerable Roman remains.

A good road runs from the town — a lively, swinging place — in the north some 50km to the south-eastern tip, and minor roads climb steeply to attractive mountain villages and dip down to long and sandy beaches. NTOG, Kos: 0242/28.724. Tourist Police, Kos: 0242/28.227.

Just north of Kos, **Kalymnos** is renowned for the bravery of its sponge-divers who set off each spring for the coasts of Egypt and Libya, marked by a week-long fare-well. The sponges (a good, light-weight take-home present) are sold throughout the island. Mountain-ous and rocky with lush green valleys, the island has natural thermal springs. See: Neolithic settlement at Emborio; legendary cave (2km from capital); archaeo-logical museum.

Patmos has an 11C monastery dedicated to St John, who wrote the Apocalypse in a cave there. Orange groves lead up to Hora, notable for its white houses with vaulted door-ways and interior carved wooden partitions. See: monastery church (frescoes and temple), treasury (Byzantine and later icons, jewellery and ecclesiastical relics), library. Festivities: 15 August, folk-dance festival. Traditional sweets offered

Sponge fishermen, Kalymnos

include *confits* and *diples*. For centuries Patmos owned the neighbouring **Lipsi**. This little-known island has an annual festival on 24 August when it is said that all dried flowers will come to life again.

Halki, whose inhabitants are mainly fishermen and sponge-divers, is famous for its poignant love-songs. In 1983 it was declared 'an island of peace and friendship of young people of all nations'. **Simi**, almost tucked into an inlet in the Turkish coast, is half barren and rocky, half covered with pines and mulberries. A day trip from Rhodes enables you to see the Monastery of Archangel Michael (Byzantine frescoes). **Tilos** is a carpet of spring-time flowers. Mules and donkeys are still the most favoured means of transport on the single unmade road. **Nissiros** is 42 sq.km of drama, its pure white icing-sugar-like houses strident against the black volcanic rocks. A massive, but inactive, volcano towers over all. See: remains of Acropolis; Byzantine fort; Monastery of St John and, if you are lucky, the *perioli* dance at a wedding feast. **Leros**, mountainous with picturesque valleys and a craggy coastline, has the largest natural port in the Mediterranean. Festivities: Last Sunday in Lent, carnival with chariot parade and wine festival; feast of the Madonna, 15 August. **Kassos**, between Crete and Karpathos, has an exceptionally rural atmosphere due, perhaps, to the informality of its roads. See: Selai cave near Ag. Marina with remains of ancient walls. Festivities: folk-dance festival, 17 July.

The most easterly of the Dodecanese group — to the east of Rhodes — is **Kastellorizo**, also known as Megisti, only 9 sq.km in total area. See: folkloric exhibition in Turkish mosque; grotto of Parasta (a boat trip). The most westerly is **Astipalea**, its 110km coastline zig-zagged with small bays and sandy coves.

The North-Eastern Aegean Islands

The islands were settled around 1100 BC by Pelasgians and Ionians fleeing from the Peloponnese. By 7C and 6C BC they were centres of advanced civilisations, and independent and powerful maritime states. They were not, however, united, and fell one by one to a succession of invaders, notably the Genoese and Turks.

All the group are linked by the inter-island ferry run from Piraeus, and the largest ones — Samos, Hios, Lesvos and Limnos — have airports.

They have been famous for the quality of their wines since Homer's day, producing a full-bodied red table wine and a sweet, heavy dessert wine. Samos wines are perhaps best known, the red muscat-type being of such depth that it is referred to as *mavros* (black).

Samos (468 sq.km) birthplace of Pythagoras, was, the locals like to tell you, a great power 'when Athens was a young man'. The good road network through densely wooded countryside makes it possible to span the centuries in a single day, visiting Pythagorion, the ancient capital; the 2,500-year-old tunnel of Euphalinos built to carry water from the mountains; the site of the temple to Hera; the ancient marbles at Tigani; and the Palaeontological museum at Mytelene. Oh, and the numerous small fishing hamlets and tree-fringed beaches. Festivities: 6 August, a folk festival crowned by the 'dance of Samos'. Tourist Police: 0273/27.333. Port Authority: 0273/27.890.

To the east of Samos, **Icaria** (267 sq.km) is renowned for its connections with Icarus, the man who thought he could fly, and for its ancient radioactive thermal springs. See: considerable remains of Roman baths at Therma. This is mountain-goat country, and the meat is a speciality in the tavernas. Other specialities: honey from the *koumaro*, arbute berry, fruit and nuts of all kinds, and *raki*, a strong colourless spirit. Tourist Police: 0275/22.222, Port Authority: 0275/22.207.

Hios (858 sq.km) claims Homer as one of its sons, and has (near Vrondades) the School of Homer on a rock platform. The north is mountainous, rising to 1,230m, the south covered with citrus fruits, figs, grapes, olives and the mastic gum tree. See: 11C Monastery of Nea Moni; ruined temple to Apollo on site of 6C BC city, acropolis at Eborio, and countless picture-postcard villages. Tourist Police: 0271/26.555. Port Authority: 0271/22.837.

Lesvos, or Mytilene (1,630 sq.km) is large and pleasantly green with golden beaches, caves, grottoes and a petrified forest. It was the home of the poetess Sappho, and Aristotle lectured at its school of philosophy. At the capital Mytilene, you can be one with the jostling crowd and, practically anywhere else, 'get away from it all'. Tourist Police: 0251/22.776. Port Authority: 0251/28.827.

Limnos, where earth and fire were worshipped in ancient times, has a turbulent past in the shape of a once-active volcano. At Poliohni, traces of Neolithic and Bronze Age settlements; at Hephaistia, remains of 5C BC theatre, at Hlio, remains of ancient sanctuary, and grotto. Tourist Police: 0276/22.200. Port Authority: 0276/22.225.

Samothrace is most easily reached by boat from Alexandroupolis or (once a week) Kavala. The island has one of the tallest mountains in the Aegean, Fengari (moon) at 1,600m. In its shadow, Sanctuary of the Great Gods, site of Caveirian mysteries. See: 2C BC theatre and many contemporary remains. Tourist Police: 0551/41.203. Port Authority, 0551/41.305.

The Sporades

It's no secret that for one Grecophile, at least, Skiros is the gold-medal-holder of the group (see tour on p. 95). Skiathos, Skopelos and Alonissos, complete the quartet which forms an arc off the east coast of Evia. You can reach these 3 islands by ferry from Agios Konstantinos (166km from Athens, facing the west coast of Evia on the Lamia highway) and from Volos (334km from Athens, north and east of Lamia), and in summer occasionally from Paralia Kimi. An airport on Skiathos makes short work of island-jumping in this group. Port Authority: Ag. Konstantinos, 0235/31.759; Volos, 0421/20.115.

Skiathos has it all — a 30m wide pine grove fringing 1,000m of silvery beaches — behind which, a lagoon — 70 sandy inlets, and 9 tiny off-shore islets, plus Kastro, the ancient walled town where the whole population moved in 16C. Festivities: 26 July with folk dances. Tourist Police: 0424/42.005. Olympic Airways: 0424/42.200.

Skopelos, by no means upstaged in the matter of beaches, has 360 churches, chapels and monasteries — 123 of them in the capital. The houses, startlingly white, step down to the harbour. The locals have a charming 'friendship' custom. After offering visitors crystallised prunes, almond cake and *raki* they present a sprig of fresh basil which means, 'please come again'. Festivities: 6 August, Transfiguration Day. Tourist Police: 0424/22.235.

Alonissos is a sun, sand and sea paradise with only 10km of roads but a good round-the-beaches motor-boat network. The centre of the island is submerged, leaving islets, grottoes and precious little of the ancient city. Tourist Police: 0424/65.205.

The Ionian Islands

With Corfu and Lefkas, explored on pages 121-34 and 52-6, Zakinthos, Kefalonia, Ithaca and Paxos make up this group in the Adriatic. All can be reached by car-ferry from the mainland, Corfu, Kefalonia and Paxos from Patra, north Peloponnese (Port Authority, 061/277.622); Zakinthos from Kylini, north-western coast of that peninsula (Port Authority, 0695/22.417); Corfu also from Igoumenitsa, Epirus (Port Authority, 0665/22.235); and Paxos also from Parga, Epirus. Corfu, Zakinthos and Kefalonia have airports. Lefkas can be reached by road from the mainland.

Zakinthos, also known as Zante, its Venetian name (the Venetians also called the island 'flower of the Levant'), is the most southerly. It has sulphur springs near Xinthia cave. Another spectacular cave, Blue Grotto on the north coast, is reached by boat. Climb to the Venetian fortress to see the green carpet of olives and vines on the country estates. See: museum of paintings with Byzantine and Renaissance subjects. Tourist Police: 0695/22.550.

Kefalonia is an island of endless beaches, a fine naval tradition and spectacular caves. See: Drongarati cave near Haliotata, and Melissani cave, concealing an open lake. Festivities: 15 August when, according to local tradition, harmless snakes with a black cross on their heads appear for that day only. NTOG: 0671/22.847.

Ithaca, tucked into the eastern wing of Kefalonia, caused Odysseus to endure 10 years of hardship in order to return. And for what? The marble cave (above Vathi, the capital) where he hid gifts from the Phaeacians, sandy beaches, sheltered coves, olive groves and now, pretty fishing hamlets and tiny chapels.

Paxos, 'the island of flowers' south of Corfu, is only 19km long and has a population of 3,000. It is characterised by small sandy bays, rocky coves, sea caves and, in the summer, a splash of water-sports of all kinds. Festivities: 15 August, on Panagia isle, and the capital, Gaios.

BOOKS

Note: Some of these are out of print and obtainable only from libraries.

Aegean Quest, *Eric Forbes-Boyd* (Dent) A romantic search for Venetian Greece.

The Michelin Green Guide: Greece A useful sightseeing guide with emphasis on history and archaeology.

Blue Guide Greece (Benn) Comprehensive volume dealing almost exclusively with history, architecture and archaeology.

Fodor's Greece A region-by-region guide ranging from historical facts to hotel lists.

The Traveller's Journey is Done, *Dilys Powell* (Haag) Recalls the author's early travels to Greece in the 1920s and 1930s with her archaeologist husband.

An Affair of the Heart, *Dilys Powell* (Haag) A nostalgic and realistic view of Greece which opens the reader's eyes to the beauty and the human tragedy — war and civil war — of the recent past.

Mani, *Patrick Leigh Fermor* (Penguin) The bitter family and tribal feuds, the bleak towers, the wild countryside — a portrait of the southwestern Peloponnese.

Roumeli, *Patrick Leigh Fermor* (Penguin) A portrait of the Samaria Gorge.

The Odyssey, *Homer, translated by E.V. Rieu* (Penguin Classics) The story of Odysseus' epic voyage from Troy to his kingdom of Ithaca.

The Iliad, *Homer, translated by E.V. Rieu* (Penguin Classics) A prose translation of the epic poem, which retains the quality of timeless tragedy.

The Islands

The Companion Guide to the Greek Islands, *Ernle Bradford* (Collins) A wealth of information especially for the sea traveller and yachtsman.

Greek Island Hopping, *Dana Facaros* (Hippocrene, USA) A matter-of-fact and chatty book, with history and present-day life closely interwoven.

The Webb & Bower Dumont Guide: Greek Islands A time-warp handbook of Greek mythology and history.

The Greek Islands, *Lawrence Durrell* (Faber) This well-known Grecophile's very personal and highly evocative view. He describes Nero as having 'islomania'; he has it, too.

Prospero's Cell, *Lawrence Durrell* (Faber) Written 1945 about Corfu, every sparkling ripple across the bay, every breath of wind through the olive trees, every glass of zarian wine. Pure magic.

Reflections on a Marine Venus: A Companion to the Landscape of Rhodes, *Lawrence Durrell* (Faber) The island seen through the eyes of its most poetic observer, in the late 1940s.

My Family and Other Animals, *Gerald Durrell* (Penguin) A captivating account of Corfiot life as it was lived by the eccentric Durrell family — including the animals. Not to be judged by the pale and wan TV version.

Natural History

Flowers of Greece and the Aegean, *Anthony Huxley and William Taylor* (Chatto & Windus) Nearly 500 colour plates and botanical descriptions facilitate identification.

Travels with a Wild Life Artist, *Peter and Susan Barrett* (Columbus) Watercolour paintings and jottings that evoke the colour and scent of the flora, the flutter and scamper of the fauna.

Food

Greek Food, *Rena Salaman* (Fontana) The author, an Athenian, describes *mezithra* sheep's cheese as 'a process of overlapping waves of pleasing tastes'. The same could be said of her book.

Greek Cooking, *Pamela Westland* (Ward Lock) Dishes first tasted in a monastery, others cooked in an island cottage at sunrise — a personal collection of recipes from a travel notebook.

Language

Greek Phrasebook, *N. Sangos and Jill Norman* (Penguin).

Colloquial Greek, *Katerina Harris* (Routledge) The book leads quickly and readily from the alphabet to simple and practical sentences.

Modern Greek for Everyday Use, *A Palafoutis* (published in Athens) A phrasebook with travel guide supplement.

Greek for Tourists and Travellers, *N. Eliopoulos* (published in Athens).

Modern Greek for Everyday Use, *A. Palafoutis* (published in Athens) A say-it' elementary grammar.

Just Enough Greek/Traveller's Greek, *D.L. Ellis and H. Rapi* (Passport Books/Pan Books). An essential phrasebook for getting by in Greek.

Just Listen 'n Learn Greek/Breakthrough Greek, *Eleni Marcopoulos-Gambarotta and Jennifer Scamp* (Passport Books/Pan Books). Complete cassette and coursebook programme for learning Greek.

For a wide selection of books on Greece and the Greek language: Zeno, booksellers and publishers, 6 Denmark Street, London WC2H 8LP, and Hellenic Book Service, 122 Charing Cross Road, London, WC2H 8LP.

INDEX

Note: Page numbers of the entries in **bold** type indicate the start of a complete route. Place names with the abbreviation Ag. (Agia or Agios, Saint) are listed together alphabetically, as are mountains (Mt.).

Abbreviations 11
Abdera 119
Acrocorinth 17
Adravasti 146
Aegina 169
Aetorrahi 71
Afanou 161
Afrates 149
Ag. Deka 148
Ag. Dimitrios 24
Ag. Fotia 145
Ag. Fotini 150
Ag. Galini 148
Ag. Georgios 128, 139
Ag. Gordis 132
Ag. Ilias 125
Ag. Ioannis 85, 150
Ag. Isidoros 164
Ag. Kiriaki 54, 167
Ag. Lavendris 86
Ag. Lavra Monastery 37
Ag. Matheos 132
Ag. Minas 66
Ag. Nikitas 55
Ag. Nikolaos 53, 109, 166
Ag. Orestiko 102
Ag. Petros 55
Ag. Roumeli 152
Ag. Stephanos 129
Ag. Varrara 147
Agnanda 70
Agnoundas Monastery 18
Agria 86
Agriles 153
Agrinio 46
Akorotiri 172
Alepohori 24
Alexandros 54
Alexandroupoli 119
Ali Meria 86
Aliki 113

Aliveri 93
Almiro 35
Alonossos 176
Amarinthos 93
Ambelakia 80
Amfilohia 45
Amfissa 48
Amigdali 140
Amorgos 172
Anaharavi 125
Andou 138
Andritsena 30
Anilio 85
Ano Korakiana 125
Ano Perdina 65
Ano Volos 84
Antirio 43
Aperi 166
Apidia 24
Apolakia 163
Apolona 160
Apostoli 149
Arachova 50
Aratos 118
Archangelos 61
Areopoli 33
Argolid 15
Arhangelos 160
Arilas 129
Aristi 66
Arisvi 118
Arkadades 129
Arkasa 167
Arkitsa 91
Armenades 129
Arnea 110
Arnissa 104
**Around the Dikti
    Mountains 140**
Arta 67, 70
Artemissia 88

Artemissio 91
Aspotiades 129
Aspouss 97
Asprangeli 65
Asini 19
Astakos 45
Asteri 26
Astipalea 174
Astris 113
Aviotes 129
Azokeramos 146

Bamdakardos 154
Bassae, Ancient 30
Benitses 133
Bitola 104
Books
    Food 178
    General 177
    Islands 177
    Language 178
    Natural History 178
Bralos 48
Byron, Lord 44

Cape Dukato 55
**Central Greece and Lefkas
    41**
Choristi 117
Conversion tables, Metric
    12
Corfu 121
Crete 135
Cyclades, The 170

Dafni 110, 129
Danilia 130
Delos 171
Delphi 49
    Ancient 49
Demonia 25

Index

Derreziana 69
Derveni 29
Diafani 167
Dikela 119
Dikti Cave 138
Dion 81
Diros Caves 34
Dispilio 102
Distos, Ancient 93
Dodecanese, The 172
Dodona, Ancient 68
Domeniko 82
Douli 129
Dragoni 30
Drakia 86
Dramesii 69
Drepano 19
Driving and parking 4
Dukades 130
Durrell Country (Corfu) 123

Eastern Province (Crete) 143
Eastwards to Thrace 114
Eating out 5
Edessa 104
Edipsos 91
Elasson 82
Eleonas 48
Eleousa 160
Elia 26, 69
Elliniko 25
Elonis Monastery 24
Elos 26
Embona 164
Epano Episkopi 146
Epano Kalamona 159
Epanohori 153
Epidavros, Ancient 18
Epirus 57
Episkepsis 125
Eretria 93
Ermioni 19, 169
Ermones 131
Epta Piges 160
Etolia and Akarnania 42
Evia and Skiros 87
Evros Wetlands 119
Exo Mouliana 145
Exo Potami 140

Faliraki 161
Feraklo Castle 160
Festos 136, 148
Festos and the Amari Valley 147
Fila 95

Filakio 149
Finiki 167
Flamouriana 142
Flomohori 33
Floria 154
Florina 104
Fokida 46
Food and drink 6
Fotina 82
Fourfouras 150
Fournes 152

Galanovrisi 82
Galata 19, 169
Galataki Monastery 90
Galaxidi 50
Garalades 130
Gasatika 125
Gastouri 133
Gefira 24
Genardi 163
Genio 54
Gerakari 150
Geraki 24
Gerakini 107
Gerolimenos 33
Getting there 2
Giannades 131
Githio 32
Glifada 132
Gliki 60
Gomati 109
Gonies 138
Gortina 148
Gortyns 148
Goulediana 149
Gournes 138
Gournia 144, 145
Gouvia 125
Gravia 48
Gravouna 120
Greece, the regions and the routes vii
Greek language 11
Gytheio 32

Halandritsa 38
Halki 174
Halkidiki 106
Halkis 88, 93
Hania 84, 154
Haraki 160
Helatos 70
Hiliomodi 22
Hios 175
Hiring transport 3
History — the chronology 10

Hlomos 132
Hohlakies 146
Hora Sfaki 152
Horeopiskopi 129
Hortata 55
Hourmeriakos 142
Hrisi 143
Hristos 143
Hydra 169

Icaria 175
Ierapetra 140, 143, 144
Ierissos 109
Igoumenitsa 59, 60, 63
Ilia and Ahaia 35
Iliassos, Ancient 155, 159
Introduction 1
Ioanina 63, 64, 67, 71, 75
Ionian Islands, The 176
Iraklion 138
Island groups, The 169
Istiea 91
Itanos 146
Itea 50
Ithaca 176
Ithomi 29
Itilo 34

Kafalatos 154
Kafalonia 176
Kafirea 92
Kakopetros 154
Kala Nera 86
Kalagoni 53
Kalamafka 143
Kalamata 35
Kalambaka 77
Kalami 126
Kalamitsi 55
Kalavarda 160
Kalavrita 38
Kalentzi 71
Kalinistra 38
Kalives 114
Kaloneri 102
Kalpaki 66
Kalymnos 173
Kambos 35
Kaminaki 139
Kamiros, Ancient 159, 164
Kamiros and the North (Rhodes) 156
Kamiros Skola 164
Kanali Beach 61
Kandanos 153
Kanoni 133
Kapa 78
Kapi 160

Kardamili 34
Kardara 51
Karditsa 78
Karies 110
Karitena 29
Karitos 94
Karpathos 156, 164
Karusades 129
Kassandra 107
Kassiopi 126
Kassos 174
Kastania 78, 105
Kastellorizo 174
Kastoria 102
    Lake 102
Kastro 97
Katakolo 36
Kataratikis 38
Katavia 163
Katerini 81
Kato Garouna 132
Kato Gatzea 86
Kato Glikovrisi 26
Kato Horio 144
Kato Klitoria 37
Kato Korakiana 127
Kato Makrino 46
Kato Vlasia 38
Kato Zakros 146
Katohi 44
Katsimbala 29
Kavala 115
Kavousi 145
Kelaria 146
Kera 138
Keramoti 112
Kere 149
Kerlaki 150
Kimi 95
Kimolos 113
Kinira 113
Kiparissia 31
Kissos 85, 149
Kita 33
Kithnos 170
Klipio 163
Klitoria, Ancient 37
Knossos 136, 137, 138
Kokkala 33
Kombelos 78
Komotini 118
Kontaraina 54
Korissia, Lake 132
Kos 173
Kosmos 24
Kota 103
Koudoumalia 139
Kouloura 126

Kouroutes 150
Koutselio 71
Kozani 101
Krasi 138
Krini 120
Kritinia 163
Kritsi 142
Krokees 26
Kroustas 142

Laconia 22
Laerma 164
Lafki 126
Lagia 33
Lagovouni 37
Lahania 163
Lakones 128
Lala 36
Lambia 37
Lambinu 85
Lamia 46, 48
Langada 34
Lardos 163
Larissa 79
Lasithi Plain 137
Lato 142
Leconia 86
Lefka Ori 152
Lefkada 53
Lefkadia 105
Lefkanti 95
Lefkas 52
Leonidi 23
Lepoura 94
Leptokaria 81
Leros 174
Lesini 45
Lesvos 175
Leucas, Ancient 53
Liapades 130
Lidoriko 51
Ligia 53
Limenaria 113
Limenas 112
Limeni 34
Limni 90
Limnos 175
Linaria 96
Lindos 161, 162, 164
**Lindos and the South
    (Rhodes) 161**
Lipsi 174
Lira 25
Lissos, Ancient 153
Lithines 146
Litohoro 81
Loutra 113
Loutses 126

Loxada 78

Macedonia and Thrace 99
Magazia 97
Makrades 126
Makri 119
Makriammos 113
Makrinitsa 84
Makrirahi 85
Malaki 86
Maleme 154
Males 143
Malia 136, 137, 138
Malona 160
Mani 31
Mantoudi 90
Marandohori 54
Margarita 62
Maries 114
Maritsa 159
Marmari 94
Marmekato 139
Maronia 119, 146
Masari 160
Mataranka 46
Mavromati 78
Mavrommati 29
Maza 153
Mega Papingo 66
Megalapoli 29
Megalapolis, Ancient 29
Megali Panagia 109
Megali Prespa 104
Melambes 148
Menetes 167
Meronas 150
Mesa Lasithi 139
Mesa Potami 139
Mesanagros 163
Mesavali 154
Meskla 152
Mesopotamos 61
Messembria 119
Messini 28
Messinia 27
Messolongi 44
Mesti 119
Metamorfosi 24
Meteora 76
Metropoli 78
Metsova 76
Mezapos 34
Mihalitsi 61
Mikines 21
Mikrą Papingo 66
Mikra Prespa 103
Mili 143
Milies 85

Index

Milopotamos 85
Milos 170
Minas 159
Mirriotissa 132
Mirthios 149
Mirtos 143
Mistra 26
Mitikas 45
Mixorouna 149
Mohos 140
Monemvassia 25
Moni Thari 164
Monistraki 20
Monodendri 65
Monolithio 70
Monolithos 163
Mouressi 85
Mournies 151
Mouse Island 133
Mouzaki 78
Mt. Ataviros 164
Mt. Athos 109
Mt. Filerimos 159
Mt. Holomon 107
Mt. Melitonas 109
Mt. Mitsikeli 65
Mt. Ossa 80
Mt. Pandokrator 125
Mt. Parnassos 50
Mt. Parnon 23
Mt. Profitis Elias 160, 167
Mt. Stavrotas 55
Mt. Taigetos 26
Mt. Timfi 63
Mt. Tomaros 68
Mykinae, Ancient 21
Mykonos 173
Mytilene 175

Nafpaktos 51
Nafplio 19
National Tourist
    Organisation of Greece
    9
Nauossa 105, 172
Naxos 172
Nea Figalia 30
Nea Karvali 120
Nea Marmaras 108
Nea Mirtos 143
Nea Plastiras 78
Nea Stira 94
Neapoli 102, 140, 141
Necromanteion 61
Neohori 110
Neraida 78
Nestor's Palace 31
Niata 24

Nidri 54
Nikiana 53
Nikiforos 117
Nikitas 108
Niklitsi 69
Nikopolis, Ancient 61
Nimfes 129
Nissiros 174
Nithavri 150
North West (Corfu) 127

Ohthonia 94
Oiniadi 45
Olinthos 107
    Ancient 107
Olympia 34
    Ancient 34
Olympos 79
Olympos (Diafani) 167
Omalos 152
Omolio 80
Opening times 8
Orei 91
Ormilia 108
Ormos Panagias 109
Ormos Prinos 114
Osia 65
Othos 166
Ouranopoli 109
Ovia 38

Pagi 128
Palekastro 146
Paleohori 110
Paleokastritsa 128
Paleokastro 110
Paleros 45
Panagia 113
Pandelimon 130
Pandokrator, Mt. 125
Paradisia 29
Paradissos 120
Paralia Kimi 95
Paramithia 60
Paranesti 117
Parga 62
Paros 172
Parthenon 108
Passanon, Ancient 57
Pastida 159
Patra 38
Pefkari 113
Pelekas 132
Pelion 82
Peloponnese 13
Perama 133
Perama Caves 64
Perdika 62

Perigiali 54
Perithia 126
Perivolia 30, 151
Petalia 126
Petaloudes 159
Petralona 30
Phaistos, Ancient 136, 137,
    148
Philippi, Ancient 117
Pilalimata 146
Piles 166
Pinakates 86
Pinakiano 138
Pirgadikia 109
Pirgos 36, 143
Pirgos Dirou 34
Pirihos 33
Platamona 81
Platani 20
Platania 160
Platanies 154
Platanousa 70
Plataria 62
Plati 138
Platonovrisi 38
Platsa 34
Pleuron 44
Poligiros 107
Polimilos 106
Polipotamos 94
Politika 90
Pondikonissi 133
Portaria 84
Poros 54, 169
Porto Carras 108
Porto Koufo 109
Porto Lagos 119
Poseidonion 165
Potamia 113
Potamos 132
Potos 113
Preveza 61
Prina 142
Priolithos 37
Prokopi 90
Prosilio 35
Psahna 90
Psakoudia 107
Psihro 138
Public Holidays 9

Rahoni 114
Rethiminon 147, 150
Rhodes and Karpathos
    155
Rhodes Town (Rhodos)
    156, 158, 161
Rio 39

Rivio 46
Roads and maps 3
Roda 129
Rodavgi 70
Rodini Park 158
Rodovani 153
Ropa Plain 131
Rousatiana 139
Rovies 90
'Rupert Brooke' Islands 95
    grave 98

Salakos 160
Salamis 169
Samaria Gorge 150, 152
Samos 174
Samothrace 175
Santorini (Thira) 170, 172
Sapes 119
Saronic Gulf Islands 169
Sarti 109
Serifos 170
Seroni 159
Sgombou 125
Sgourades 125
Siana 163
Siatista 101
Sidari 129
Sifnos 170
Sigos 125
Sikea 24
Sikia 109
Simi 174
Sinarades 132
Siros 171
Sitea 145
Sithonia 107
Sivota 62
Sivros 54
Skala 26
Skala Marion 114
Skala Potamia 113
Skala Ranoniou 114
Skiathos 175
Skiros 95, 96, 97, 175
Skopelos 176
Skripero 130
Sofiko 17
Sokraki 125
Sotira Monastery 95
Sougia 153
Southern Tip (Corfu) 130
Sparta 26
    Ancient 26
Spetses 169
Spili 149

Sporades, The 175
Stagira 110
Stanos 46
Stavropigi 35
Stavros 133
Stavroupolis 117
Stefanovouno 82
Steni 90
Stes 166
Stira 94
Stratoniki 110
Stratos 46
    Ancient 46
Sybrita, Ancient 149

Tavronitis 154
Taxiarhis 110
Temploni 131
Temenia 153
Temple of Aphaia Athena
    169
Temple of Bassae 30
Thassos 111, 112
Theologos 113
Theriso 153
Thermo 46
Thesprotia 59
Thesprotiko 69
Thessaly 73
Thira 172
Thissoa 30
Tholo 31
Thronos 149
Tilos 174
Timbaki 148
Tinos 171
Tiranavos 82
Tiryns, Ancient 20
Toroni 109
Touring information 9
Toxotes 120
Tripiti 109
Tsambika Monastery 160
Tsangarada 85
Tsoukalades 56
Tolo 10
Trahia 19
Trahila 34
Trigona 76
Trikala 74, 77
Tripotama 37
Tris Boukes 98
Tsoukalades 56
Tzermiado 139

Vafeika 119

Vai 146
Valanion 129
Vale of Tempe 80
Valira 29
Valley of the Butterflies
    159, 172
Varnakova Monastery 51
Vasiliki 144
Vasses 34
Vassiliki 54
Vegoritida, Lake 104
Vergina 105
Veria 105
Vigla 104
Vikos Gorge 65
Vistonas 128
Vistonis, Lake 119
Vitsa 65
Vizari 149
Vizitsa 85
Vlaherna, Monastery of
    133
Vlaho 54
Vogatsiko 102
Volada 166
Volos 83, 86
Vonitsa 45, 53
Votonisi 75
Voukelies 154
Vouniatades 132
Vounihora 52
Vourvourou 109
Vrises 140, 152

**Western Crete — The
    Gorges 150**
Western Macedonia 100
Where to stay 4
White Mountains 152

Xanthi 117

Zagoria 63
Zagorohorio 63
Zaharo 31
Zakinthos 176
Zakros 146
Zalongo 61
Zante 176
Zarakes 94
Zenia 140
Zevgaraki 46
Zitsa 67
Zoodokos Pigi 105
Zouvra 152